WEB OF LIES

Aoife Gallagher is a research analyst at the Institute for Strategic Dialogue, a non-profit think tank working to push back against the rising tide of disinformation, extremism and polarisation. Previously she worked as a journalist at the online news agency Storyful.

WEB OF LIES

The lure and danger
of conspiracy theories

Aoife Gallagher

Gill Books

Gill Books
Hume Avenue
Park West
Dublin 12
www.gillbooks.ie

Gill Books is an imprint of M.H. Gill and Co.

Designed by Typo•glyphix
Edited by Sands Publishing Solutions
Proofread by Ciara McNee Editorial
Printed by Clays Ltd, Suffolk
This book is typeset in 13/18pt, Bembo Std

*The paper used in this book comes from the wood pulp of
sustainably managed forests.*

A CIP catalogue record for this book is available from the
British Library.

5 4 3 2 1

For N.

Contents

Jet fuel ~~can't~~ *doesn't have to* melt steel beams

I N 2008, when I was 19 years old, I was introduced to a film called *Zeitgeist*. It was an intriguing production, laced with hypnotic imagery, smooth narration and rhythmic music. The film was split into three parts. The first was about Christianity. It claimed Jesus was a fictional character and that the Christian faith was mainly based on a combination of ancient astronomy and parts of other religions. It was quite convincing, especially for someone who had stepped away from the Catholic Church.

The second part was about September 11. This *really* interested me. Exactly 10 weeks before that fateful day, on 26 June 2001, I was standing on the observation deck of the South Tower of the World Trade Center gazing over the skyline of New York City while on a family holiday. I was 12 years old. Like everyone who has a memory of the events of 9/11, I couldn't look away as the news replayed the videos of the planes hitting the Twin Towers. The spot I had stood in only weeks earlier folded into a mushroom cloud of its own debris, and thousands of people ran for their lives as thousands more died. We had *just* been there. As a result, throughout my teenage years I was quite obsessed with watching anything and everything about 9/11, so when *Zeitgeist* presented me with an alternative theory about what happened that day, I was all ears.

One of *Zeitgeist*'s main claims was that ignited jet fuel from the planes wasn't hot enough to melt the building's steel beams; it suggested instead that the Twin Towers had actually fallen in a controlled demolition. It questioned whether an aeroplane had even hit the Pentagon, suggesting rather that it was a missile, and it even raised doubts as to whether Flight 93 had really crashed in Pennsylvania. These claims were all tied together by questioning whether the Bush administration knew in advance that the attacks were going to take place – even suggesting that they were the ones responsible. I was intrigued. It seemed plausible. By the time I watched *Zeitgeist*, it was also apparent that the premise for the Iraq War was based on a lie. If they lied about weapons of mass destruction, what were the odds they would lie about 9/11?

The third part of *Zeitgeist* claimed that a small cabal of international bankers really controls the world, using debt to keep us enslaved, and instigating disasters (including 9/11) in order to strip people of their liberties. The ultimate aim, according to the film, is to implant the entire population with microchips and create a one-world centralised economy and government to track and monitor every individual. In 2008, the world was in the throes of a global financial crisis. The idea that rich bankers were scheming to keep us all in debt rang true to me, as I'm sure it did for many others who watched *Zeitgeist* at that time.

After watching the whole film, I remember feeling empowered with this new information, like I had access to secrets that other people were not aware of. I remember feeling like a fog had been lifted and that many injustices about the world had been explained. My father had often told me that it was good to think outside the box and that following the crowd wasn't always the answer. This seemed like the ultimate way to think differently.

After *Zeitgeist*, I watched another slickly produced film called *Loose Change*. This one was solely about September 11 and built on many of the same themes outlined in *Zeitgeist*. Hearing the same claims made again reinforced the idea that something definitely didn't add up about the official narrative of what happened that day.

Thinking back, as much as I was sucked in by these films, it's hard to tell whether they had an impact on the way I lived my life. I had friends who also watched them, and it made for some very deep and interesting conversations after a few drinks. I had always considered myself quite anti-establishment, and the themes of the films definitely bolstered that. I remember rewatching them a couple of times, but I never branched out much further beyond those two films.

Fast forward to 2016. I had just finished a master's in journalism and got a job with Storyful, a social media news agency. 'Post-truth' was the word of the year. The UK had voted for

Brexit, and Donald Trump was elected in the US in a wave of 'fake news' and conspiracy theories. The bread-and-butter work of Storyful journalists is to verify online video content from breaking-news scenarios so that news organisations can use it, safe in the knowledge that what the video shows is accurate. I was learning how to use online tools to do this, while also figuring out how to identify and track misinformation and conspiracy theories online. One day *Zeitgeist* popped back into my head, so I decided to give it a watch.

I started with part two, the 9/11 segment. I was approximately six minutes into it when I heard a voice that I recognised. I shook my head and had a little chuckle to myself. It was Alex Jones, the notorious founder and presenter of *InfoWars*, one of the most popular far-right conspiracy theory shows on the planet. As a 19-year-old, I wouldn't have recognised Jones's voice, but 28-year-old me did. *Zeitgeist*, it turned out, borrowed quite a bit of footage from *Terrorstorm*, a documentary about 9/11 made by Jones the year before. Jones also happened to be listed as an executive producer on a follow-up film to *Loose Change*.

Alex Jones is arguably the most successful conspiracy theorist of modern times. For over 25 years he has been bellowing purple-faced rants in a caricature-like fashion to his ever-increasing audience, warning of impending doom at the hands of the globalists/New World Order/Illuminati/Satanists. Whatever the event, Jones has a conspiracy theory for it. The Oklahoma City bombing? Inside job. Deadly flood/hurricane/tornado? Government-controlled weaponised weather. Boston Marathon bombing? Inside job. Bill Gates's philanthropic work? Mass eugenics. HIV? Government eugenics. Climate change? A hoax. September 11 attacks? You guessed it: inside job.

In 2012, Jones took his spurious claims to new depths in a story that epitomises the callous nature of his thinking. A school shooting at Sandy Hook Elementary School in Connecticut left 26 people dead, including 20 children aged between six and seven years old. It was the second-deadliest school shooting in US history. Jones, in typical fashion, claimed the horrific event was a false flag (a hostile action orchestrated to make it look like it was the work of someone it wasn't) designed by the government to take firearms away from Americans. He said that no one died and that the victims and their families were 'crisis actors' hired by the government to play the part of victims. In one particularly cruel segment, he mocked the parents who spoke on TV after losing their children, saying they were faking their emotions. The victims' parents have been harassed with abuse and death threats for years as a result of Jones's claims. In November 2021, Jones was found liable to pay damages to the families after they took a number of cases against him.

For these reasons and many more, Jones's involvement in both *Zeitgeist* and *Loose Change* raised huge red flags for me, and I started down my own rabbit hole to look into the claims made in the films. It turns out that jet fuel doesn't have to melt steel beams for them to lose their structural strength. The 'evidence' the film used to suggest the towers fell in a controlled demolition was actually air and debris being expelled as the building collapsed on itself in a process experts call 'pancaking'. Dozens of eyewitnesses at the Pentagon described seeing an aeroplane hit the building, none saw a missile. I could go on

– and I'll talk about other tactics used in those films to suck viewers in a bit later – but it's safe to say that almost all the claims they make have been thoroughly debunked by experts.

Do I have all the answers to what happened on 9/11? I don't. Do I still think it was an inside job? I don't. The claim that the US government was somehow involved in the events of that day was supported by all the other debunked claims, leaving nothing but speculation and suspicion to prop up the 'inside job' theory. It convinced me at the time, however, and it certainly convinced many others who continued down the rabbit hole from there.

Since then, my work – at both Storyful and where I work now, a counter-extremism think tank called the Institute for Strategic Dialogue (ISD) – has been focused on understanding how disinformation (false information spread to deliberately mislead people), misinformation (false information spread without the knowledge that it is false) and conspiracy theories spread online, and how all these elements are weaponised by extremist groups and political movements.

In many ways, the 9/11 truther movement provided a blueprint for how conspiracy theories would form and spread in the twenty-first century. People gathered in online communities, consulted bad experts, swapped evidence and ideas and did their own research. Amateur filmmakers took those ideas and turned them into easily digestible movie formats that spread far and wide in an ever-growing online ecosystem of truth seekers.

My hope with this book is that those who read it will gain an understanding of where these movements come from and why people fall for them. In many ways, they are not new. Many parts of these movements are using theories that have been recycled for centuries and given a new coat of paint for the internet age. Others are unique to the cultures of the online world. It is an international force, much of it influenced by the US, but it has infected countries around the world, and Ireland is not immune. I also hope in some way to inoculate people against their rhetoric, so that you can recognise the language and tactics in the future and know how to avoid falling down the rabbit hole.

A couple of things before you dive in. There are a lot of nasty topics covered in this book – mass shootings, child sexual abuse, racism, homophobia, transphobia, xenophobia and misogyny – so be prepared. Some names and details have been changed to protect people's privacy. Also, please try to forget everything you think you know about government conspiracies and secret societies if it comes from *The X-Files* and Dan Brown novels. They are what they are: great works of fiction.

To everyone reading this because they believe I'm a propaganda arm for British Intelligence/Bill Gates/George Soros, thanks for reading.

Chapter 1

The Mind

A CONSPIRACY IS A SECRET PLOT BETWEEN two or more individuals for some kind of nefarious purpose. Conspiracies are real and happen all the time. They include anything from secret plans between two people to rob a local shop, to plots between powerful people and institutions to deceive the public for their own selfish ends.

The oil and gas giant ExxonMobil knew that burning fossil fuels was leading to climate change as early as 1977, and it subsequently spent millions of dollars promoting doubt and denial in order to protect its profits. In 2013, Edward Snowden revealed that the National Security Agency (NSA) was spying on US civilians on an unprecedented scale. For 40 years, hundreds of Black men were recruited to take part in a study about the effects of syphilis and promised free healthcare for the condition. The Tuskegee Study, as it was named, was actually designed to track the full progression of the disease, and participants were not given treatment, even after effective medicines were found. Dozens of the participants died before the scandal was exposed.

These conspiracies were revealed because of a whistle-blower, leaked information or government or journalistic investigations. Evidence revealed the wrongdoing, and the conspiracies were exposed and fell apart, although the consequences remain. These are but a small sample of the horrendous incidents that lay bare the very worst of humanity and that have contributed to distrust and suspicion across the world. Black communities in the US are wary of taking part in medical trials as a result of the Tuskegee Study. The entire world now has to deal with the consequences of rampant climate change denial, and the NSA revelations showed what lengths the US government would go to in the name of 'national security'.

These conspiracies have been proven to be true. Conspiracy theories, on the other hand, are speculative by nature. Political scientist Joseph Uscinski defines a conspiracy theory as a way to explain a certain event or phenomenon by invoking a sinister plot orchestrated by powerful actors, who are acting in secret for their own benefit and against the common good.[1]

I'm not going to tell you that every conspiracy theory is nonsense. That would be unwise. After all, we should be suspicious about the extent to which people will use power, wealth and influence for their own selfish ends, or to protect profits and business. There have been times when conspiracy theories have been proven true – the most famous example being the Watergate scandal. US President Richard Nixon went to huge lengths to cover up his involvement in the break-in and bugging of the offices of the Democratic National Convention before investigations exposed the truth, resulting in his impeachment and resignation as president. Following the revelations that revealed the truth, Nixon's involvement was no longer a theory, but a proven conspiracy.

While Watergate was a plausible conspiracy theory, many of the claims that have pulled people down the rabbit hole in recent years are based on implausible ones. In his book *The Nature of Conspiracy Theories,* Michael Butter makes the point that Watergate provides proof that many conspiracy theories are 'inconsistent with reality'. 'If the American president – commonly dubbed the most powerful man in the world – cannot even spy on his political opponents … how can anyone be supposed capable of faking the moon landing, 9/11 or the refugee crisis and keeping it secret for years or even decades?'[2]

These kinds of conspiracy theories suggest elaborate degrees of coordination and cooperation between world governments, multi-million-dollar corporations and global institutions. In order for them to be true, there need to be thousands, if not millions, of people involved who are either incompetent enough to be ignorant to their involvement, or happy to forsake their morals and work towards the destruction of human liberties. Most importantly, they need to keep it a secret. In the words of Benjamin Franklin, 'Three may keep a secret, if two of them are dead.' Many far-fetched conspiracy theories are simply impossible for this reason. Because of the need for the highest levels of secrecy, the more people involved in a supposed conspiracy, the more likely it will be to fail due to exposure.

Dr David Robert Grimes, a physicist, cancer researcher and author who has dedicated considerable time to debunking scientific myths and conspiracy theories, tested this hypothesis. He began by assuming that the Covid-19 pandemic was orchestrated as a ruse in order to implement a mass vaccination campaign. Being conservative, he included only public health bodies, researchers and drug companies as co-conspirators (and not politicians and the media). Using some fancy maths and statistics to compare the pandemic conspiracy theory to proven conspiracies – including the NSA spying and Tuskagee study – Dr Grimes estimated that the conspiracy would unravel within about 10 weeks.[3] Although maths is no substitute for reality, the conclusion remains valid: the sheer number of people who would need to be in on the secret would mean it could not be sustained for a significant period of time and would be destined for failure.

The issue discussed in this book is really related to a conspiracy-theorising mindset – when people start seeing conspiracies in everything and cannot be assuaged by evidence that proves their theory wrong; when critical thinking and common sense are replaced with overwhelming suspicion that twists people's sense of reality, sometimes leading to a spiral of paranoia and dissociation from everyday life. These conspiracy theories tend to be based on a combination of speculation, illogical reasoning, cognitive biases and seeing connections where they don't exist, as opposed to any kind of verifiable evidence. They are often impossible to disprove, as doing so means trying to prove that something *isn't* happening.

Conspiracy theories also tend to be self-sealing, meaning that any evidence that critiques, counters or proves a conspiracy theory false is routinely subsumed by supporters and, for them, becomes proof that the conspiracy theory is real. For example, when reports and investigations confirmed that 9/11 was the work of 19 al-Qaeda terrorists under the direction of Osama bin Laden, 9/11 truthers interpreted this as further proof that the US government was in on the act and attempting to cover up their involvement. This means conspiracy theories can survive through time, which is why people are still touting the same conspiracy theories that have been around for decades, if not centuries.

As Michael Barkun points out in his seminal book *A Culture of Conspiracy*, 'Conspiracists' reasoning runs in the following way. Because the conspiracy is so powerful, it controls virtually all of the channels through which information is disseminated … Hence information that appears to put a conspiracy theory in doubt must have been planted by the conspirators themselves in order to mislead.' This is why it is often impossible to debate a die-hard conspiracy theorist.

Which begs the question, who constitutes a conspiracy theorist? The easy answer is that every single one of us is a conspiracy theorist, and I would bet decent money that everyone reading this book engages in conspiratorial thinking. They don't have to be far-flung theories like the New World Order trying to impose a one-world government. There are everyday occurrences that will provoke this kind of thinking. For example, if you order a drink in a bar that tastes weak, you may theorise that the bar owners are watering down spirits to increase profits. Our brains are built to theorise like this. Sometimes there is good reason to be suspicious; other times,

you're simply trying to rationalise a situation using the information you have available.

Conspiracy theorising therefore falls along a spectrum,
illustrated cleverly by the Conspiracy Chart created by disinformation researcher Abbie Richards.[4] Some instances simply
involve asking questions about events that still have an air of
mystery surrounding them – speculating on the truth about
UFOs, for example. Others can be relatively harmless, even
though they are unequivocally false: for example, theories that
Avril Lavigne died in 2003 and was replaced by a body double.
But over the past few years, the world has unfortunately become
familiar with the effects of harmful conspiracy theories. Anti-
vaccine conspiracy theories can make people refuse life-saving
medical treatment or increase the risk of spreading a disease to
people around them. Others, such as those associated with
white nationalism or Islamophobia, are used to scapegoat
minority communities, encourage hate and can radicalise
people to violence.[5] Studies have shown that exposure to conspiracy theories makes people less willing to reduce their carbon
footprint or engage in politics. In recent years, however, conspiracy theories have also been seized upon by political figures,
such as former US president Donald Trump, and they have
weakened the foundations of democracy in the US as a result.
At a personal level, they can leave people detached from reality
and unable to maintain relationships and friendships.

A common refrain that can be heard both online and in real
life is that conspiracy theorists are crazy, or stupid, or idiots or
any other pejorative term. Some parts of the media have a habit
of leaning into this, giving people an excuse to mock and

belittle them. In some ways, this reaction is understandable; conversing with someone who believes things that are so inherently untrue can be extremely frustrating. However, a default dismissal runs the risk of further isolating people who already feel like they have been shunned by wider society. It can encourage them to double down on their beliefs and radicalise them into more extreme positions.

The truth is that conspiracy theorists come from a cross section of society. Some are old, some are young. Some never finished school, while others are doctors or PhDs. Some are unemployed, and others are successful business owners. They have families, friends and people who love them. From looking at these movements for almost five years, my belief is that, for the most part, the people who get pulled into them are not 'bad' people. Many are victims of really powerful and compelling stories of fiction that play on our biases, feed into our suspicions and fears, and trigger certain cognitive processes in our brains.

But conspiracy theories have the ability to take caring, empathetic people and expose them to a version of reality that makes them promote hatred and irrationality. Conspiracy theories are an inherent characteristic of all kinds of extremist movements, from religious fundamentalists and cults to far-right and far-left ideologies.[6]

The conspiracy theories used by extremist movements tend to play on dangerous stereotypes and are used to attack and malign groups of people based on characteristics such as race, ethnicity, gender, religion or sexual orientation. Although we all subscribe to certain in-groups based on things such as where we live, our jobs or our hobbies, extremist movements are obsessed with narrowly defining their in-group identity (for example, in terms of religion, nationality or ethnicity), and they feel threatened by those they see as belonging to out-groups. Extremist movements tend to view their in-group as superior and therefore engage in antagonistic behaviour towards out-groups – be that migrants, the LGBTQ+ community, women, Jews, Muslims or Christians, etc. to assert that superiority[7].

For example, the majority of Irish far-right groups can be described as ethno-nationalists – they define Irish nationality in terms of ethnicity. In this case, the out-group consists of people of different ethnicities living in Ireland, even if they were born here. Former Lord Mayor of Dublin and Green Party politician Hazel Chu, for example, was born and raised in Ireland to parents originally from Hong Kong. She is the constant subject of racially charged abuse at the hands of the Irish far right, because she does not meet their strict definition of what it means to be Irish, and they see her success as a threat.

Conspiracy theories within extremist movements serve as justification for hatred and violence against out-groups. For example, the white nationalist Great Replacement theory claims that there is an elitist plot set up to replace native populations with migrants. In recent years, this conspiracy theory has been used as justification for the mass killing of minorities, including the murder of 51 Muslim worshippers in Christchurch, New Zealand, in 2019.

Since the Covid-19 pandemic, far-right movements have been successful at infiltrating conspiratorial communities that attract more moderate support – for example, anti-vaccine and anti-5G conspiracy communities. Because belief in one con-spiracy theory often has a snowballing effect – when you believe in one, you're more likely to believe in others – it means that far-right groups have willing audiences primed to lap up their hate-filled agendas. Discussions have taken place in Irish Covid-19 conspiracy communities about the vaccines being tools to kill off native populations and replace them with migrants – a clear example of how anti-vaccine and Covid-19 conspiracy theories can act as a gateway to more extremist ideologies such as white nationalism.

A matter of trust

What exactly draws people to conspiracy theories in the first place? Professor Jan-Willem van Prooijen, a behavioural scien-tist and expert in the psychology of radicalisation, extremism and conspiracy thinking, explained that feelings of fear and uncertainty are often a trigger. Such feelings cause people to ruminate, to try to find the cause of their negative feelings and make sense of the situation they find themselves in. He says this is likely part of our evolutionary psychology of self-preservation: it's a survival instinct.[8]

These triggers also explain why conspiracy theorising tends to increase following events that elicit fear, such as September 11 and the Covid-19 pandemic. Often very genuine fears and concerns are the root cause of conspiracy theorising. Health concerns and fears over medical interventions, or anxiety over technological developments that may infringe on our privacy, are legitimate feelings that can be easily manipulated by conspiracy theories.

Professor of Social Psychology Karen Douglas told me that people tend to turn to conspiracy theories when certain psychological needs are not being met in their lives. First on this list is the need for knowledge. 'People have a need for knowledge. They want to be certain and know what the truth is,' she said. 'If those needs aren't being satisfied with regular explanations, conspiracy theories might seem appealing.' She noted that this is especially true in times of fear and uncertainty, when people are trying to make sense of events. 'If you're feeling uncertain about something and someone tells you, "Well, this is how it actually happened", this will make you feel a little bit better because you now have that knowledge to explain the uncertainty.'

Conspiracy theories play on people's lack of knowledge on certain subjects. I'm not an expert on engineering, so when I watched *Zeitgeist* and *Loose Change* and heard someone confidently say that jet fuel doesn't melt steel beams, and therefore the collapse of the Twin Towers was pre-planned, I was convinced. This is also true for political conspiracy theories, which may play on people's naivety about the electoral process, for example, while science-related conspiracy theories are particularly good at exploiting the average person's lack of knowledge of how science is conducted.

Professor van Prooijen made the point that feelings of uncertainty cause us to fear the worst, and our perception of other people at this time can impact how we understand a situation or interpret information. He said that a concept called the myth of self-interest plays an important role here, meaning that people 'overestimate the extent to which the behaviour of others is driven by self-interest'. In other words, we sometimes have a tendency to assume that people are driven by selfishness, when in fact they may be driven by a want to care for others.

For example, if you hear that an Irish politician has decided to donate their salary to charity, you may believe that they've done this in order to make themselves look good, instead of being driven by a genuine desire to help people. Our perception of these kinds of situations is also down to our biases: if you happen to like the politician in question, you'll likely believe this was a genuine act. If you dislike the politician, you may believe it was driven by self-interest.

Which brings us to another very important topic: trust. The level of trust – or, more accurately, distrust – people have in institutions is a major driver of conspiratorial beliefs. Every country and region in the world has to deal with the failures and corruption of political leaders, greed of corporate overlords or incompetency from the institutions meant to protect them. That's not to mention real conspiracies that undermine public trust. Often, these incidents are followed by a lack of justice, which cements the idea in people's heads that there is one set of rules for the elite classes and another for regular people. People are left scarred, battered and bruised by these actions, and conspiracy theories feed on these wounds and often find a home among the most disillusioned in society.

This leads into the second unfulfilled need that can lead people to embrace conspiracy theories: the need for people to feel safe and secure in the world and feel autonomy over their decisions. Professor Douglas explained that people are more likely to be drawn to conspiracy theories when they feel powerless, anxious or out of control, which is another reason why conspiracy theories tend to flourish during times of crisis. 'They give people a sense of understanding about why they're out of control,' she said. This is often done by blaming powerful groups, people or institutions in which they may already have high levels of distrust.

I spoke to a number of people whose loved ones lost businesses and livelihoods as a result of the 2008 recession and subsequently fell into Covid-19 conspiracy theories. Their personal losses contributed to a deep-seated distrust in authority figures. During the pandemic, some of those same authority figures were telling people to close their businesses and stay at home, and this didn't sit well. When conspiracy theories were presented to them that claimed the authorities were actually lying about Covid-19 and were instead using the pandemic as an excuse to introduce authoritarianism, it fit in with their past experiences and seemed plausible.

Many people with deep conspiratorial beliefs have lost trust in everything that could be considered mainstream: the media, healthcare, science, universities, fact-checkers. They are told all those sources of information are controlled, or pushing a certain narrative or agenda. Instead, they say they only trust their own intuition. They do their own research.

The third unmet need Professor Douglas described are social needs. People have a desire to feel good about themselves and the groups they belong to. One way people can try to meet this need, she said, is to feel like they have access to secret knowledge that other people don't have. Secret knowledge is a key part of most conspiracy theories. 'When people feel that they know what's going on, they can feel superior to others, which is why many in conspiracy theory movements tend to call other people "sheep",' she explained.

The online world is the perfect tool for attempting to feed this need. Before the internet, conspiracy theorists would have to track down a specific book, or VHS tape, likely not sold in high-street stores. It took effort. Now, conspiracy theories are readily available online, and there are countless communities of like-minded people to join and discuss your new-found secret knowledge with.

Overall, during times of crisis, conspiracy theories tend to give people quite simple answers to complicated situations, which fit in with the way they view the world. In researching this book, I talked to many people who have 'lost' loved ones to conspiracy theories in recent years and I noticed a common theme: trauma. Many of them talked about their loved ones dealing poorly with loss or not properly addressing hardships in their lives, which seemed to leave them vulnerable to the lure of conspiracy theories.

The pandemic was a source of stress and trauma for everyone, to some extent. Faced with a complex situation that involved understanding virus transmission, how the virus affected people differently, how this translated to hospitalisations and pressure on the health service, or the risks of long Covid, many blamed the entire situation on elite groups trying to control their populations. The knowledge feels empowering. It gives people a sense of control and, to many, a purpose: to fight back against the perceived injustices.

What do *you* believe?

Sometimes I sit and think about the fact that I am just one of around eight billion people living on an enormous spinning rock that is, in turn, rotating around an even bigger ball of fire in the middle of the vast expanse of nothing. It's quite terrifying, right? Thinking about something like that too often can make you feel insignificant and powerless.

The world is simultaneously a terrifying and wonderful place. It can be full of pain and suffering, while also being mesmerisingly beautiful. For every person on this planet, it's our first time here, and we're all trying to find our way. In order to navigate life, we often rely on our beliefs. Some people believe the stars can tell the future, or that the lines on our palms can be read to interpret things about our personalities. Others think that saluting when you see a single magpie will stave off sorrow, or that having a certain crystal in your pocket will reduce anxiety. I know plenty of people who, three to four times a year, will blame their woes on Mercury being in retrograde. Millions of people across the globe believe that all our actions are judged by a god and that we will be rewarded in an afterlife if we behave a certain way in this one.

Beliefs, as Professor van Prooijen explained, are 'unproven convictions about the state of reality'. They are different from facts, but beliefs serve a very important purpose by helping us to deal with uncertainty. They can instil in us a sense of calm and hope, which is increasingly important in a high-stress world. In fact, it has been found that religious or spiritual belief can lead people to live longer and healthier lives, because it can reduce the body's stress response and give people a sense of purpose and an optimistic outlook on life.

For the most part, these kinds of beliefs have a positive impact on our lives and don't cause us any harm. I have a crystal sitting on my desk in front of me. Do I think it has magic powers? No, but when I find myself getting stressed, I can convince myself that it's helping to calm me down. Many people will say that's nonsense, but what does it matter if it's not causing me or anyone around me any harm? Plus, it's pretty.

But like many things in life, people can take their beliefs to an extreme. Religious extremists of all faiths have used their belief in gods to justify violence against people for centuries. When belief starts to override common-sense decisions around healthcare, for example, this can also lead to harm. If, God forbid, I get diagnosed with cancer and turn down medical treatment in favour of healing crystals, that would be a harmful decision based on my beliefs.

In many ways, conspiracy theories are regular beliefs where a grain of truth has been distorted and taken to an extreme. For example, many people would agree to some extent with the following statements:

→ The media doesn't always tell the truth.
→ The government doesn't always have your best interests at heart.
→ Pharmaceutical companies sometimes care more about making money than helping people to get better.

We *should* somewhat agree with those statements, since scepticism is healthy. We shouldn't blindly trust every word of the media, or every move the government makes, or every pharmaceutical advertisement. We should be aware that those working in all these entities are human and make mistakes. We should be aware that some news stories can be sensationalised, or that commercial or staffing pressures can lead to a drop in reporting standards, errors of fact or errors of judgement. Some pharmaceutical companies *do* engage in unethical marketing practices to sell more products, and have caused grave harm to people as a result.

We should be aware that some politicians can spin the truth and are sometimes more concerned with doing whatever they can to stay in power, or satisfying corporate interests, than with working in the interests of the citizens they represent. That's not to say that we should accept that this is just the way things are. Those with power, wealth and influence should always be scrutinised, questioned, criticised and held to account for their decisions and mistakes.

To conspiracy theorists, however, there is rarely room for nuance. They often develop a Manichean view of the world – that is, one in which things are simply divided into good and evil. QAnon, a wild conspiracy theory movement, is built on the belief that Democrats and liberals are evil, murderous child abusers who want to control the world, and that Trump and his allies are the saviours. Extremist movements and fascism are also rooted in such 'us versus them' thinking.

In the case mentioned above, a dedicated conspiracist will believe that the media is always actively lying to them, that the government is working to destroy their life and that Big Pharma only wants to make people sick. This means that politicians, journalists and those working with pharmaceutical companies aren't just incompetent or immoral – they are demonstrably evil. Scepticism has been replaced by deep cynicism.

Michael Barkun outlines what he sees as the three principles found in almost every conspiracy theory:[9]

1. *Nothing happens by accident:* Conspiracy implies a world based on intentionality, from which accident and coincidence have been removed. Anything that happens occurs because it has been willed.

Within QAnon, for example, there is a common refrain of 'nothing is a coincidence', and followers of QAnon are encouraged to look for intentionality in seemingly random and unconnected events. In one case of many, QAnon followers were directed to look into the death of Loretta Fuddy, a Hawaiian health director who died in a plane crash in 2013. The implication was that the crash was not an accident, and QAnon followers were told to figure out what had *really* happened.

2. *Nothing is as it seems:* Appearances are deceptive, because conspirators wish to deceive in order to disguise their identities or their activities. Thus, the appearance of innocence is deemed to be no guarantee that an individual or group is benign.

In Ireland, when the decision was made in January 2022 to lift the majority of Covid-19 restrictions, conspiracy communities lit up with their thoughts on why this was. The reality was because the population was highly vaccinated and case numbers were not translating to increasing hospitalisations. The following conversation took place in an online conspiracy theory community that day:

> *Gerry: It's over, we've won.*
>
> *Harry: I'm more frightened of this. We haven't [won] anything.*
>
> *Mark: We won nothing, we lost more …families divided, children mentally and physically abused by those trusted to protect them … elderly relatives left to die in homes to protect the narrative … I feel relieved myself, but we have to keep up the pressure more than ever now.*
>
> *Lesley: Yes, but let's take our time to take this in, and enjoy the relief for now, regroup and keep going with the fight.*
>
> *Mark: Absolutely, but as [has] been said in the voice chat, this was a dry run for something bigger.*
>
> *Doc: This is far from over, Gerry. They're dangling another freedom carrot. Worst is yet to come.*
>
> *Anna: My thought as well, too easy. They will not give up. What happens when the[y] switch on the cuig g [5G].*

In the above case, there is little agreement on what is happening, but a common understanding that what they're being told isn't the entire truth and that something else is planned. There is often a general consensus that world events are false flags that are coordinated in order to distract people from something bigger going on.

> **3. *Everything is connected:*** Because the conspiracists' world has no room for accidents, pattern is believed to be every-where, albeit hidden from plain view. Hence the conspiracy theorist must engage in a constant process of linkage and correlation in order to map the hidden connections.

People who were engrossed in Covid-19 conspiracy theory communities were told beyond doubt by the figureheads in the movement that the vaccines were dangerous, so when the roll-out began in 2021, they began looking for proof of this, and they found it everywhere. Any vaccinated person who died for any reason was suspected of being a vaccine-related death. One person in an Irish group chat on the online messaging platform Telegram said they were noticing more car accidents since the roll-out of the Covid-19 vaccines. 'Anyone else joining these dots?' they asked.

Celebrity deaths, such as that of Prince Philip and actress Betty White, were attributed to the vaccine, despite both of them being 99 years old and old age being a much more likely cause of death. The sudden deaths of a number of young teens in Ireland were blamed on the vaccine by the Covid-19 con-spiracy communities. These communities used the names and images of these teens, without permission, to promote protests, and their heartbroken families were harassed by those involved in the movement and accused of covering up the truth about their deaths.

These three principles – that nothing happens by accident, nothing is as it seems and everything is connected – come together to form the conspiratorial mindset. The self-sustaining nature of this mindset and the fact that, frequently, blame is attributed to the same small group of people or institutions – Bill Gates, the media, the government – means that when someone buys into one conspiracy theory, they're likely to buy into more.

There are a number of inherent cognitive functions that we share which make us all susceptible to the lure of conspiracy theories. One of these is pattern perception, or our tendency to see meaningful connections between things. Pattern perception is absolutely essential to our survival. As Professor van Prooijen explained, 'the capacity of the human mind to automatically look for and find patterns is highly functional, as it enables them – among other things – to predict the consequences of their actions.' Pattern perception in our everyday life is often unconscious. You hear a song on the radio that you like and you start singing along, because your brain detects the pattern. If you're walking along a quiet country road and hear a car coming in the distance, your brain tells you to be alert.

But this ability of our brain to perceive patterns can also misfire, in a process called illusory pattern perception. In these cases, we infer connections between things that are, in fact, random. An example of this is how our brain sees shapes in clouds, or the face of the man in the moon. In 2004, a Florida woman cashed in on this when she sold a burnt cheese toastie on eBay that seemed to be emblazoned with the face of the Virgin Mary, scooping $28,000. Illusory pattern perception is also common in gambling. For example, you may believe that you have better odds of landing a heads in a coin toss if you've just flipped three tails. 'The next one *has* to be heads.' In reality, the odds are always 50/50, and the sequence you believe you are seeing is random.

Professor van Prooijen gave another example of detecting patterns in randomness: ascribing coincidences to mysterious forces. If an old friend pops into your head and later on that day they happen to call you, you'll likely think, 'That can't be a coincidence?' As Professor van Prooijen pointed out, you don't think about all the times you thought of an old friend and they *didn't* call you.

Illusory pattern perception plays a central role in a belief in conspiracy theories, a key part of which involves making connections between coincidences. Conspiracy theory documentaries such as *Zeitgeist* and *Loose Change* feed our brain's love of patterns. They bombard the viewer with information – some of it true, some of it speculative, some of it based on poorly constructed 'evidence', some of it coincidental. The viewer barely has a chance to process one claim before another is thrown at them. When all the poorly sourced information is pointing in one direction, your brain's pattern perception takes over, and you start to think that their theory has truth in it, even though there is little actual evidence for it.

Illusory pattern perception is absolutely central to certain parts of modern conspiracy movements such as Pizzagate and QAnon. The central premise of the Pizzagate conspiracy theory involved interpreting sinister meanings from innocuous mentions of pizza and other foods in the leaked emails of John

Podesta, Hillary Clinton's campaign manager. Similarly, QAnon followers are told to look for symbols used by elites and celebrities that seemingly prove they are involved with the Illuminati.

Another example is seen in the old adage that correlation does not equal causation. In other words, just because the prevalence of two things rise or fall at the same time does not mean that they are connected, or that one is causing the other. For example, a student at Harvard found a perfect correlation between the number of films Nicolas Cage has appeared in each year and the number of people who have drowned in swimming pools, but we don't blame Nicolas Cage for those deaths.

The anti-vaccine movement will point to the fact that autism diagnoses have increased with rising numbers of childhood vaccinations since the early 1990s. The scientific consensus is clear that vaccines don't cause autism,[10] but this claim is one that just won't die. What the anti-vaccine movement often avoids mentioning is that, before the early 1990s, autism was not well understood. For decades, in fact, it was thought to be caused by bad parenting. As more research went into the condition, it became easier to recognise. Researchers of autism have acknowledged that, as greater research and resources were devoted to learning about the condition, the number of diagnoses of autism would increase over time too.

Vaccine/autism claims are further confounded by the fact that the signs of autism often become prominent at the same age children get some vaccinations. When parents notice changes in their child's behaviour after getting a vaccine, the vaccine seems like the perfect culprit. But even before vaccines were blamed for autism, parents would still search for reasons for their child's changed behaviour. A doctor who worked with autistic children for years pointed out that they would blame things like a recent fall, an accident or even removed tonsils as the cause of the change. It's hard to fathom the heartbreak that comes with seeing your child regressing in their development. There is an understandable reflex to find something to pin it on, and pattern perception is the perfect vehicle for this.

Just as our pattern perception can be distorted to make us see connections where they don't exist, so too can another cognitive function known as agency detection. Agency detection refers to the way our brain finds intentionality in the actions of others and, like pattern perception, it is a key part of our day-to-day life. Professor van Prooijen described how agency detection is part of a broader mental capacity called 'theory of mind', which allows us to figure out what other people are thinking or feeling. This, he explained, is why we know it's wrong to laugh at a funeral. 'Thanks to theory of mind, people develop a good sense of when to speak up, when to shut their mouth, when to apologise, when to turn the volume of their music a bit lower and so on.'

When humans were still hunter-gatherers, agency detection was key to our survival. If we heard a rustle in a bush and dismissed it by mistakenly attributing it to the wind when in fact it was a predatory animal, it could cost us our lives. This means that in today's world, our agency detection can be overly sensitive and, like illusory pattern perception, it can mistakenly attribute agency, known as illusory agency detection.

Examples of how illusory agency detection contributes to some gentle irrationalities in everyday life include anytime you've placed blame for an action on an inanimate object. Stub your toe and blame the door? Curse at your car for not starting? Neither the door nor the car are alive or have the ability to decide to hurt you or ruin your morning, yet a distortion in our agency detection causes us to momentarily blame them.

In conspiracy theories, illusory agency detection is everywhere. Every time a conspiracy theorist blames an innocent person or entity for doing something that they haven't done (which is often), they are seeing agency where it doesn't exist. Anti-5G activists regularly blame 5G technology or other forms of wireless communication for headaches and other ailments, despite evidence that this is not the case. The 2013 plane crash mentioned earlier, which killed Hawaiian health director Loretta Fuddy, is an example of this too. Conspiracy theorists point to the fact that Fuddy was the only person to die in the crash, and that she was involved in the release of Barack Obama's birth certificate during the 'birther' controversy, a conspiracy theory bolstered by Donald Trump during Obama's 2008 presidential campaign that claimed the president-to-be wasn't born in the US.

This was catnip to conspiracy theorists, who immediately claimed that Fuddy had been assassinated because she knew too much. In reality, the plane's engine malfunctioned, and the pilot made an emergency landing in the water. An investigation found that 65-year-old Fuddy was wearing a faulty life jacket meant for a child when she entered the water, was seen to be hyperventilating by other passengers and died of heart failure. This evidence was dismissed by conspiracy theorists, who instead placed the blame on someone in Obama's administration – a clear example of illusory agency detection.

This is another example of the self-sealing ability of conspiracy theories. When Loretta Fuddy released Obama's birth certificate, showing unequivocally that he had been born in the United States, in an ideal world, this should have satisfied the people alleging some sort of conspiracy. Instead, they claimed the birth certificate was fake and that Loretta Fuddy was in on the secret. *Nothing is as it seems*, remember?

The other feature this story highlights is called proportionality bias, or the assumption that big events must have big causes. When something big happens to important people, we tend to assume that it must have been caused by something big. Loretta Fuddy had an important job, and her job was made all the more prominent (especially among conspiracy theorists) after her approval of Obama's birth certificate. A conspiracy theorist will think, 'What are the odds that Loretta Fuddy died in a plane crash? There must be more to the story.' But take into account the fact that Fuddy lived and worked in Hawaii, a state made up of islands with well-established daily flight routes between them. Fuddy was travelling on a routine taxi commuter flight from the island of Molokai to Honolulu the day she died, a flight that officials in Hawaii likely take quite often. Therefore, the odds of her dying in a plane crash were likely higher than a regular person who flies on average a few times a year.

Professor van Prooijen gave another great example of proportionality bias. Take, for example, that the president of a large country dies of the flu. Because the president is human, and therefore as fragile and susceptible to the flu as anyone is, it is within the odds of reason that the flu could be the thing to kill them. But to many people, something so normal killing someone so powerful will lead to suspicions that *something else* happened. Sometimes, big events just have small, regular causes.

False pattern and agency detection are also prevalent in religious, spiritual and supernatural beliefs. A common belief across major religions is that events on earth happen as a result of interventions from a god, therefore believers in religion are more inclined to see events as being by design – that is, part of a pattern. This is such a prevalent belief that we refer to natural disasters as 'acts of God'. If you are religious and say a prayer for your loved one to return home safely, you will connect their safe return to the prayer (pattern) and thank God for answering it (agency).

Although there is a cognitive explanation for religious belief, it does not mean that religious belief is all nonsense. Most religious belief at its core is about treating people with kindness. As Justin L. Barrett, a psychologist and an observant Christian who has spent considerable time looking into the cognitive science of religion, told *The New York Times* in 2007, 'Suppose science produces a convincing account for why I think my wife loves me – should I then stop believing that she does?'

Studies have shown that correlation between general religious belief and conspiracy belief is not huge, yet also not insignificant. According to Professor Karen Douglas, although the data does suggest that religious believers are more likely to believe in conspiracy theories, the correlation is fairly weak.[11] 'These sorts of beliefs do go together, but not in as strong a way as you might think,' she told me.

There is some evidence that more devout religious belief is correlated with conspiratorial belief. For example, a study from

2021 conducted among Polish Roman Catholics found that those with more fundamentalist religious beliefs were more inclined to believe conspiracy theories about Covid-19. This in turn, led to what the researchers termed 'maladaptive behaviour', such as ignoring public health guidelines. In the US, a YouGov poll conducted by *The Economist* in 2021 gave similar results, showing that belief in QAnon and other conspiracy theories was highest among devout white evangelicals.

This tracks with what I see within conspiracy communities that have a religious bent. The belief within Christianity that struggles in life are against the dark, spiritual forces of evil translates well into the conspiratorial belief of evil forces secretly controlling the world. QAnon, for example, has an entire strand that is themed around evangelicalism, complete with a number of preacher-like influencers dedicated to spreading the word of QAnon in a style akin to spreading the word of God. As a result, QAnon has 'infected' and torn apart evangelical communities, especially across the US. Pastor Ben Marsh spoke to *CNN* about the impact of QAnon on the evangelical community, saying that pastors across the country were 'driven to their knees in prayer … because they didn't know what to do' about the hold the cult-like movement had on their congregations. QAnon promises the Storm, an apocalyptic event when the truth will be revealed about the evil Democrats, followed by a time of transformation and glory. This reflects the main themes around the Rapture, or the End Times, which is a prominent feature of many branches of Christianity, but especially evangelicalism.

The evolution of a religious strand of the New World Order conspiracy theory also has roots in these kinds of evangelical beliefs. Some devout Christians have claimed that the End Times would bring in the rule of the New World Order, which will be led by the Antichrist. They also claim that the Mark of the Beast will indicate people's allegiance to Satan. During the Covid-19 pandemic, claims of the vaccine being the Mark of the Beast became widespread within conspiratorial communities, often spread by evangelical Christian conspiracy believers. In Ireland, the Christian radio station LifeFM regularly featured some of the country's best-known anti-vaccine and Covid-19 conspiracy theorists, who were allowed to tout their bizarre and false claims about the pandemic unchallenged on air. The station was founded by Anna Daly who is a member of Aontú, a socially conservative political party with a strong anti-abortion stance. Daly herself told her listeners that there was a sinister plot at play to embed people with 'implantable chips'.

This brings up another interesting concept: the world of prophecies, or more accurately, failed prophecies. According to various groups, the New World Order has been on the verge of taking over the world for decades. QAnon is full of prophecies that have failed to come to fruition, yet people still follow it. The reason for this is tied to a theory known as cognitive dissonance, which was first explored in the classic 1956 social psychology book *When Prophecy Fails* by Leon Festinger, Henry Riecken and Stanley Schachter.

They studied a group called the Seekers, led by housewife Dorothy Martin, who claimed to be receiving messages from an alien population on a planet called Clarion. The aliens told her that most of North America was going to be destroyed in a great flood on 21 December 1955, and that she and the Seekers would be saved the night before the flood by a spacecraft. Martin and her small group of believers gathered on the night of 20/21 December waiting for the spacecraft to arrive. Needless to say, it didn't come. The group were distraught, believing that they would be wiped out the following day in the flood. Hours later, Martin claimed to receive further messages from the aliens telling her that the Seekers' belief had caused them to call off the apocalyptic event.[12]

Although several people left the group after this revelation, many of the hard-core Seekers – those who had left jobs and relationships and given away their money and possessions as a result of their commitment to the prophecy – doubled down on their beliefs and began proselytising. This, Festinger et al reasoned, was a result of cognitive dissonance, or the theory that holding inconsistent beliefs at the same time can cause major discomfort, so people find ways to rationalise them in order to maintain the consistency of their belief system. Simply put, we don't like making mistakes or being wrong, so we'll try to convince ourselves that we were, in fact, right. A classic example is seen in a smoker who knows smoking is bad for their health but rationalises this by saying, 'Smoking helps me to relax.' Conspiracy theorists, and especially those who have dedicated themselves to their beliefs, experience cognitive dissonance quite a lot, which is why evidence disproving conspiracy theories often doesn't work. They will simply find a way to rationalise this by making it part of the conspiracy theory so that their beliefs remain intact.

Speaking of aliens, there is also a well-established link between New Age beliefs and conspiracy theories. New Age beliefs can include everything from wellness practices like meditation and yoga, to spiritual healing, psychics and even belief in the supernatural and UFOs. New Age beliefs are concerned with physical and mental healing, self-improvement and spiritual enlightenment. Because they are so wide-ranging and focused on self-improvement, each person's interest in the New Age tends to be personal to them. As Matthew Remski, host of the podcast *Conspirituality* and a cult survivor, told me, 'New Age practices cannot be pinned down to any single doctrine. It is very subjective and self-authorised. You'll find shared practices between people and communities, but those practices can always be individualised.'

Some New Age movements are very good at tricking our cognitive processes. Take horoscopes, for example. People who follow horoscopes will seek to find personal meaning in their predictions, which always tend to be general, vague and open-ended, so they can be easily applied to just about anyone. To test this, look up a horoscope that isn't yours and tell me if you can relate to it. This tendency to relate to generalised depictions of our personalities is known as the Barnum effect, named after the showman and circus owner P.T. Barnum (who is the basis for the film *The Greatest Showman*).

Barnum statements, as they are known, are also used by people reading tarot cards, as well as in astrology. Here are a few examples of Barnum statements:

→ You have a great need for other people to like and admire you.
→ At times, you have serious doubts as to whether you have made the right decision or done the right thing.

→ At times, you are extroverted, affable, sociable, while at other times you are introverted, wary, reserved.

They feel relatable, right?

The link between New Age beliefs and conspiracy theories is one that has come into sharp focus in recent years, to the point that a term was coined to describe it: conspirituality. Conspirituality is exactly what it sounds like: New Age movements based around concepts of spirituality and wellness that have mixed with belief in (mostly right-wing) conspiracy theories. It is not a new concept: a number of leading Nazis were obsessed with yoga, alternative medicine and astrology, and they often spoke about engaging in a cosmic battle against the forces of evil – that is, the Jews. But it has been given more attention since the Covid-19 pandemic, when online communities dedicated to alternative health practices, yoga and spiritual growth became overwhelmed with conspiratorial content. People sought to figure out why these movements, which would commonly be thought of as antithetical, were suddenly converging.

The term conspirituality was coined by two researchers – Charlotte Ward and David Voas – in a 2011 paper[13] in which they accurately describe it as 'a means by which political cynicism is tempered with spiritual optimism'. Ward and Voas pointed to the emergence of British conspiracy theorist David Icke as an adopter of conspirituality in the late 1990s. Icke famously declared that he had a spiritual awakening to the fact that, in his eyes, the world is run by a shadow government made of shapeshifting reptilians. Ward and Voas also pointed to *Zeitgeist*, the film I watched in my late teens, which spoke about the need for a spiritual awakening from our established power systems.

Ward and Voas used Michael Barkun's three principles of conspiratorial thinking (nothing happens by accident, nothing is as it seems, everything is connected) to show how these overlap with New Age beliefs that see events on earth as being controlled by some higher power, or energy. As Matthew Remski explained, 'There is a very strong notion of some higher truth emanating from somewhere that one can be in touch with at any given time.' Remski also said that there is a very strong belief in the idea that everything is connected, as well as an emphasis on the power of intentionality and the idea that your thoughts can impact, change and shape reality. Many spirituality movements are also deeply sceptical about established institutions, so it is understandable that these concepts could align with conspiratorial thinking, which also promotes a blanket distrust of institutions.

Wellness and alternative health treatments, often used in conjunction with spiritual practices, have frequently been susceptible to pseudoscience due to their sceptical outlook on Western medicine. Gwyneth Paltrow's Goop, for example, has been regularly criticised for using women's genuine disillusionment with modern medicine to sell a range of overpriced products that have often been described as 'snake oil'. In 2018 the company had to pay a $145,000 fine for claiming that inserting jade eggs into the vagina could help with depression, regulate menstrual cycles and prevent uterine prolapse. In the same year, Goop was reported to the UK advertising regulator for breaching more than 113 advertising laws by promoting false and often harmful claims about the products they were selling, including a 'natal protocol' for pregnant women that contained such a high amount of vitamin A that it could potentially harm an unborn baby.

Some alternative health and wellness movements promote an extreme form of clean living, and urge people to choose natural therapies as opposed to conventional medicine. This is part of a wider phenomenon that is often called the 'appeal to nature', or the idea that everything that is natural must be good for you, and everything that is unnatural, or synthetic, must therefore be bad. It's an appealing aesthetic, and one that has become quite engrained in many populations, especially as we have learned more about what it takes to be healthy. However, in practice, it makes little sense.

As Dr David Robert Grimes pointed out to me, 'arsenic, Ebola and uranium are all natural, but you don't put them on your breakfast cereal.' The rejection of modern medicine within these movements has often been accompanied with conspiratorial-like claims that real cures and therapies are being hidden by pharmaceutical companies or health institutions. For this reason, the anti-vaccine movement was enmeshed with the wellness world for a number of years and took easily to bogus Covid-19 cures and wilder claims about the entire pandemic being a hoax.

It's hard not to overemphasise the harm that these movements can cause if they persuade people to reject life-saving medical treatment. One study with more than one million participants found that people with curable cancer who used alternative medical treatments (including herbs, vitamins, homeopathy, naturopathy and specialised diets) were twice as likely to die than those who didn't use alternative treatments.[14]

The treatment offered by a Mayo-based homeopathic practitioner was responsible for at least two deaths in the early 2000s. In 2001, Mineke Kamper convinced 55-year-old Jacqueline Alderslade to give up the steroid drugs she was on for asthma. Mrs Alderslade died of an asthma attack 10 days after first seeing Kamper. Just over a year later, Kamper was linked to the death of 49-year-old Paul Howie, who died of an untreated cancerous tumour in his throat. Howie had been persuaded by Kamper to avoid conventional medicine and hospital in favour of homeopathy. The allure of living an all-natural life can be appealing, especially when coupled with a distrust in modern medicine, but the results can be devastating.

The overlap in alternative health and conspiracy theories was seen clearly during the pandemic with the release of *Plandemic*, a slickly produced conspiracy theory film released in May 2020. The film, mostly based on the testimony of one discredited doctor, claimed that the pandemic was planned, that death rates were being manipulated on purpose, that cures were being suppressed and that the vaccines (which had yet to be developed) would be dangerous.

The film was viewed over eight million times in one week. One of the earliest promoters of the film was alternative health doctor Dr Christiane Northrup, who shared the film with her over half a million followers on Facebook on its release. From there, the film spread across the world of wellness gurus and alternative health influencers and beyond, poisoning the minds of countless people who watched it and believed it.

That's not to say that anyone with an interest in spirituality, wellness or alternative health movements is causing themselves or others undue harm. There are many aspects of these movements that can contribute to increased health, comfort, resilience and quality of life. But it is more than clear that these beliefs can also be taken to extremes. Like everything, there is a fine balance to strike.

One pill makes you larger

'Fuck both of you.' That was the response of Lilly Wachowski, director of the 1999 science fiction classic *The Matrix*, to a 2020 exchange between Elon Musk and Ivanka Trump on Twitter, where they enthusiastically discussed taking the 'red pill'. In the 21 years since the release of the film, the red pill reference has become seared into modern culture. In *The Matrix*, Morpheus holds out his hands and gives Neo a choice between taking a blue pill or a red pill. Morpheus says, 'You take the blue pill, the story ends, you wake up in your bed and believe whatever you want to believe. You take the red pill, you stay in Wonderland, and I show you how deep the rabbit hole goes.' The term 'red pill' has since been co-opted by various movements to describe a paradigm shift in someone's vision of reality, or an 'awakening' to some previously hidden or uncomfortable truth. In *The Matrix*, Neo takes the red pill and discovers that he had actually been living in a computer-generated simulation.

This concept of red-pilling, or awakening, is central to modern online conspiratorial and extremist movements. Red-pilling is based on belief, not fact, and it thrives on those who are disillusioned with life, giving them a way to project their dissatisfaction. Anti-feminists, men's rights activists (MRAs) and pick-up artists (collectively known as the manosphere) were among the first online subcultures to popularise the term, which is used to describe waking up to the notion that feminism and liberalism are toxic and that men are the ones who are actually oppressed in life. Red-pilled anti-feminists and MRAs believe in sweeping conspiratorial-tinged stereotypes, such as the belief that all women are cheaters and that society is against men, so they develop toxic strategies to fight back against this.

The manosphere went on to fuse with online trolls, white nationalists, neo-Nazis and fascists to form the alt-right, which also utilised the red-pilling metaphor. Robert Evans wrote about the alt-right's red-pilling for *Bellingcat* in 2018. According to Evans, the seeds of the alt-right were sown by the red-pilling of men into anti-feminism, and from there it grew to encompass other extremisms, including Islamophobia and white nationalism. Donald Trump is often credited with people's awakening to the alt-right. The ultimate red pill in alt-right or far-right movements is buying into anti-Semitism: the belief that Jews control the world and are therefore the root of all our problems. For many, this also means denying that the Holocaust happened and believing that 'Hitler did nothing wrong'.

From the alt-right, the red pill metaphor became baked into the wider conspiratorial world, especially through movements like QAnon, which evolved out of the same online spaces as the alt-right. By the time 2020 came around and the pandemic struck, QAnon had meshed with the wider anti-vaccine and conspirituality movements, and red-pilling had become a term used to signify a realisation that the mainstream – be that the media, the government, science or healthcare – were all constantly lying. Red-pillers had been awoken to a new version of reality, where nothing was as it seemed.

The term 'Great Awakening', which became a rallying cry within QAnon, has also been used to describe a number of Christian revivals in the past. Matthew Remski explained how this concept of awakening is attractive to New Age spiritualists, who believe that humanity is undergoing a paradigm shift in consciousness and are often searching for a way to transcend to a higher level of knowledge and understanding. In a blog post, Remski describes how it is often seen as paradoxical: 'The conversion experience was overwhelming, it almost killed them with disillusionment and despair. But now they were on the other side, and the world would never be the same. They had been dreaming, and now they were awake.' This ties in with Ward and Voas's description of conspirituality as political cynicism mixed with spiritual optimism.

The red pill simultaneously closes people's minds to facts agreed upon by the vast majority of the public and opens them to any other explanation for how the world works. Often, in many conspiratorial communities, there is little agreement about the specifics of what is actually going on. What they've bonded over is their rejection of the mainstream and their embrace of the conspiratorial mindset. One study that highlights how contradictory the conspiracists' world view can be showed that the more that participants believed that Princess Diana had faked her own death, the more they believed that she had been murdered[15].

This acceptance of conspiracy as an explanation for any kind of event means that red-pilled people are easily led further into extremist movements. This is plain to see when neo-Nazi propaganda documentaries are shared and accepted as the 'ultimate red pills' with QAnon, anti-lockdown and anti-vaccine communities. These films rewrite history, and present Hitler as the saviour who was trying to rescue the world from the scourge of the Jews – the pinnacle of neo-Nazi red-pilling.

There's really no way to sugar-coat it: 'taking the red pill' is a euphemism for becoming radicalised. Just how radicalised depends on the person, but having such a profound shift in your sense of reality can have undue consequences both for the red-pilled person and the people around them. Lilly Wachowski's 'Fuck both of you' response to the then-president's daughter and a tech billionaire's willingness to flirt with these elements is pretty spot on, in my opinion.

What's the frequency?

Shaun had a rough start to 2020. Just before the pandemic shut the world down, one of his lifelong friends died tragically, and Shaun didn't cope well. I talked to Jen, his best friend. They've known each other for over 14 years. 'He's a really popular, affable guy. He wears his heart on his sleeve, and everybody loves him, but he does not manage his feelings. He is very good at compartmentalising and has a tendency to turn to alcohol,' she told me.

Just weeks after the death of his friend, Shaun was plunged into the solitary life that came with the lockdowns. He lives on his own in a one-bedroom flat in Cork, which Jen described as being akin to a prison cell. He has a customer-facing job, so when the lockdown struck he had no work and nothing but himself and the four walls of his tiny flat for company. Because of the lockdown and everything that went along with it, Jen didn't see Shaun for over six months, but they kept in touch over text.

'He started talking about 5G and Wi-Fi and how they were harmful, and he was sending me videos of people measuring the radiation off these telegraph poles in Dublin.' At the beginning of the pandemic, fears around 5G hit an all-time high, with many claims based on the fact that Wuhan had installed 5G towers before the outbreak began (*everything is connected*). Although 5G had also been rolled out in many other places, conspiracy theorists seized on this and ran with it. Across the world, mobile phone towers were damaged and set alight because of fears that 5G was somehow causing or spreading Covid-19. It's difficult to explain how impossible that is. It's like trying to explain why jumping on a trampoline might cause it to start raining. There is simply no connection between the two.

The core belief of the anti-5G movement is based on a misunderstanding of what constitutes harmful radiation. Harmful radiation is known as ionising radiation and unharmful is non-ionising. Just like 4G and 3G, 5G operates on frequencies that are well inside the safe zone for non-ionising radiation.

The videos Shaun was sending to Jen are a common feature in the anti-5G movement and usually show someone measuring levels of non-ionising radiation beside phone masts to claim the levels are dangerous. Thankfully, Jen was aware of the science behind this and tried to explain it to him calmly.

She didn't call him dumb or stupid. She would simply ask him questions to try to get him to reason himself out of it. 'He was very aggressive about it and very defensive of his opinion,' she said. 'Eventually he would come around and tell me he was glad I said it because he realised he was being ridiculous.'

But it soon became clear that her calm explanations weren't working. During the first lockdown, Shaun got rid of his television, his Wi-Fi router, his microwave and his Xbox for fear they were causing him some kind of harm, leaving only his smartphone for entertainment and company.

Shaun's beliefs started to get more extreme, and he was texting Jen an endless stream of contradictory messages, ranting about what he thought was going on: one day 5G was causing Covid-19, the next the virus was fake, and another day it was made in a lab. 'I wanted to listen to him and support him. He had no one else to talk to, and I thought I could just let him rant and get it out of his system.' Jen's approach was caring and considerate, but his anger took her aback. 'I couldn't understand why he was so angry at me. He just kept telling me that I couldn't see what was going on.'

When the vaccine roll-out began, Shaun was adamant he wasn't getting it. 'He believed the vaccines were poison and that they were going to do something really bad to his body.' Every conversation became about Covid and the vaccines. He was obsessed, and it was impossible to reason with him as he was constantly repeating the same points. His drinking had also increased. As much as she wanted to support him, Jen had to draw a line in the sand: no more conversations about Covid-19, vaccines or 5G.

But things kept escalating. Shaun's elderly parents had to give him an ultimatum: he couldn't come to see them unless he got the vaccine. Shaun's mother was immunocompromised, and they couldn't take the chance because Shaun was back at work and seeing customers every day. Jen says this hit him hard. 'He's a Mammy's boy. They speak every day, and for a few weeks they kind of cut contact.'

Shaun gave in and got the vaccine. 'He had worked himself up so much about getting it that the day after he had a severe anxiety attack. He genuinely believed something really bad had gone into his body.' In the days and weeks after the vaccine, he became paranoid that any mark, bruise or rash on his body was a side effect. 'For a couple of months, he was very down about the fact that he got the vaccine and blamed his parents for making him do it.'

Jen said she knew something was shifting in him before Christmas: 'Something started to really push him over the edge. He was losing his grip on reality.' Shaun had become obsessed with spirituality, crystals and energies, and he was convinced he had healing powers. During one conversation, he told her that he could see the buildings vibrating as he walked down the street and that he was receiving messages through movies that told him something big was about to happen. 'It really upset me to see him like that. I genuinely thought he was starting to lose his mind.'

Shaun's spiritual obsessions started to affect his work, and he was becoming inappropriate in front of customers. In January

2022, Shaun's boss asked him to take some time off, which he was insulted by. Jen thought she could convince him to get professional help, but he said no, he didn't think there was anything wrong with him. His drinking got worse again.

At this point, Jen had to step back. She felt she had tried everything. 'I couldn't keep feeding into it and saving him when he didn't want the help.' It was taking a huge mental and emotional toll on her.

When I spoke to Jen, she hadn't talked to Shaun in almost a month and said she barely recognises her best friend. 'He was the cheeriest, happiest, funniest guy you'll ever meet. He's like a magnet to people, but he's not the same person I knew before,' she said. 'He's angry. He's defensive. He's isolated himself. He doesn't have the same zest for life that he once did. He's a dark soul now, and I never thought I'd say that about him.'

'I love him so much. He's my best friend. He's not a bad person, but he's very sick at the moment.'

It's only natural

Lydia Greene grew up in Edmonton, the capital city of Alberta, Canada, before moving to a small mountain town with her husband to raise their three kids. It's quiet and isolated, she said, but she loves it and has embraced everything the outdoors has to offer: gardening, hiking, camping – you name it. When I spoke to her in February 2022, her youngest son periodically ran past in the background and popped in front of the camera to give his mum a hug and kiss. He was adorable. Lydia told me that she was training to become a nurse practitioner. 'I want to provide primary care for my community because our town has a hard time keeping doctors,' she said. She was friendly, caring and dedicated to doing the right thing, for both her family and her community.

But for around 12 years, Lydia's dedicated and hardworking nature had been directed elsewhere. In 2008 she had her first child, a daughter. Like all first-time mothers, she wanted to do everything perfectly. When she had a hard time breastfeeding, she joined a natural parenting forum online for advice. They had discussion topics for everything from organic cloth diapers and attachment parenting, to tips on how to make all your baby food from scratch. When her daughter was eight weeks old, Lydia took her to get her first vaccine. She knew there were people on the forum who were against vaccination, but she didn't really pay much attention to that. She got the flu vaccine when pregnant, and although she was nervous about her child's first vaccine (like any parent), she knew it had to be done.

After the vaccine, her daughter started crying. 'She had this really nasty crying spell afterwards, where she was just screaming and screaming, then sleeping, then screaming. It was a really rough couple of days.' Lydia called the nurse, who dismissed her concerns as those of a first-time mom being overly worried. 'I felt blown off and quite embarrassed,' she said. 'It just didn't sit right with me.'

So, she turned to the internet and to her natural parenting group, who convinced her that her daughter had a reaction to the vaccine, called the DTP cry. 'They told me that my daughter's brain was probably inflamed, and that was why she was screaming.' At that point, she said she felt scared. 'I had found a reason for why she was crying so much, and I had also found a way to make sure it never happened again.'

At this point, Lydia's beliefs could be described as vaccine hesitant. It's important to differentiate between those who are hesitant about vaccines and those who are anti-vaccine. Hesitancy is understandable and can come from myriad reasonable fears that people have about vaccines, from side effects to a fear of needles. If a vaccine-hesitant person finds the right person to assuage their worries, they can be convinced to proceed with vaccination. If they come across the wrong information, the kind that Lydia was reading, this can easily descend into anti-vaccine beliefs.

Lydia said she reluctantly took her daughter for two more vaccines, but after that she stopped. 'After being exposed to too many anti-vax things, I just stopped vaccinating. I couldn't bring myself to do it.' Lydia had gone from vaccine hesitancy to being a full anti-vaxxer, and she refused to give her daughter, or her two younger children, any more vaccinations.

Lydia distinguished between being vaccine hesitant and being anti-vaccine by the belief in conspiracy theories: 'When you're using conspiracy theories to justify your position, I think that's a lot harder to overcome.' She explained how, when you're in the conspiratorial mindset, it is easy to explain away any evidence that disproves your position. She gave the example of a famous Danish study that analysed data from every child born in Denmark between 1999 and 2010, a total of over 650,000 children, to assess whether the MMR (measles, mumps and rubella) vaccine was linked to autism. The results were unequivocal: the vaccine was safe. There was no increase in developmental disorders among the vaccinated compared to the unvaccinated. 'I explained that,' she said, 'by deciding that it was "corporate science", that it had been bought and paid for.'

Lydia's belief in these conspiracy theories is even more remarkable when you know that she once worked as a quality-control chemist for a pharmaceutical manufacturing plant. She explained how stringent the pharmaceutical process was and how every product was tested for safety and quality. As she aptly put it, 'You couldn't fart in the lab without documenting it.' I asked her how she reasoned the knowledge she gained from working in pharmaceuticals with her new-found belief in science-related conspiracy theories. Lydia's belief in conspiracies ran so deep that she convinced herself that even she had been a part of it: 'I told myself that I was part of the system and that I was a cog in the machine working for an evil company.'

Lydia suffers from a severe form of Crohn's disease, an auto-immune condition. The things she was reading online at the time had convinced her that autoimmune conditions were brought on by vaccines. And not just autoimmune conditions – also autism, allergies, asthma, diabetes. 'I thought, "I want to protect them [her children] from that",' she said. 'It plays on your fears as a parent because they tell you that everything is a vaccine's fault.'

Lydia said she started questioning everything about evidence-based medicine, convinced that *that* was what was making children sick and leaned further into natural parenting and alternative medicines. It wasn't easy, but it wasn't meant to be. Lydia explained how the entire natural parenting movement is sold as 'doing it the hard way'. Lydia is a hard worker, so this resonated with her. 'Nobody ever said "You took the easy way" as a compliment.'

She didn't want to be seen as a 'lazy parent' for feeding her kids commercially bought baby food, and she didn't want to give in to the ease of vaccination. 'Skipping vaccination is hard, but you are reassured that if your kid is breastfed, eats healthily and has a strong enough immune system, then you have nothing to worry about.'

Lydia explained how there is an emphasis put on individualised knowledge within these movements. When you buy into the conspiracy theories and the idea that conventional medicine is actually harmful, you no longer trust the system or anyone in it, so you have to believe in your own ability to heal yourself. 'I started to believe that my Crohn's disease wasn't just something my body did, it was something *I did* to my body, so I held the power to cure it.'

Over the years, Lydia had tried multiple diets to attempt to treat her Crohn's. One time, she went vegan for a year. 'I kept removing more and more food groups, and my disease flared up so severely that by the time I saw my GI [gastroenterologist] I had several fistula tracts going in and out of my intestine.' This was serious, and her GI told her that she would need surgery unless she took medication. She reluctantly accepted and was feeling better within days. Even this didn't change her mind on alternative medicine, though, and when she felt better, she went right back to alternative medical cures. 'It's like going back to a shitty husband or something.'

You might be asking at this point what *did* get her out. As it turns out, it was the pandemic. For countless people, the pandemic and the fear that came with it were what pushed them into conspiratorial thinking. For Lydia, it was different. The fear of what the pandemic would bring didn't push her further into conspiracy theories – rather, it caused her to realise she had been duped for years.

'When Covid happened, I was really worried that society was going to crumble and that we weren't going to have access to proper healthcare, or even clean drinking water.' Lydia was aware that diseases tend to resurge in times of economic disaster; for example, she knew that when Venezuela's economy collapsed in 2010, there had been outbreaks of measles and diphtheria. Lydia started questioning her choices and wondered whether she should get her kids vaccinated against some of the more serious diseases, but not all of them.

As she was researching online, she came across a site called Vaxopedia. Run by a doctor, the site is dedicated to helping parents to get educated about vaccines. Lydia slowly started to realise that her long-held ideas were not true. Even the claims about the DTP cry that initially scared her into vaccine hesitancy – and further into the anti-vaccine movement – were not true. She discovered that the crying her daughter endured was likely caused by localised pain as a result of the needle. Lydia found doctors and paediatricians online who would willingly answer her questions with kindness and compassion, dispelling the myths she held in her head that painted them as evil caricatures. It took her a few months, but she slowly started vaccinating her children and challenging all her beliefs about alternative medicines.

Fear pushed Lydia into the anti-vaccine movement, but fear also got her out. Her realisation that she had been so wrong now means that she is dedicating her life to reaching people who have fallen for the same theories as her. She hosts a podcast and runs a website called Back to the Vax, based on this mission; her decision to become a nurse was also driven by this. She also gives university webinars to healthcare workers to offer them advice on how to talk to vaccine-hesitant people without dismissing their worries. 'The last thing you want nervous parents to do is to turn to the internet.'

Now Lydia sees vaccines as being the same as any other medical treatment. 'Some people are allergic to penicillin. Does that mean that my child should never have penicillin?' She encourages people to talk to their doctors and avoid the scare stories online, which overblow the risks of side effects and never discuss the legitimate risks that go with avoiding conventional medical treatments.

When love and hate collide

When Jason started questioning the Holocaust and talking about the need to preserve the white race, Andy started to worry that his little brother's beliefs were getting dangerous. 'He started saying that we [white people] are a superior race, that there was no question about that. It was white supremacist stuff, but obviously he would never call it anything like that.'

Jason, who is four years younger than Andy, had been down the rabbit hole for a while. In fact, they had both started the journey together watching 9/11 conspiracy theory films in the mid-2000s: 'We watched all the videos on YouTube back in the very beginning. It was interesting at the time, you know?'

I sure do. Andy and I shared our stories about discovering *Zeitgeist* and *Loose Change* and how, at the time, we found them entertaining and compelling. You'd talk to people about them at house parties and share your opinion on what you thought was really going on in the world. Andy and Jason bonded over them, and one year, for Jason's birthday, Andy bought him a box set about unexplained events that covered classic conspiracy theories like the Roswell UFO crash.

Whereas Andy saw them as an interesting phenomenon, Jason was determined to find answers and dig further into what he was seeing. He believed that 9/11 was an inside job orchestrated by the Bush administration, and following this thread led him to the world of secret societies, namely the Illuminati.

From there, Jason became somewhat obsessed with the symbology related to these secret societies. When you start looking for this kind of symbology, you see it everywhere, because the symbols are quite common – triangles, eyes, pyramids. It feeds into our brain's use of illusory pattern perception and into the conspiracist mindset, where everything is connected. He would point them out in Beyoncé and Britney Spears music videos or in pictures of celebrities doing a gesture with their hands over their eyes. Jason believed it was the Illuminati signalling to the world that they had infiltrated pop culture. 'The symbology held more weight for him than it did for me. I found it interesting, but he saw it as something to be challenged on and find out the truth about.'

I asked Andy why he thought this was. He explained that Jason had lost his best friend in a tragic accident when he was 18. 'It had a profound effect on him.' Andy thinks that Jason's trauma has never been properly addressed, and this made him vulnerable. At the time, he was searching for answers to more than just conspiracy theories.

Although Jason had a degree and a highly specialised master's, he left a good job at a tech company and found himself living at home with his parents, in a small town in the south of Ireland, and working a low-paid job. 'He just wasn't really able for it,' Andy told me. Then Jason decided to go travelling, a decision Andy encouraged, thinking it would help to get him out of his slump.

Jason went to New Zealand for a year and travelled around Southeast Asia on the way home. When he got home, Andy said, all Jason had were the clothes on his back: 'The poverty he saw in Vietnam and Cambodia really tormented him.' Jason had given away all his clothes and belongings to people he met who needed them. 'That's just his nature,' said Andy.

Jason's compassionate and caring nature made it all the more difficult to comprehend the direction his conspiratorial beliefs took him in the years following. 'Jason is a very kind, soft person. He would do anything for you and is such a good-natured guy. It's hard to rationalise that the same person could then develop all these oppressive ideas,' Andy said.

It was after a break-up that these ideas started getting darker. Jason started following Alex Jones and his UK equivalent, David Icke, believing that atrocities such as the Sandy Hook Elementary School shooting and the Boston Marathon bombings were false flags. He also supported Trump and his Make America Great Again mantra, attracted to the anti-establishment senti-ment Trump espoused and his hatred for Hillary Clinton.

But it was the day that Jason started splitting hairs over the number of people killed in the Holocaust that Andy became really unnerved. 'This has gone beyond a joke,' he thought. Jason would discuss wild theories about Hitler, the kind that are propagated by neo-Nazis to claim that Hitler was set up and did nothing wrong.

Jason would send Andy videos, encouraging him to watch them: 'He'd say, "Just watch it and see what you think afterwards."' The videos talked about an apparent Islamic plot to take over the West through refugees, a common theory espoused by far-right Islamophobic groups.

Before this development, Andy and Jason would debate each other about all sorts of issues. Andy liked being able to challenge Jason, so he would read a lot about different conspiracy theories himself. Andy described these conversations as 'quite jovial but also quite serious'. They both had pretty strong opinions, but in general the discussions were healthy and weren't about forcing each other to think a certain way.

But when these discussions turned to issues around race, they would take a nasty turn. 'They would get to a point where you just couldn't keep the tone. You couldn't keep it friendly anymore because he would say something really shitty,' Andy said.

Jason was becoming withdrawn. He couldn't have conversations about what was going on in the news because he would say it was 'brainwashing'. Russia Today, a Kremlin-sponsored news channel known for disseminating Russian disinformation to international audiences, became one of Jason's primary news sources. He also became very religious, devoting himself to a cult-like evangelical Christian group.

There were fleeting moments of clarity, however. Andy told Jason that the hateful things he was saying didn't fit with the person he was, reminding him that he was kind and good-hearted, and that spouting prejudices about certain races or demographics didn't sound like the person he knew. 'He would say, "Okay, yeah, I can see that" and he would simmer for a bit.' During these moments, Andy thought he was getting through, but they wouldn't last for long.

'We always had a really healthy relationship. I say "had" because it's changed now,' Andy told me.

The pandemic was a turning point. Jason never believed that the virus was real or something to take seriously. His beliefs about it would change all the time. First, it was a plot by Bill Gates, then it was related to 5G and then it was a eugenics plan through enforced vaccinations, or a plan to make the world infertile. Jason didn't wear a mask or keep to any restrictions, and he attended anti-lockdown protests in Dublin organised by far-right groups and alternative health campaigners.

When the vaccine roll-out began, he refused to get it, but he also convinced their mother, a cancer survivor, that she didn't need it. 'He was in her ear, telling her she was fit and healthy and there was no need to put that stuff in her body,' Andy said.

In November 2021, Jason and Andy's mother caught Covid-19. She was in a bad way, unable to leave her bed for nearly two weeks. Andy had to convince her to go to hospital after finding out that her blood oxygen levels were dangerously low. Once in hospital, she was put on the highest level of oxygen for 10 days. It was touch and go, with nurses saying that if they had left it even another few hours before coming to hospital she likely would have died.

Things haven't been the same since. 'We still spend time together, but just not on the same level. We used to get into deep conversations, but now I'm just happy to simmer across the top,' Andy said. Jason's descent down the rabbit hole completely changed their relationship and had a huge effect on the whole family. Andy says Jason's personality has changed, as has the way he interacts with people. He's become stiff and serious when he used to be open and funny.

'I've lost years of my life trying to understand this. It's like losing someone to an addiction.'

* * * *

While it may seem to those who believe in them that conspiracy theories make them feel better, Professor Douglas told me that they likely make people feel worse. There is no evidence that conspiracy theories fulfill the unmet psychological needs that make people turn to them in the first place. In fact, they tend to increase the feelings of powerlessness and uncertainty. Take this post from a woman in a UK-based Covid-19 conspiracy channel:

> It's bloody scary what they have as a global plan for us … Once you know you can never return to the normal reality. I personally have had sleepless nights (2 years) and still waking to a nightmare. But once you understand there's no going back. Firstly, stand your ground. Protect your

children. We will win. The more people that wake from this
trance of normal mainstream media. The better our chances as
a human race.

This ties with Michael Barkun's view of the conspiratorial mindset, which he says magnifies the power of evil while simultaneously promising a world that is meaningful, as opposed to random. As he says, this is 'both frightening and reassuring'.

In many ways, we're all just trying to deal with the fact that we're a tiny dot on a spinning rock hurtling around a ball of fire. We all feel powerless against what seems like an endless stream of corruption and injustice. Instead of dealing with the chaotic and random nature of evil in the world, it can be a lot easier to believe it's all connected, that it's all coming from a central hub and that all we need to do to make it better is fight back against that central power. The attraction of a definitive answer to the world's problems is hard to resist.

The danger with modern conspiratorial movements is that they have become a mass movement against injustices that are simply not happening, and they are being weaponised by political groups and extremist activists, and the effects are spilling over into the real world. Many, including the woman who made the post above, feel like they have a duty to fight back against the evil forces. Evidence won't calm them down, and often neither will persuasion from friends and family. They've taken the red pill. They've found others who have taken the red pill, and they are convinced above anything else that they are right.

Chapter 2

The Plan

The illuminati wants this to happen.

That is what the great reset is all about.

Their plan is to crash the entire global economy, then when every nation is broken and starving, the helpless people will welcome in the new world order as their only hope.

That's not what happens though.

The illuminati is going down, and when that happens, it is the end of all jewish power and the entire world will be free of the jew!

THE ABOVE MESSAGE WAS POSTED ON a conspiracy theory message board on 11 October 2021 in response to people losing their jobs for refusing the Covid-19 vaccine. In 78 words, the anonymous user outlines a super-conspiracy theory involving secret societies, a violent battle between the forces of good and evil, and a plan to destroy and dominate the world. The only way to stop it, they say, is to stop those at the forefront of this plan – the Jews.

There is no original or groundbreaking thinking in this post. In fact, it could easily have been written 100 years ago. Theories involving the supposed malevolent actions of secret societies that have the power to shape world events through their control of entities such as the media and financial and electoral systems have existed for decades, if not centuries. It is the core belief of many conspiratorial movements.

These super-conspiracy theories are often dramatic, compelling tales that present a simplified explanation of reality and easily separate the good from the evil. But in this simplicity, they ignore the chaos, complexity and unpredictability of the world, ultimately portraying an unrealistic version of life.

But where did these theories come from? Why have they been so prevalent over time? Why are the Jews constantly linked to sinister plans of world domination? How have these theories played out in Ireland?

The enlightened ones

On 1 May 1776, Adam Weishaupt, the dean of the law faculty at the University of Ingolstadt in Bavaria, Germany, met with four students for the first meeting of what would be a new secret society. At that time, the Age of Enlightenment was at its peak across Europe. This period, in the seventeenth and eighteenth centuries, was a time when intellectual and philosophical thinking advanced significantly. Great thinkers began to promote scientific reasoning, tolerance, rationality and scepticism over traditional ideas around religion and politics that were often based on superstition and irrationality. Secret societies were a common way of promoting these Enlightenment ideas while avoiding the scrutiny of the ruling eyes of the Church, which did not take kindly to them.

Weishaupt's society, which he named the Order of the Illuminati, was no different. The university was under Jesuit control, and Weishaupt was known for his liberal, often radical and anti-clerical views, to the point that his salary had been withheld by the Jesuits, who claimed he was a 'dangerous free-thinker'.[1]

The Illuminati was hierarchical and modelled on another secret society, the Freemasons. The Freemasons, an organisation that still exists today, dates back to the Middle Ages and was originally a society for stonemasons, hence the compass and square as its symbol. In the seventeenth and eighteenth centuries, the Freemasons opened their doors to members (mostly men) unconnected to the profession, and lodges spread across Europe and the US. They began promoting Enlightenment ideas, making them a cause of contention among the Catholic ruling classes. Secret passwords, handshakes, ceremonies and rituals reinforced a sense of identity between members in lodges all around the world and created an air of ancient mysticism that survives to the present day[2].

Even though the Freemasons have lifted their veil of secrecy in recent years, an air of suspicion has followed them through the ages due to their association with powerful figures. Many people are not satisfied with the seemingly innocent explanation for their (somewhat strange) activities.

Conspiracy theories today often encourage people to look for symbols associated with the Freemasons and Illuminati. These are meant to prove that certain people are involved in these secret societies and are doing their bidding, both secretly and while flaunting it to the world. These symbols commonly include celebrities photographed covering one eye with their hand, or making a triangular shape with their index fingers and thumbs.

The eye and triangle symbols are meant to represent the Eye of Providence, commonly referred to as the 'all-seeing eye of God'. The symbol can be seen on the US dollar bill and has been wrongly associated with the Illuminati for decades. There is no evidence that the Illuminati ever used this symbol, although it was used by the Freemasons. Variations on the Eye of Providence have been found throughout history. It is believed that the version we know today stems from a misinterpretation of Egyptian hieroglyphics that mistranslated a symbol of a single eye into the word 'god'. It then became popular in the 1700s, where it made its way on to the Great Seal of the United States and subsequently to dollar bills, but there was no Freemason involvement in its design. The Freemasons began using it widely only *after* it held more mainstream appeal. As art historian and BBC reporter Matthew Wilson astutely noted: 'the repeated use of the Eye of Providence ... is proof not of a concerted conspiracy, but of its enduring brilliance as a piece of logo design'.[3]

Back in the 1700s, Freemasonry proved extremely popular throughout Europe and the US and attracted thousands of members, whereas Weishaupt's Illuminati got off to a slow start, growing to only 60 members in its first four years. Weishaupt was, by all accounts, a very difficult and contentious man. He held contradictory convictions, believing in an egalitarian society while also ruling with a dictatorial force over an organisation based on hierarchy. He had visions of radically changing the world, and Illuminati members were expected to adhere strictly to the Order. Historian Vernon Stauffer said that Weishaupt's thirst for domination 'converted the order into a despotism against which men who had been taught by their leader that they shared with him the innermost secrets of the organisation, rebelled'.

The Order hit a new stride when an alliance was forged between the Illuminati and the Freemasons, and by the early 1780s it had grown to between 2,000 and 3,000 members, spread across a number of countries in Europe. But in 1784 the Bavarian monarchy issued the first of a series of edicts against any societies that were not approved by law. Another two decrees followed in 1785 specifically naming the Illuminati and Freemasons, and a final one in 1787 made recruiting into the Order punishable by death. Those who were found to be members of the Illuminati were fired from their positions, student members were dismissed from university and the Order was no more. Weishaupt fled Bavaria and found refuge in the city of Gotha.

The final nail in the coffin came when the house of a prominent Illuminati member was raided and documents containing membership lists and secret communications were found and made public. The information elicited fear and shock from the public when they learned of the Order's defence of ideas such as atheism, abortion and suicide. These notions were completely at odds with the prevailing religious establishment. According to Stauffer, 'So intense and widespread was the fear which the order engendered ... that it was impossible that its shadow should pass immediately.'

Two years later, in 1789, rioters and revolutionaries stormed the Bastille prison in Paris, marking the start of the French Revolution. The revolution was a watershed moment, and the course of history in France and the rest of Europe was radically changed over the 10 years that followed.

In the midst of this major political and social upheaval, people desperately tried to figure out *how* such a significant revolution had been possible. In 1797, two books, written independently of each other, put forward a theory that would have lasting consequences for centuries to come.

Augustin Barruel, a former Jesuit monk, outlined his thoughts in *Memoirs Illustrating the History of Jacobinism*. In it, he put forward a theory claiming that the French Revolution had been the result of a decades-long plot in which Enlightenment thinkers and anti-monarchists had colluded with the Illuminati and the Freemasons to overthrow the monarchy and Catholicism: 'Everything was foreseen, premeditated ... all had been prepared by men, who alone held the clue to these conspiracies conceived in [the meetings of] secret societies ... The grand cause of the Revolution ... is all to be found in one chain of plots.'[4]

The second book to make similar claims came from John Robison, a British physicist, mathematician, philosopher and former Freemason, in his *Proofs of a Conspiracy Against All the Religions and Governments of Europe*. In his own theory, Robison, like Barruel, denounced the revolution as a secret Illuminati plot. He claimed that Weishaupt had revived the Order under a new name shortly after it had been dissolved, and it had 'this time taken so deep root that it still subsists without being detected, and has spread into all the countries of Europe'.

Like all conspiracy theories, those of Robison and Barruel were based on a grain of truth, but the dominant role they gave to the Illuminati and Freemasons in planning the revolution was wildly exaggerated. Barruel claimed that the organisations had hundreds of thousands of members, when Illuminati membership never reached more than 3,000 and Freemasons totalled around 100,000 across the whole of Europe and the US. It's true that the spread of Enlightenment thinking was a factor in France's drive towards revolutionary change (liberty, equality and fraternity were Enlightenment ideas, as well as the slogan for the revolution). Weishaupt certainly also had an insatiable thirst for power, but his plans were ultimately thwarted when the Order was banned and he fled. Also, Freemasons fought on both sides during the revolution. Even the prominent counter-revolutionary and Freemason Joseph de Maistre called Barruel's accusations 'foolish' and 'false'.

In reality, the French Revolution was triggered by a complicated series of events, including vast economic and societal crises that the monarchy had failed to tackle. The population of France had increased enormously throughout the 1700s, and poor harvests resulted in food shortages in the 1780s. Unemployment was also at a high, as was state debt. To top it off, the monarchy decided the way to deal with the rising debt was to increase taxes on the poor peasant classes (which made up 98 per cent of the population), while the clergy and nobility classes continued to live in luxury. Pinning all the blame on a sinister plot of secret societies simply failed to grasp the complexity of the situation.

Nevertheless, Robison's and Barruel's books proved extremely popular. Robison's in particular had a profound impact in the US and contributed to a widespread Illuminati scare in New England in 1798 and 1799. Although the Illuminati was a functioning society for just 11 years, the fear it generated allowed it to live on for centuries to come.

The spectre of communism

In 1847, Karl Marx and Friedrich Engels wrote in the opening of *The Communist Manifesto,* 'a spectre is haunting Europe – the spectre of communism'. At the time of the pamphlet's publication, the world was going through a period of profound social change. The Industrial Revolution had transformed working life from rural agrarian societies to urban factory-driven industries where workers slogged in often dangerous conditions. Potato blight led to famines – most notably, of course, in Ireland, but also in parts of mainland Europe – and these were accompanied by rising food prices. Ideas such as democracy, nationalism, communism and liberalism were seen as disruptive and radical, yet they were proliferating despite efforts to clamp down on them. Because of this, Europe saw a series of political revolutions that, in the words of historian A.J.P. Taylor, 'took no one by surprise'.

The Communist Manifesto had little impact on these (largely unsuccessful) revolutions, but it grew to be a pivotal influence within political activism over the following decades. The scourge of capitalism was becoming more apparent. Workers were realising that they were cogs in the machine, increasingly subjected to longer working hours and higher production rates. The divide between the workers and the industry owners was widening. Marx and Engels outlined what they saw as an inevitability: the capitalist system was destined for failure, and workers worldwide would eventually rise up against the exploitation. A socialist revolution would erupt and lead to a new type of classless society – communism – in which the means of production and property would be collectively owned and distributed to people according to their needs. The days of capitalism bleeding people dry would be over. 'Working men of all countries, unite!' the *Manifesto* urged.

It wasn't until 1917 that the world saw these ideas put into practice. In Russia, after years of famine and inequality and with the country decimated by World War I, the Russian tsarist monarchy was defeated and a provisional government installed. In October 1917, Vladimir Lenin and his Bolshevik party successfully overthrew the provisional government, promising Russians 'peace, land and bread', and became the first communist party ever in power.

A five-year civil war followed, resulting in victory for the Bolsheviks and the creation of the Union of Soviet Socialist Republics, the USSR. During the civil war, the Bolsheviks engaged in a bloody and ruthless campaign against their political enemies. Dubbed the Red Terror, this saw the execution and imprisonment of tens of thousands of people – some records say more than a million. This intolerance for dissent and use of terror as a means of control laid the foundations for the tactics employed by the USSR for decades to come.

Lenin deviated from Marxist teachings quite significantly in his quest to bring about a communist society. Most notably, instead of a revolution instigated by the working classes uniting, Lenin wished for one brought about by an authoritarian vanguard political party. Marx had also said that a socialist revolution could only take place in an advanced capitalist nation, which Russia certainly wasn't. Lenin and his successor, the even more ruthless Josef Stalin, employed strategies to force a largely agrarian economy to become a modern industrial one. Although this modernisation was successful, it came at a huge price. Millions of people suffered and died under their rule through famines, slave labour, reigns of terror, imprisonment, the forced collectivisation of land and the mismanagement of resources.[5] Communism in action was proving itself to be a deadly, oppressive force.

Across Europe and the United States in the early 1900s there was a rising anti-communist movement, pushing back against the influence of the Bolsheviks, who were inspiring communist and socialist parties around the world. There was anxiety about what a communist takeover could entail, but along with the real threats came those that were imagined and born out of fear. Just as with the French Revolution, the world was looking for an explanation for the Bolshevik takeover, and in 1921 a British woman named Nesta Webster reignited an old theory.

Webster was a writer who had moderate success as a novelist and women's rights activist in the 1910s before becoming one of the UK's most influential conspiracy theorists and campaigners for fascist organisations. After reading the story of two aristocrats during the French Revolution, Webster began to believe that she herself was the reincarnation of someone who had lived through the period. This was spurred on by her interest in Buddhism, causing her to re-evaluate her entire life.[6] It's probably fair to say that she had an 'awakening' of sorts.

In 1920, Webster published *The French Revolution: A Study in Democracy*, in which she argued that the revolution could not have been the result of a populist uprising. Instead, she said it had been the design of the Illuminati and Freemasons 'working for revolution and the destruction of Christian civilisation'. She was convinced that Adam Weishaupt had been able to wield enormous power to influence the direction of history. Because she was an established author, the book was widely reviewed but generally wasn't well received, with reviewers criticising her reliance on conspiracy theories and poor sources.

A year later, Webster wrote *World Revolution: The Plot Against Civilisation*, in which she took these theories further. Not only had the Illuminati and the Freemasons planned the French Revolution, she said, but they were still operating in secret through influential political forces and were responsible for the Russian Revolution and the Bolshevik takeover of Russia. She further claimed that communist movements worldwide were part of this sinister plot to destroy civilisation and that many people had been duped into being pawns in their scheme.

In 1924, Webster published her most influential book: *Secret Societies and Subversive Movements*. In this, she added a key element to the theories she had previously developed. The Illuminati, the Freemasons and the communists weren't the only ones pulling strings; the real power, she said, came from the Jews.

The oldest hatred

Anti-Semitism can be defined as many things. At a very basic level, it is the hatred of or discrimination against Jews, but it manifests in different ways – from religious anti-Judaism rooted in Christianity's centuries-long animosity towards Jews, to racial anti-Semitism based on pseudoscience that presents Jews as an inferior race and, further, to conspiratorial anti-Semitism that portrays Jews as an all-powerful, money-hungry entity with plans to dominate the world.

This prejudice is known as the 'oldest hatred' due to its pervasiveness throughout history. For centuries, Jews have been persecuted and discriminated against. They have been blamed for tragedies, disease and countless crises. This eventually culminated in the murder of six million Jews across Europe during the Holocaust. Anti-Semitism has proven highly adaptable, revising itself countless times for hundreds of years and rearing its ugly head within political movements, extremist circles and conspiracy theories right up to the present day.

But why the Jews? Where did this hatred come from, and how has it played out throughout history?

Within the Christian faith, anti-Judaism goes back to the death of Jesus Christ, when Jews were cast as the 'Christ killers' who rejected Jesus as the Messiah and sent him to his death.[7] In AD 70, a large part of the Jewish population of Israel, seen as the homeland of the Jews, was either massacred or exiled after the Romans destroyed the Second Temple in Jerusalem. Jews then began to flee across the world.

As Christianity became the state religion of Rome in the fourth century, hostility towards Jews only increased, resulting in the destruction of synagogues, the passing of laws that banned marriage between Christians and Jews, and restricted religious devotion. This hostility continued into the Middle Ages, when Jews were blamed for spreading diseases and poisoning wells, and came to a head during the Crusades, a series of religious wars between 1096 and 1291 that were often instigated and supported by the Catholic Church in its determination to secure control of holy sites from Muslims in the Middle East. During this period, Jews were frequently the subject of persecutions, killings and pogroms (violent race-related riots) in Europe, resulting in large numbers of Jews fleeing countries such as England, France and Austria.[8]

Anti-Jewish sentiment took a significant irrational turn at this time, too, when baseless claims about Jews ritually murdering Christian children began to circulate, originating from the unsolved death of a young boy called William in Norwich, England, in the year 1144. Without evidence, William's death was blamed on a local Jewish population that had moved to the area a decade earlier. A book written by a monk about William's life and death contained a story, allegedly told by a Jew who had converted to Christianity, in which he claimed that William's murder was part of an annual ritual sacrifice held by Jews to show their contempt for Jesus. This claim was absolutely baseless, but soon after the additional detail was added that the ritual involved drinking the blood of children, and so the myth of 'blood libel' was born.

From Norwich, false accusations of blood libel spread across the world, causing unknown amounts of death and destruction. Often this would result in the entire Jewish population of a town being hunted and brutally executed on made-up charges. This myth has since been repurposed as an integral part of QAnon.

It was also during this time that one of the most damaging Jewish stereotypes began to take hold – that is, the relationship of Jews with money. Hateful clichés, which have often featured in popular culture, have presented Jews as greedy and money-hungry, while also being stingy and cheap. William Shakespeare's character Shylock in *The Merchant of Venice* is a Jewish money-lender who demands his 'pound of flesh' before being forced to give up his wealth and his religion. In Charles Dickens's *Oliver Twist*, Fagin, the criminal who teaches children to make a living from pickpocketing, is based on a hackneyed representation of a Jewish person.

This stereotype developed as a result of restrictions placed on the occupations Jews could hold during the Middle Ages, which also extended in some circumstances to them not being allowed to own land. These limitations pushed Jews into less desirable occupations, such as moneylending, which Christians were prohibited to do because it was seen as sinful. Jews became highly adept in the world of finance as a result, and were often employed by the noble classes – in positions known as court

Jews – to provide these services. Court Jews were granted special privileges because of their position, distinguishing them from the regular Jewish population. They were allowed to live outside of the ghettos to which many Jews were confined and were taxed at the same rate as Christians. Some were also granted titles. Their status, however, did not make them immune from scorn, and these privileges – and the financial power they held – contributed to further animosity between Jews and Christians.

Mayer Amschel Rothschild was one such court Jew, and his rags-to-riches story has provided fodder for anti-Semitic conspiracy theories right up to the present day. Born in the Jewish ghettos of Frankfurt in 1744, Mayer learned the ropes of banking as an apprentice in a bank in Hamburg and specialised in dealing in rare and collectable coins. He became a trusted financial adviser to Crown Prince Wilhelm of Hesse and protected his fortunes during Napoleon's invasions by loaning them to the British Crown. These investments paid off for Mayer, who gained generously from them, allowing him to create the Rothschild banking dynasty by setting up offices in London, Naples, Vienna and Paris run by his sons. The business focused on loaning money to governments and the aristocracy, providing a similar service to that of today's International Monetary Fund (IMF). These activities, however, contributed to the conspiratorial tropes about the Rothschilds still circulating today, which claim they have financed both sides of every war since the 1800s.

The Rothschilds were without doubt one of the richest and most powerful families in Europe at the time, but their influence waned significantly following World War II. The Nazis seized much of the assets of the Austrian Rothschilds, a fact that has morphed in the conspiratorial world to mean the Rothschilds 'funded the Nazis'. The formation of the IMF also depleted their power and influence. Although descendants of the dynasty maintain significant wealth today, the conspiracy theories attributed to them, such as claims that the family controls all the banks of the world are, as *Skeptoid* podcast's Brian Dunning puts it, 'about 100 years out of date'.[9]

By the early 1500s, Jews had been expelled from England, France, Germany, Spain, Portugal and Russia, with many either dying while attempting to leave or fleeing to Poland, the Netherlands or northern Italy. The irrational hatred continued to grow. In 1543, Martin Luther, the figure behind the Protestant Reformation, wrote a bitter screed against the Jews, encouraging people to burn down their synagogues and homes, rob them of anything of value and ultimately annihilate them.

Violent attacks, false accusations and blatant prejudice against Jews continued through the sixteenth and seventeenth centuries, but the Age of Enlightenment and its thinking around tolerance and freedom brought a change in attitudes and a debate over the best way to integrate Jews into society. This debate was known as the 'Jewish question'. France became the first country, following the French Revolution in 1790, to emancipate Jews and grant them equal rights as citizens. Other countries in Europe began to follow suit. Now with full legal rights in many countries and access to education, as well as social and professional opportunities, many Jews prospered.

However, not everyone welcomed the equal participation of Jews in mainstream society.

History professor Shulamit Volkov explained that, prior to emancipation, the fear of and prejudice against Jews was the result of them being seen as different: they belonged to another religion, they had different social and cultural norms, and consequently they were marginalised. But the prejudice didn't vanish with emancipation; it simply changed form. Now the danger was seen in the fact that Jews were the same as everyone else and were trying to mingle in general society. Their success made them more visible and thus spurred on a new form of hatred.

In a fresh attempt to frame Jews as different and inferior, racial anti-Semitism was developed in the late 19th century. Paramount to this new hatred was both the use of the language of science, known as race science, and a concept known as social Darwinism. Based on Charles Darwin's theory of natural selection, social Darwinism posited that certain races of people were superior and others inferior, and that successful people were part of an innately 'better' race. The concept is now agreed to be scientifically groundless (yet is still touted by white supremacist groups today), since genetic differences between humans across the world are tiny. However, in the late 19th and early 20th centuries, it was seen as credible, and it was used to promote the idea that Jews were a distinct and inferior race.

It was also during this time that the term 'anti-Semitism' was coined, denoting a new ideology. It was popularised in Germany in the 1870s to represent a distinct movement of people who felt threatened by Jewish success and wished to push back against Jewish emancipation by declaring Jews as racially distinct. The word 'semitic' is in fact a linguistic term to denote languages spoken in the Middle East and parts of Africa, but during this time it became synonymous with Jewishness.

One of the most bitter and hostile displays of anti-Semitism following Jewish emancipation occurred in France at the end of the nineteenth century. Captain Alfred Dreyfus, a French artillery officer of Jewish descent, was convicted and sentenced to life in prison for sending military secrets to the Germans. But Dreyfus was innocent, and the evidence presented at his trial was bogus. A divisive period followed, with public opinion split between support and opposition. This was accompanied by vile anti-Semitism that swept across the country as a result. Dreyfus was finally exonerated in 1906, 11 years after his conviction. The Dreyfus affair and the horrific anti-Semitism that went with it had a long-lasting impact on France.

The hatred on display during the Dreyfus affair had an acute influence on an Austro-Hungarian journalist named Theodor Herzl, who saw it as a sad indication that Jewish emancipation and assimilation were impossible and that anti-Semitism could never be defeated. Herzl subsequently dedicated himself to a new movement calling for the restoration of a Jewish state in Israel. That movement became known as Zionism.

Despite anti-Semitic stereotypes that viewed all Jews as homogenous and bound by common interests, they were in fact a diverse group of people with different political, religious and cultural beliefs, as well as class variations. Jews in the Russian Empire, for example, were mostly poor and powerless, yet were still a despised minority. They could only officially become Russian by converting to Russian Orthodox Christianity and were not fully emancipated there until after the 1917 Russian Revolution. The Russian press blamed the Jews for the assassination of Tsar Alexander II in 1881, and pogroms spread throughout the country. An estimated two million Jews fled the Russian pogroms between 1880 and 1914, settling in the United States, Palestine, Canada, Britain and Ireland.

The approximately 3,000 Jews who arrived in Ireland in the late 1800s and early 1900s settled in areas of Dublin, Cork, Belfast and Limerick and created Jewish quarters in these cities. Although many Jews spoke in a positive way about their welcome in Ireland and the compassion shown for those fleeing persecution, Ireland did not escape the anti-Semitism that was so pervasive across Europe and beyond. Dr Brian Hanley, Assistant Professor of Twentieth Century History in Trinity College Dublin, told me, 'Ireland wasn't unique. There was nothing especially bad about the Irish, but the anti-Semitism that was pervasive throughout contemporary Europe was also found here.' In his book *Architects of the Resurrection*, R.M. Douglas writes, 'While physical attacks on Jews were comparatively infrequent … lesser forms of intimidation – menacing graffiti, anonymous death threats, the daubing of Jewish-owned premises with offensive messages – were considerably more common.'[10]

There were those who felt threatened by the newly arrived population. This was evident in an 1893 editorial published in the *Lyceum* magazine by Father Thomas Finlay, who wrote about the need of the native Irish population to defend itself against the possible economic danger that Jews could bring, based on their association with moneylending. 'Our first duty is to ourselves and to our own people, and no sympathy with the suffering and persecuted Jews can avail to free us from this obligation,' he wrote. In the editorial, Father Finlay referred to Jewish stereotypes, claiming that Jews were able to amass great power through their association with moneylending and speculated that Jews were attempting to take over Irish farms. He concluded by stating that Jews were welcome in Ireland, but only if they were honest. If they came 'as a parasite', however, their reception would be less than hospitable.[11]

A particularly nasty and often repeated example of organised hate directed towards Jews came in Limerick in 1904. The incident, often referred to as the Limerick pogrom, made international headlines at the time. Although not a pogrom in the traditional sense, in that it bore little resemblance to the violent and murderous riots of Eastern Europe, it was the closest Ireland came to such horrific scenes. The vitriol directed at the Jews left a long-lasting stain of anti-Semitism and resulted in a number of Jewish families fleeing the city. The sparks that ignited this incident came from the mouth of Redemptorist priest Father John Creagh, who delivered a fierce tirade against the Jews in the city from the pulpit, after shopkeepers had grown hostile to the Jewish pedlars, or travelling salesmen, who they claimed were providing 'unwelcome competition'.

Calling them 'Christ killers' and referring to claims of blood libel, Father Creagh said there was 'no greater enemy to the Catholic Church' than the Jews. 'They were sucking the blood of other nations, but those nations rose up and turned them out and they came to our land to fasten themselves on us like leeches,' he said. He ended his sermon by calling for a boycott of Jewish businesses in Limerick. Following this, the congregation began intimidating, threatening and assaulting the Jewish community, which lived mostly on Colooney Street in the city, causing many to lock themselves in their homes. The boycott and incitement went on for two years and was supported by people such as Sinn Féin founder Arthur Griffith, whose newspaper the *United Irishman* had regularly promoted anti-Jewish tropes.

An article in the London-based *Jewish Chronicle*, a newspaper still in circulation today, described the fear within the community at the time. 'My pen trembles as I sit down to write to you about the situation of the Jews in Limerick … When I witnessed the organised attacks today and heard the mob yell "Down with the Jews: they kill our innocent children", all the horrors of Kishinev came back to me.'

The Kishinev pogrom of 1903 was a particularly horrific massacre that took place in modern-day Moldova, in which 49 Jews were killed and dozens more injured. Michael Davitt, the leader of the Land League and a journalist, travelled to Kishinev and reported on the massacre. In his book *Within the Pale: The True Story of Anti-Semitic Persecution in Russia*, he described the horrific murder, rape and torture endured by the Jewish population there. 'I have taken pictures … of the shed in which the young girl of thirteen was assaulted, and killed with four men, of groups of little girls and women who passed through the two nights of horror in the quarter where the Moldavian fiends committed the worst deeds, and of houses in which numerous murders were committed.'[12] Davitt was therefore sympathetic to the struggles endured by the Jewish community and he regularly defended the new arrivals in Ireland from hate and intolerance.

In response to the news of the Limerick boycott, Davitt wrote in the nationalist paper the *Freeman's Journal*, 'I protest as an Irishman and as a Catholic against the barbarous malignancy of anti-Semitism which is being introduced into Ireland under the pretended regard for the welfare of the Irish people.'

A less discussed but even more horrendous series of events occurred in Dublin in 1923, when two Jewish men were shot dead in targeted anti-Semitic attacks in the city. Bernard Goldberg, a jeweller and father of four, was shot on St Stephen's Green on Halloween night, and two weeks later Emmanuel 'Ernest' Kahn, a civil servant, was gunned down when walking home after playing cards. Kahn was accompanied by a friend who was also shot but managed to escape.[13] He told police at the time that they were stopped by two young men who asked, 'Are you a Jew?' before telling them to run, at which time they were fired upon.

The killers were members of the Free State army and escaped prosecution, with at least one fleeing the country to Mexico. Evidence from the time suggests that there was an effort to cover up the crimes, and Dáil transcripts from 1934 suggest that one of the killers went on to become a member of the anti-communist paramilitary and para-fascist group the Blueshirts, which provided security for the pro-Treaty Cumann na nGaedheal before merging with the party to form Fine Gael.

The masterplan

In 1903, a pamphlet first published in Russia had one of the greatest impacts on anti-Semitism and the world of conspiracy theories right up to the present day. For many people, the *Protocols of the Elders of Zion* provided 'proof' of the Jewish conspiracies they believed in and gave further reason to scapegoat, antagonise and slaughter Jewish populations worldwide.

Written as a first-person narrative, the *Protocols* profess to outline the minutes of a meeting of a secretive group of Jewish elders. The pamphlet weaves a twisted tale that spells out a centuries-old plot by Jews to dominate the world. It claims that the concepts of liberalism and freedom are myths created by the Jews to deceive the masses, and that the success of ideas from Darwin and Marx was 'prearranged' by the Jews. The *Protocols* also state that Jews control the media, the financial world, and education and electoral systems. They supposedly have so much power that they can start wars. The pinnacle of this plot is a political and economic masterplan that will result in the formation of a Jewish one-world government that will destroy Christianity and freedom forever.

Anti-Semites fully embraced and promoted the *Protocols*. Here, after all, was a document that proved what they had thought all along: that Jews were inherently evil, and their presence on earth brought nothing but destruction. And they had laid out their plan in plain text for the whole world to see!

There was, however, a major problem. The *Protocols* were completely made up. Numerous passages from the text were found to be plagiarised from a fictional political satire written by

French publicist Maurice Joly titled *The Dialogue in Hell Between Machiavelli and Montesquieu*. Other parts were taken from an anti-Semitic novel written by a German named Hermann Goedsche. The author of the *Protocols* is unknown and still debated to this day.[14] Russian mystic Sergius Nilus is most often credited with first publishing the document. His stories about where the *Protocols* were discovered contain many contradictions. Initially Nilus said they had been given to him by a prominent Russian conservative who had apparently received them from an unknown woman; she in turn had stolen them from an influential Freemason. Then he claimed that his friend had stolen them directly from Jews in France. Then he said they came from Switzerland.

The fabricated nature of the *Protocols* is also obvious upon reading them. Although purportedly written by Jews, the *Protocols* presented Jewish people as evil and deceitful, with powers that the devil could only wish for. Consider this quote, for example: 'The weapons in our hands are limitless ambitions, burning greediness, merciless vengeance, hatreds and malice.' They describe old anti-Semitic stereotypes as fact and often refer to non-Jews as 'animals'. The document was obviously written in a way that appealed to anti-Semites, to confirm all their suspicions and present it as coming straight from the mouths of the Jews they so despised. It also provided a conspiratorial explanation for the success Jews had gained since emancipation.

The fact that the *Protocols* was a forgery did not deter its spread, and it soon became a popular weapon for placing the blame for all past and present revolutions at the hands of the Jews, especially after the 1917 Russian Revolution and World

War I. As journalist Herman Bernstein aptly put it: 'The method is simple. Was there a revolution in Russia? Blame the Jews. Was there a revolution in Germany? Blame the Jews. Who made the French Revolution? The Jews. Who caused the World War? The Jews. Who profited by the war? The Jews.'[15]

The *Protocols* provided the foundations for the Judeo-Bolshevism myth that Nesta Webster would go on to write about, suggesting that communism was part of a Jewish plot. Many Jews in Russia did support revolutionary change. After all, they had been institutionally persecuted, attacked and killed by the tsarist empire for centuries. Several leading Bolsheviks were also Jews, but this number is often grossly exaggerated, and records show that in 1917, only 5 per cent of the Bolshevik party was Jewish. This reduced to 4.34 per cent in 1927, and by the mid-1930s, after Stalin's campaign of terror known as the Great Purge, Jews had been largely eliminated from any senior positions.[16]

In 1920, Winston Churchill, then British Secretary of State for War, spoke about the Judeo-Bolshevik conspiracy theory in a feature he wrote for the *Illustrated Sunday Herald*. In the piece, he referred to the work of Nesta Webster and claimed that there had been a Jewish plot in place for the overthrow of civilisation since the days of Weishaupt's Order of the Illuminati, through to the French Revolution, Karl Marx and the Russian Revolution.

Churchill was generally seen as an ally of the Jews, and he distinguished between the Jews he saw as a threat and those he didn't. But his belief in a worldwide Jewish communist conspiracy reflects the acceptance of anti-Semitic attitudes towards

Jews at the time and the pervasiveness of the conspiracy theory outlined in the *Protocols*.

In 1920, Henry Ford, one of the richest men in the world, brought the lies espoused in the *Protocols* to the US by publishing a series based on them in the newspaper he owned, the *Dearborn Independent*. The articles, called 'The International Jew', were also printed in book form under the same name, selling more than half a million copies in the US.

Ireland was going through a period of monumental political and social upheaval in the early 1900s following the Easter Rising and the War of Independence. 'During the Irish Revolution, the British right saw the revolution as part of an international Jewish, or Bolshevik, conspiracy,' Dr Brian Hanley told me. In 1920, for example, London newspaper the *Morning Post* published a series of articles called 'The Cause of World Unrest' based on the *Protocols*, attempting to link the Irish uprising to a Judeo–Bolshevik plot. Nesta Webster also believed that Jews were the cause of revolution in Ireland, and Henry Ford's *Dearborn Independent* claimed, in another 1920 article, that the Bolsheviks were behind the IRA.

Certain elements of this conspiracy theory were more widely believed than others. Éamon de Valera, a key revolutionary who would go on to found Fianna Fáil and become Taoiseach, and later President of Ireland, was often falsely accused of being a Jew during this time. Dr Hanley said that this belief was 'very widespread' and initially came from the British and the unionists. It was bolstered by the fact that de Valera was born in the US to an Irish mother and Spanish father, meaning he was often accused of being a 'foreigner'.

Claims of de Valera's 'Jewishness' became a flashpoint again after his bitter dispute with John Devoy, a prominent Fenian living in the US in 1920. After this split, Devoy unabashedly referred to de Valera as a 'half-breed Spanish-American Jew' in his paper the *Gaelic American*. In the early 1930s, this slur was levelled at de Valera again by pro-Treatyites, eventually leading to him addressing the allegations directly on the floor of the Dáil.

Similar to every claim related to Judeo-Bolshevism, reducing the Irish Revolution to a Bolshevik plot fails to account for the complexity of the situation, not to mention the hundreds of years of struggle in Ireland that led to the revolutionary events of the early 1900s. But, as there often is, there was a small grain of truth to the claims. 'Bolshevism,' Dr Hanley told me, 'was reasonably popular in nationalist Ireland when it was associated with being anti-war and being against the British Empire. During the revolution, there was grassroots enthusiasm for Bolshevism within the republican movement.'

James Connolly, one of the leaders of the Easter Rising in 1916, was a socialist and Marxist who was pivotal in workers' rights movements and was a founding member of the Labour Party. Connolly was seen as a hero to Lenin, and the events of the Easter Rising were inspiring to the Bolsheviks. Lenin described the Rising as 'a blow delivered against the British imperialist bourgeoisie in Ireland' and the Bolsheviks often pointed to it as an example of national self-determination.

The role of Jews in the Irish revolutionary movement is somewhat complex. As Dr Hanley explained to me, 'Jewish people who came to Ireland from Eastern Europe in the early 1900s were coming to a part of the United Kingdom, and many wouldn't have understood the need for the rebellion.' They saw the UK as a place to escape persecution. But there were a small number of prominent Jews involved in the republican movement, most notably Robert Briscoe, who went on to become a Fianna Fáil TD and Lord Mayor of Dublin. Dr Hanley noted that Briscoe's Jewishness was 'a factor in both how he was received and perceived by peers'. Dr Hanley said there was 'considerable paranoia' surrounding some of Briscoe's activities, especially those undertaken in the US where it was assumed he was working with communists. Artist Estella Solomons, who was a member of Cumann na mBan and used to provide her Dublin studio as a sanctuary for men on the run, was another noteworthy Jew supporting the nationalist cause. Jews overseas, particularly in the US, also expressed support and raised funds for the fight for Irish independence.

Although there was often an attempt to frame Ireland as somewhat immune to anti-Semitism during this time, Dr Hanley refutes this notion saying that in fact, anti-Semitism was 'so pervasive that most people would have regarded it as normal'. Nationalist anti-Semitism, Dr Hanley said, 'was a real phenomenon, influenced variously by religious, social and political trends', and although the tale outlined in the *Protocols* had little widespread impact within republican circles, elements of it still shone through. For example, Count George Noble Plunkett wrote a letter to Éamon de Valera in 1921 warning him against forging close alliances with Jews, claiming that Jews and Freemasons had colluded to cause World War I and that they controlled the British press. Maud Gonne, the suffragette, revolutionary and muse of W.B. Yeats, believed in Freemason conspiracy theories and has been described as 'noisily anti-Semitic'. Arthur Griffith, mentioned above for his support of the Limerick boycott, had previously written in the *United Irishman* that the 'three evil influences of the century were the Pirate, the Freemason, and the Jew'.

It was in Germany that these ever-increasing and more intricate displays of anti-Semitism would coalesce into a deadly force. Following the country's defeat in World War I, Germany was on its knees. The Treaty of Versailles, a peace agreement signed after the war, imposed huge penalties on Germany and laid blame for the war almost solely at Germany's feet, humiliating an already broken nation. In right-wing circles, to counter this humiliation, a new claim began to spread: that Germany's defeat was down to revolutionary socialists who had betrayed the country on the home front. This became known as the 'stab in the back' myth. It quickly developed profound anti-Semitic elements that falsely claimed that Jews involved in the war had been working against the interests of the country as spies and profiteers – meaning that the German defeat was ultimately down to the Jews.

The period after World War I in Germany was a time of extreme political, social and economic instability. There to take advantage of this volatility was the Nazi Party, led from 1921 by Adolf Hitler, a World War I veteran who felt humiliated by Germany's defeat in the war and believed wholly in the 'stab in the back' myth. The party was explicitly anti-Semitic, anti-communist, anti-democratic and obsessed with ideas of 'racial purity'. It also found inspiration in Mussolini's Fascist Party in Italy, even going so far as to borrow elements such as the straight-armed salute. Mussolini's successful March on Rome, which put his Fascist Party into power in 1923, encouraged Hitler to attempt his own coup d'état. But the Munich Beer Hall Putsch was unsuccessful, and Hitler was imprisoned for eight months for his attempted coup. During his incarceration, Hitler wrote *Mein Kampf*, a political autobiography that outlined his vision for the future of Germany.

In *Mein Kampf*, Hitler described his journey into anti-Semitism and how he eventually came to see Marxism and Judaism as the world's 'two perils'. He discussed his belief in the *Protocols*, the authenticity of which he said was cemented by the media's repeated statements declaring it a forgery – an indication of the self-sealing nature of conspiracy theories and Hitler's embrace of the conspiratorial mindset where *nothing is as it seems*. He explained his belief in the superiority of the German 'Aryan' master race and decried those who 'mingled their blood with that of an inferior race'. Hitler used these beliefs to justify what he saw as a need for the extermination and imprisonment of inferior races in order for Germany to succeed.

The Nazi Party's popularity increased significantly throughout the 1920s, and it eventually rose to power in 1933, quickly passing laws that gave Hitler dictatorial control and allowing him to put the ideas in *Mein Kampf* into practice. Non-Jewish Germans were forbidden from marrying Jews, and Jews were stripped of the rights they had gained through emancipation. The *Protocols* became a key element of Nazi propaganda and was used to indoctrinate the Hitler Youth. *Mein Kampf* became required reading, and claims of blood libel and the 'stab in the back' myth were widely promoted. Hitler forced the sterilisation of minorities that he saw as inferior; he also murdered political enemies, Jehovah's Witnesses, members of the LGBTQ+ community, Roma Gypsies, the handicapped and the mentally ill. Then, in what he and the Nazi Party saw as 'the final solution to the Jewish question', Hitler ordered the systematic mass murder of more than six million Jews, wiping out two-thirds of the Jewish population of Europe during the Holocaust.

Reds under the bed

During World War II, the United States and the Soviets put their differences aside in order to join forces to defeat the Nazis. Almost as soon as the war was over, however, tensions between the two superpowers resurfaced in a period known as the Cold War. Once again, the fear of international Bolshevik infiltration took hold. The USSR had seized control of much of Eastern Europe following the war, so while this fear was certainly not baseless, it was often expressed through paranoia, public hysteria and conspiratorial thinking.

In 1947, US president Harry S. Truman signed an executive order designed to root out communist infiltration in the US government. Two years later, the Soviet Union tested its first nuclear weapon, and two years after that, Ethel and Julius Rosenberg were tried and sentenced to death in a New York court for spying for the Soviets. In 1949, Chairman Mao Zedong declared China a communist country. US foreign policy at this time was refocused on defeating the spread of communism abroad. In 1950, the Korean War broke out and saw the US taking the side of South Korea against the communist and Soviet-affiliated North Korea. In 1954, the Vietnam War brought more of the same. All of these events contributed to a growing panic within the US administration about communism creeping into American life, and this filtered out into the general public. This threat was often talked about in apocalyptic terms, as a matter of life and death, by the administration at the time.[17]

In 1950, Senator Joseph McCarthy attracted a flood of press attention when, speaking at a meeting of the Republican Women's Club in Virginia, he revealed a piece of paper with a list of what he claimed were 205 communists working for the US State Department. Despite the fact that McCarthy could provide no evidence for his claims (in fact, McCarthy's secretary later stated that the sheet of paper didn't even contain any names), this sparked a campaign to expose suspected communists or communist sympathisers that would have deep ramifications in the lives of regular Americans.

What followed was a crusade that can only be described as a witch hunt in which thousands of people – including state employees, members of the media, those working in higher education, artists, intellectuals and filmmakers – were accused of being communists and called to testify before investigative committees. The grounds on which people were suspected of being affiliated with communism were outlandish and flimsy. Women who kept their maiden name after marriage were suspected, as were people who owned certain kinds of art or those who claimed sexual and racial discrimination against their employers. In general, so-called McCarthyism targeted people who held liberal or left-of-centre views and rarely succeeded in finding any actual communists. As a result, thousands of people lost their jobs and were included on 'blacklists'. It was reported that an untold number of people took their own lives for fear of having to testify before the committees. Although it is agreed that the communist threat at the time was not entirely fictitious, the reaction to it was greatly exaggerated.

McCarthy's fall from grace came almost as quickly as his rise. In 1954, during Senate subcommittee hearings that were broadcast on live television, McCarthy accused a number of people of aiding the Communist Party and exposed himself as a liar. The Senate condemned McCarthy at the end of the year, and he died of suspected alcoholism in 1957.

Ireland did not escape the effects of this kind of paranoid anti-communist fever, despite the fact that, as Professor of Modern History Enda Delaney points out, 'communism as a political force was never likely to have widespread appeal in Ireland'.[18] Although left-wing activists were often inspired by communist ideas, issues of sovereignty and other constitutional concerns related to the struggle for independence took precedence. This was even stated by the CIA, which, as Professor Delaney pointed out, was 'rarely known for its tendency to understate "red" fears'.

In fact, a more serious threat to Irish democracy at the time came from those who were influenced by fascism. Following the civil war, accusations of Bolshevism were used as a political weapon, especially by the pro-Treaty party Cumann na nGaedheal, which attempted to smear the anti-Treaty Fianna Fáil and the party's leader, de Valera, as Bolsheviks during the highly contentious 1932 election, which saw Fianna Fáil elected to government. The Blueshirts formed in the same year to provide protection for Cumann na nGaedheal and were explicitly anti-communist. Under the command of former Garda commissioner Eoin O'Duffy, the Blueshirts attracted tens of thousands of members, including many holding anti-Semitic views.

Membership was limited to Irish-born Christians, with O'Duffy stating that Jews had to be excluded because they 'are the instigators of communism'. The group was heavily influenced by European fascism leading to their adoption of the straight-armed salute and distinctive blue uniform that gave the group its name. O'Duffy even attempted a March on Dublin in 1933, modelled on Mussolini's successful March on Rome a decade earlier, but his plans were quashed by de Valera's government, which feared an insurrection and then suppressed the group.

Ned Cronin, who was O'Duffy's successor as leader of the Blueshirts, stated in 1934 that 'if a dictatorship is necessary for the Irish people, we are going to have one. It will be better than the so-called democratic Government we have, run by foreigners and Jews.' As historian John Newsinger explained, 'There should be no doubt that if the Blueshirts had been successful, Irish parliamentary democracy would have been replaced by some kind of authoritarian government reflecting the balance of forces between the conservatives and fascists in the movement.'[19]

After the Blueshirts merged with Cumann na nGaedheal to form Fine Gael, O'Duffy went on to lead the party briefly, although he was removed from his position for increasingly volatile rhetoric. Throughout 1935, he spoke at European fascist conferences and set up his own Mussolini-inspired fascist party. Driven by devout anti-communism and fascist beliefs, in 1936 he gathered several hundred Irish men to fight in the Spanish Civil War on the side of Franco, but they were ordered out of the country by Franco after drunkenness, indiscipline and general military incompetence.[20]

In 1945, a minor fascist party called Ailtirí na hAiséirghe (Architects of the Resurrection) had even more political success than the Blueshirts with its own distinct form of Irish fascism. The group was anti-Semitic and anti-democratic, and it campaigned for Ireland to become an authoritarian Christian state where emigration was illegal. The party also promised to build an army to reclaim Northern Ireland and said the English language would be made unlawful after five years. On Victory in Europe (VE) Day in 1945, the day Allied forces celebrated the defeat of the Nazis, members of Ailtirí were central in inciting riots in Dublin city centre. The movement was also responsible for what R.M. Douglas said 'may have been the world's first instance of Holocaust denial to appear in print' when the group claimed that film from German concentration camps were '"hate-mongering" fabrications'.

Ailtirí na hAiséirghe won nine seats in the local elections in 1945, making it one of the most successful of a small wave of fascist parties at the time. The party was short-lived and fell apart as a result of infighting, although some of its members went on to have successful political careers, including the Irish Labour Party's Seán Treacy. Oliver J. Flanagan, one of Ireland's longest-serving TDs and an overt anti-Semite, was a keen supporter of Ailtirí despite not being a member of the party. Today, far-right groups in Ireland regularly share Ailtirí's speeches and documents online, inspired by their vision of a traditional, authoritarian and Christian Ireland.

Even with all this fascist activity, communism was seen as a more threatening force at the time – with much of this campaigning coming from the Catholic Church, which held immense power in the country. The repression of Catholicism by the Bolsheviks in the USSR caused the Vatican to embark on a fervent anti-radical crusade, and the Catholic Church in Ireland followed its lead. 'When the Catholic Church took on anti-communism, that had a huge impact on Ireland,' Dr Hanley told me. 'By the late 1920s, communism became absolutely beyond the pale and was far, far more unpopular than fascism.' Dr Hanley explained that for decades the Catholic Church opposed any hint of communism in Ireland, to the point that even 'the mildest form of social democracy may have been denounced as communism'.

In 1933, religious mobs descended on Connolly House in Dublin, home of the Revolutionary Workers' Groups (RWG), after the clergy delivered furious denunciations of the organisation from their pulpits. A violent riot ensued, and the building was burned to the ground. This also happened outside of Dublin, most notably when RWG member James Gralton's socialist beliefs made him the only Irishman ever to be deported from the country; his story was dramatised in the 2014 film *Jimmy's Hall*.

When looking into the Irish anti-communist movement, one particular name pops up again and again: Father Denis

Fahey. Fahey was a professor of philosophy and church history in the Irish Holy Ghost Fathers, an order that was of particular importance in education in Ireland. He believed that Jews were responsible for the 1917 Russian Revolution and that communism was a Jewish plot aimed at overthrowing the Catholic Church. Fahey published numerous works outlining his theories, some of which cited the *Protocols of the Elders of Zion,* and his writings proved particularly popular in the US, where they were promoted by notorious anti-Semitic radio host Father Charles Coughlin.[21]

Fahey was also in close contact with anti-communists abroad, particularly those in the US who were fighting back against what they saw as communist subversion in the Hollywood film industry. Between 1949 and the early 1950s, a group called Maria Duce, whose members were devotees of Fahey, organised protests against Hollywood actors visiting Ireland. One of these was Gregory Peck, one of the best-known actors of the era, who was due to visit Dublin for a fundraising event in November 1949.

Peck was summoned before an investigative committee in the US and questioned about his affiliation with a number of liberal groups. Although he had thoroughly denied involvement or sympathy with any communist organisations, he was still labelled a 'rabid Red Front Eager Beaver' by Fahey's anti-communist contacts in the US. Peck's visit to Ireland was cancelled, and evidence revealed that this was due to the intervention of the Archbishop of Dublin John Charles McQuaid, to whom Fahey had passed documents regarding Peck's supposed communist ties.

McQuaid himself was staunchly anti-communist and highly influential within the Catholic Church. He set up a 'vigilance committee' to monitor supposed communist activity in the country, targeting leftist groups such as the Irish Housewives Association, trade union movements and the Irish Association for Civil Liberties.[22]

McQuaid's most famous and impactful pushback against fears of supposed communism came in 1951. Minister for Health Noël Browne – who had previously introduced a successful vaccination programme against tuberculosis, saving thousands of lives – proposed the Mother and Child Scheme in an attempt to tackle the devastating numbers of women dying in childbirth and high infant mortality rates. The programme would have entitled all mothers and children up to the age of 16 to free healthcare.

The Catholic Church, led by McQuaid, opposed the scheme, which it saw as a form of communism that would reduce the control the Church had in society and lead to the introduction of contraception and abortion. The Church's campaign was successful and resulted in Browne resigning his position and the first inter-party government being dissolved. After this, McQuaid triumphantly stated that defeating the scheme had 'thrown back socialism and communism a very long time'.

Reduce, reuse, recycle

The 1990s brought about a new era in geopolitics. The years before had seen the fall of the Berlin Wall, the lifting of the Iron

Curtain and the thaw of the Cold War. The USSR was no more, and communism's grip on the world had come to an end.

On 16 January 1991, US president George H.W. Bush addressed the nation about the start of the Persian Gulf War. Speaking about foreign policy in a post-Soviet world, Bush declared, 'We have the opportunity to forge for ourselves and for future generations a new world order.'

Those three words – new world order – sent certain segments of US society into a tizzy. Although the phrase had been used in a political context throughout history, including by Franklin D. Roosevelt and Robert F. Kennedy, right-wing conspiracy theorists and evangelical Christians had come to associate it with a sinister plot for world domination, installing a one-world government and destroying people's freedom.

The New World Order conspiracy theory has two distinct lineages – one secular, and one associated with evangelical Christianity – although both eventually converged and came to signify the same thing: the end of days and the end of freedom.[23]

The evangelical version has its roots in the vague mentions of the Antichrist in the New Testament and the belief in millennialism, or the End Times, during which all Christian believers would be spirited into heaven in an event called the Rapture. The father of this theory was an Anglo-Irish evangelical named John Darby, who was the curate at the Church of Ireland in Delgany, County Wicklow, before he left the church to promulgate his own interpretation of the Bible. Darby believed that, following the Rapture, non-believers would be subject to seven years of tribulation and a period of harsh terror and persecution at the hands of the Antichrist. Under the control of Satan, the Antichrist would rule the world as a dictatorship until an apocalyptic battle signalled Jesus Christ's return. This interpretation has become a dominant belief among modern-day Protestant evangelicals, particularly in the United States.

Within Protestant fundamentalism, speculation about who or what the Antichrist would be became widespread. This speculation often had an anti-Semitic element, with the assumption that the Antichrist would be a Jew. Others claimed people like Mussolini or Hitler, actual dictators, could be the Antichrist. The Antichrist was often thought to be deceptive, so they could also come in the form of a peacemaker, who fools the world into thinking their plans are noble, before unleashing terror.

As well as individuals, international organisations that were suspected of trying to implement a system of control were also believed to be the Antichrist. The United Nations, which had been set up to promote and maintain peace following World War II, was a prime target, as was the European Union. Technology was also feared, so claims spread that a supercomputer in Brussels that was able to keep track of everyone was an indication of the Antichrist. The New Testament also mentioned that the Mark of the Beast would be required during the reign of the Antichrist, so paranoia about microchips, barcodes and the internet were added to these beliefs.

This came together in an overarching fear of a New World Order that would include a one-world dictatorial power and a cashless society operated through the Mark of the Beast system.

The secular version of the New World Order was popularised by one particular group in the 1960s that reused many of the age-old conspiracy theories that were popular in the early 1900s and gave them new meaning in the postwar world.

The John Birch Society was founded in 1958 by Robert Welch, a retired candy manufacturer who named the organisation after a US Air Force captain killed by communists in China. According to Welch and the society members, or 'Birchers', communists had infiltrated the US government and were working with the Soviets to destroy US sovereignty. President Dwight D. Eisenhower, they claimed, was secretly a communist agent. According to Birchers, the United Nations was a front whose main aim was to create a one-world socialist government. Welch cited the work of Nesta Webster and suggested that this plan had been in motion since the eighteenth century, and that the Illuminati had planned the French Revolution, giving way to the rise of Marxism and Bolshevism, and colluded to create the United Nations to fulfil their plan: the implementation of the New World Order.[24]

Illuminati theories were also bolstered by a long-running anarchist prank called Operation Mindfuck, the brainchild of two men – Kerry Thornley, the founder of Discordianism, a satirical religion of chaos, and Robert Anton Wilson, a Discordian and *Playboy* writer. In the 1960s and '70s, they began planting stories in a number of publications associated with hippie culture and libertarianism accusing anyone and everyone of being in the Illuminati, blaming the secret society for assassinations, and claiming that they had infiltrated various businesses and industries.

A number of different conspiracy authors built on the suggestion of an impending New World Order throughout the 1970s and '80s. One of these was Gary Allen, himself a member of the John Birch Society. In his 1971 book *None Dare Call It Conspiracy*, Allen included 'international bankers' such as the Rothschilds and Warburgs in the conspiracy, suggesting that they had financed the Russian Revolution. Although Allen rejected accusations that this was anti-Semitic, his exaggerated claims of the influence of Jewish bankers compared to non-Jewish ones with little evidence was clearly influenced by anti-Semitic stereotypes.[25] Alex Jones has said that Allen's *None Dare Call It Conspiracy* was one of the most influential books of his teenage years.

An even more anti-Semitic version of this theory was produced by Eustace Mullins, a white supremacist and Holocaust denier. Mullins was a researcher for Senator Joseph McCarthy during his anti-communist campaigns. He believed in the blood-libel myth and had written a book claiming that World War I and the Great Depression were the work of a conspiracy between international bankers and the Federal Reserve. In 1984, Mullins wrote *The World Order: Our Secret Rulers*, in which he claimed that Jews played a central role in the New World Order through their control of the Illuminati.

Other elite 'globalist' organisations were also implicated as being part of the New World Order conspiracy theory, namely the Trilateral Commission, the Bilderberg Group and the Council on Foreign Relations. Further details were added about secret activities, including mythical claims that black helicopters were a sign of a military takeover and that concentration camps were being set up around the country to imprison those objecting to the takeover.

The moulding of Christian fundamentalist and secular New World Order theories had a pivotal moment in 1991, when Pat Robertson released his book *The New World Order*. Robertson founded one of the largest Christian TV networks in the US and was a well-known televangelist with enormous influence. He had unsuccessfully campaigned to become the Republican presidential nominee in 1988. His book presented the familiar story: the Illuminati and Freemasons had planned the French Revolution, which made way for the Russian Revolution, which was financed by Jewish bankers, who were all in turn plotting a one-world government under the watchful eye of Satan. The significance of Robertson's book lay in his position as both a popular religious and political figure, and his claim that evil forces were plotting to destroy both Christianity and American freedoms. His book became a bestseller, opening up a whole new audience to New World Order conspiracy theories.

Therefore, when President Bush Sr uttered those three words while addressing the nation in 1991, there were many who believed that the New World Order's plans were so far advanced that they were now speaking about it publicly.

This belief in New World Order theories coalesced in the 1990s in the form of the Patriot movement, a hybridised collective of right-wing anti-government groups that believed in the impending apocalypse at the hands of the New World Order. Included within the Patriot movement were so-called sovereign citizens or 'freemen on the land', a group who believe in various warped and flawed interpretations of the law and use this to claim immunity from laws they don't consent to. The sovereign citizen movement was established by William Potter Gale, an anti-Semitic white supremacist and member of the John Birch Society. The tactics of these movements were repurposed by the Covid-sceptic movement during the pandemic.

Other groups under the Patriot banner included militia movements and Second Amendment activists who believed that the removal of gun rights would lead to government oppression. Then there were militant anti-abortionists, neo-Nazis and extremist apocalyptic Christians. Many of these movements embraced survivalism and began to prepare themselves for a doomsday-type event, which they believed was an inevitability.

In 1993, a group called the Branch Davidians, who followed the apocalyptic teachings of their leader David Koresh, started arming themselves in preparation for the End Times. The group was living in a compound in Waco, Texas, that was the subject of a search warrant after law enforcement became suspicious that the group was stockpiling weapons. A 51-day siege ensued, resulting in a shootout and a huge fire, in which 76 Branch Davidian members, including 25 children, were killed. The scenes were broadcast on TV and showed how unprepared law enforcement was for dealing with groups holding such beliefs. The disaster at Waco galvanised the Patriot movement and contributed to a growing feeling that the apocalypse was nearing and that the government was out to get them.

Exactly two years later, Timothy McVeigh drove a truck loaded with 2,300kg of ammonium nitrate and nitromethane to the front of the Oklahoma City federal building. Just after 9 a.m., the bomb exploded, killing 168 people, including 19 children who were in a day-care facility in the building.

McVeigh, a right-wing extremist who believed in an impending New World Order, claimed afterwards that the events in Waco had spurred him into action against the government. McVeigh was almost certainly inspired by an anti-Semitic, anti-government novel called *The Turner Diaries*, a copy of which was found in his car when he was arrested after the bombing. The book's plot follows a violent revolution that is sparked by the bombing of a federal building, followed by a race war that would exterminate all Jews, non-whites and liberals. It has since become a key text for far-right and neo-Nazi movements across the world.

Since the 1990s, the New World Order has become one of the world's most convoluted conspiracy theories and has been baked into the fabric of many modern conspiratorial movements. The strength of the theory lies in its ability to mould itself to diverse movements and events. It can be used to spread fears about any kind of initiative that requires a collective global effort.

In recent years, it has been used as a means to push back against efforts to tackle climate change or issues around sustainability. The UN's Agenda 21 – a non-binding resolution signed by 178 nations in 1992 that outlines ways in which communities can deal with issues around sustainability, pollution and overpopulation – is consistently pointed to as a sinister communist plan to destroy people's liberties in the name of environmental action. This rhetoric can be traced back to none other than the John Birch Society, which claimed Agenda 21 was a 'socialist-conceived' programme for the 'global control and restriction over your daily life, including your private property, individual rights and civil liberties'. Some groups claim that it is a depopulation plan that would result in '90 per cent of the population murdered', while others see it as part of a Satanic Jewish plan to enslave the human race.[26]

These claims found a willing audience in the US Republican Party, which in 2012 called Agenda 21 a 'destructive and insidious scheme' that was meant to impose a 'socialist/communist redistribution of wealth'. Several states created 'anti-Agenda 21' bills that aimed to push back against any efforts of sustainability. Senator Ted Cruz even said that Agenda 21 would 'abolish … golf courses, grazing pastures and paved roads'. This is all the more ludicrous when you consider the fact that it was not even a legally binding agreement. Signing it was seen as a show of good faith that countries would take these issues seriously. It didn't involve any kind of enforcement and did not have the power to make countries or communities do anything.

Agenda 21 conspiracy theories were recycled during the Covid-19 pandemic and mixed with another UN sustainable development plan called Agenda 2030. According to these theories, the pandemic is a hoax and is simply part of a years-long scheme to introduce a one-world government in the name of sustainability. The restrictions on liberties that came with lockdowns easily fed into this and then mixed with more extreme theories of vaccines as depopulation tools or 5G as a global monitoring system.

In June 2020, the World Economic Forum (WEF) launched a new initiative called the Great Reset, and the New World Order conspiracy theory was given its newest coat of paint. The

WEF is a lobbying organisation funded by the world's richest corporations, and it is best known for hosting an annual summit in Davos, Switzerland, that brings together political leaders, celebrities, CEOs and other elites to discuss a range of global issues.

The Great Reset was launched through a podcast, book, website, and slickly produced video in partnership with Prince Charles. It referenced the vast array of problems facing the world – from climate change to poverty and a loss of biodiversity – and argued that the pandemic had created an opportunity to overhaul the economy and create a more sustainable world. The initiative did not go into any specifics on how this would be achieved, leaving the Great Reset open to interpretation.

There are many genuine reasons to criticise the WEF and initiatives like the Great Reset. Should unelected wealthy elites be able to have so much influence on global affairs when profit is always their priority? Do billionaires flying their private jets to a ski resort to discuss global poverty and climate change really want to solve the issues they are clearly contributing to? Should capitalism be the method we use to solve problems that have been created by capitalism?

Many believe that initiatives such as the Great Reset are a way for major corporations to give the impression of social responsibility while continuing to damage the planet and contribute to the wealth gap. Naomi Klein, writing in *The Intercept*, described it as a way to 'create a plausible impression that the huge winners in this system are on the verge of voluntarily setting greed aside to get serious about solving the raging crises that are radically destabilising our world'.

Nevertheless, these genuine criticisms were overshadowed by irrational fears when the Great Reset was added to the mix of New World Order-tinged conspiracy theories in the middle of the pandemic.

The first group to associate the Great Reset with sinister motives was the Heartland Institute, one of the world's leading think tanks promoting climate change denial, which called it a 'socialist' plan to 'destroy the global capitalist economy'. (Before switching to promoting views leading to the destruction of the planet, the Heartland Institute was tasked with destroying people's health by pushing back against the scientific consensus that smoking causes cancer.)

The Great Reset bounced around right-wing media and became a mainstay in conspiratorial communities towards the end of 2020. There, it was mixed with Agenda 21/2030 claims about the pandemic being part of a years-long plot to implement a communist one-world government, depopulate the world, strip people of their freedoms and possessions, and control them by social credit systems all in the name of a 'fake green agenda'.

In discussions on the Great Reset within conspiratorial communities, one line is quoted over and over as a sure sign that the WEF is planning to strip people of their possessions: 'You'll own nothing. And you'll be happy.' This line is not from the Great Reset initiative; it actually comes from a 2016 WEF video that made 'eight predictions for the world in 2030' and also included suggestions like 'we won't transplant organs, we'll print new ones instead' and 'you'll eat much less meat'.

The source of the 'you'll own nothing' quote was a blog written by Danish MP Ida Auken, who, writing from a city in an imaginary future, described a world where technological advancements had made transport, accommodation and food free. 'Welcome to the year 2030,' she said. 'I don't own anything. I don't own a car. I don't own a house. I don't own any appliances or any clothes … Everything you considered a product has now become a service.'

Admittedly, it's quite a *Black Mirror*-type prediction, but Auken clarified that this wasn't her idea of a utopia or a dream future; it was simply a scenario 'showing where we could be heading – for better and for worse', and she wanted the piece to start a discussion on the topic. She probably could not have foreseen that the discussion she started would link her blog to a nefarious plan to devise a pandemic in order to strip people of all their possessions.

The other overwhelming flaw in the idea that the WEF and the Great Reset want to reshape the world into a dystopian communist society lies in the fact that in order for this to be true, the companies who benefit the most from capitalist society, like Amazon, Apple and Microsoft, would all have to be part of a plot to destroy the profit-making economy. The idea that corporations have any interest in bringing about a communist world flies in the face of everything that business, and the capitalist world, is built on.

* * * *

The same pattern has repeated itself over and over again for centuries: fear, discrimination and stereotyping leads to an irrational belief in a plot to destroy the world. While the

Illuminati and Freemasons bore the brunt of this fear for decades, its coalescence with the scourge of anti-Semitism brought a trail of death and destruction that changed the face of the world. Modern conspiracy theories that borrow the themes of the *Protocols of the Elders of Zion* often mask the role of the Jews, but scratch the surface slightly and you'll find anti-Semitism staring back at you.

David Icke, the notorious UK conspiracy theorist who once declared himself the 'son of God' and predicted the end of the world in 1997, has (poorly) masked the anti-Semitism of his theories by calling the *Protocols* the 'Illuminati Protocols'. He has said that instead of Jews running the world, it is actually run by shapeshifting extraterrestrial reptilians descended from the bloodlines of 'Rothschild Zionists'. Icke has denied being an anti-Semite and refuted the idea that the reptilians are a euphemism for Jews, but his heavy reliance on the *Protocols* says otherwise.

Perhaps the most successful repurposing of the *Protocols* in recent years has come from its utilisation in QAnon, which endorses ideas of Jewish bankers and elites controlling the world through their supposed all-powerful influence, as well as including the explicit repurposing of the blood-libel myth.

The ultimate red pill, the belief that neo-Nazis want to inspire in 'normies', is the belief that Jews control the world and are therefore the root of all the world's problems. Because a huge number of modern conspiracy theory movements, from QAnon to Covid-scepticism, utilise a camouflaged version of the plot of the *Protocols*, it only requires removing the layers, those that mask it as the Great Reset or the New World Order, and burrowing a little further down the rabbit hole to come across the 'Jewish question'.

For years, Jim Corr was known as a member of the popular County Louth band The Corrs, but in recent years his belief in conspiracy theories has superseded his musical success. Corr launched a website in 2008 inviting people to join him on 'a journey … to get to the bottom of what is really going on in the world today'. He said that 9/11 was 'the nexus doorway into the bigger picture' that revealed a 'push towards … the formation of an elite run totalitarian One World Government'. His website linked to films such as *Loose Change, Zeitgeist* and Alex Jones's *Terrorstorm*. Over the years, the topics expanded beyond 9/11 trutherism to include climate change denial, health conspiracy theories and wild claims about airport X-ray scanners.

In December 2021, Corr shared a 13-minute video on Telegram in which an unidentified man gives his opinion on what is happening in the world. Zionists, the man said, control 'Big Tech' and 'the entire media structure' and sit in the halls of the US Congress and within American institutions. Left-wing ideologies are planted by Zionists to 'subvert and destroy our nation'. Feminism, he said, turns women against men, incentivises divorce, decreases fertility and destroys the family structure. Refugee crises, immigration and Black Lives Matter are part of a Zionist plan to divide people. He then recommended a neo-Nazi documentary to 'invert your entire … understanding of twentieth century history'. The person talking in the video caveats what he says by explaining that 'Zionists does not mean all Jews', yet he is seemingly unaware that he has regurgitated some of the oldest anti-Semitic myths and wrapped them in a layer of Holocaust denial. Corr shared the video along with the caption, 'This guy succinctly describes what's been happening and what we're all facing'.

These theories have also revived the paranoid anti-communist style of McCarthyism. In the US, the Republican Party has based its campaigns in recent years on the idea that they are saving the country from socialism. Middle-of-the-road Democrats are regularly branded 'socialists' and 'communists' when they are nothing of the sort. The tactic is being used to push back against much-needed progressive change – such as universal health care – and taps into a long-standing fear of creeping communism that has been ever-present in American life since the Cold War.

Besides spreading unnecessary hatred and fear, these conspiracy theories hinder the development of much-needed global initiatives that would tackle an array of problems facing the world. Any issue that needs collective action for the greater good, from a pandemic to climate change, can easily be spun into a sinister communist conspiracy.

The desire to explain the world as being under the control of a small group of secretive and demonstrably evil elite forces has always found a willing audience, and conspiracy theories that claim as such have been the most resilient, adaptable and damaging ones ever to spread across the planet. They fail to capture the full complexity of the world – but to many who feel as though they are constantly being lied to, they feel right.

Ultimately, what these theories do is distract people from the very real problems facing the world. When you have a large number of people searching for sinister plots that don't exist, they are not paying attention to the actual problems in society and those who are causing them.

Chapter 3

The Internet

WHEN THE ARAB SPRING ERUPTED IN LATE 2010, the power of the internet and social media was in full force for the world to see. Activists used Facebook and Twitter to spread photos and videos, gathering support and momentum for uprisings and protest movements that were erupting all across the Middle East. In 2013, after George Zimmerman was found not guilty of killing Trayvon Martin, a 17-year-old Black boy whom Zimmerman had fatally shot for the crime of walking down the street, Patrisse Cullors tweeted using the hashtag #BlackLivesMatter, and a civil rights movement was born. In 2015, the #YesEquality campaign played a pivotal role in helping Ireland become the first country in the world to introduce marriage equality by popular vote. Three years later, #TogetherForYes ran an equally successful campaign during the country's referendum on abortion rights.

The ability of the online world to bring people together is truly remarkable. The internet can provide sanctuary and can help people find like-minded others. Have a niche interest you want to explore? The internet has a community for you. In the early days of the internet, it seemed like we had finally discovered the tool that would strengthen democracy and bring us all closer together. However, just as the discovery of nuclear fission led to the invention of the atomic bomb, it became apparent quite quickly that the online world could also be utilised to bring out the worst in people.

Since the early 2000s, online subcultures have exploded in popularity and birthed some of the most toxic movements the world has ever seen. Some within these communities have turned to terrorism, others have joined extremist groups or far-right political parties, and countless others have dedicated their time to spreading hate and bigotry online in the name of 'trolling'. Others have become detached from reality and can no longer maintain relationships with friends and family members because of their descent down the rabbit hole of conspiracy theories. Although these groups once kept to their own fringe corners of the online world, in recent years their influence has penetrated the mainstream. It's important to know how these communities evolved and the power they wield – both online and in real life.

It's all fun and games ...

In 2017, Anita Sarkeesian, a feminist media critic and YouTuber, was invited to speak at VidCon, an annual conference for online content creators. Sarkeesian was one of four women on a panel discussing a range of issues related to being a woman online, including the proliferation of online harassment targeting women. Sarkeesian was only too familiar with the subject, being the target of a mass online abuse campaign that had begun years earlier, after she produced a series of videos on her YouTube channel looking at gender tropes and stereotypes in video games. The videos analysed how female characters were often portrayed in games – as damsels in distress, or as sexy, bikini-wearing background characters subjected to violence – and were part of a wider discussion that was taking place about breaking down old stereotypes in the gaming industry.

For decades, gaming was a boys' sport. Games were made for and marketed to boys (even though girls were also playing), hence the popularity of violent first-person shooter games and the emergence of scantily clad female characters with unrealistic-ally large breasts.[1] As games went mobile and online, more girls and women started to join online communities, and people like Sarkeesian began critiquing these old stereotypes. She wasn't calling for censorship, or for these games to cease to exist, but to a sector of the gaming community, Sarkeesian's videos were a sign that women were invading their 'boys-only club' in a bid to destroy it. For Sarkeesian, who dared to raise her head above the parapet and speak about creating a more inclusive space for women, this resulted in years of rape and death threats, the leaking of her personal information online (a tactic known as doxxing), and bomb threats sent to events she was meant to speak at. Eventually Sarkeesian had to leave her home for secur-ity reasons.

These abuse campaigns garnered widespread attention in 2014, when they took a more coordinated form in a controversy known as Gamergate. Gamergate began when the resentful ex-boyfriend of game developer Zoë Quinn posted a blog online that accused Quinn of sleeping with gaming journalists in order to secure positive reviews of her game *Depression Quest*. *Depression Quest* represented a new era of indie video game development. It was a semi-autobiographical game, in which the main character was dealing with depression. The format was extremely basic, and the game wasn't necessarily fun to play – but it wasn't meant to be. It received mostly positive reviews for its educational value and for tackling issues around depression in a unique way. Some gamers were not happy about this and felt threatened by the growing influence of women within the industry. Soon after the game's release, Quinn started receiving rape and death threats, both online and delivered to her home address, as well as phone calls encouraging her to kill herself.

When Quinn's disgruntled ex-boyfriend suggested in his blog post that Quinn's success was due to sexual promiscuity (these claims were found to be false), it gave the bitter gamers a conspiracy theory to latch on to: feminists and their allies, known to some as 'social justice warriors' (SJWs) were colluding with the media and gaming organisations to push a feminist agenda in gaming, they claimed. 'Gamergaters', as they were called, said they were pushing back against this to protect 'ethics in gaming journalism'. This pushback took the form of an unprecedented harassment campaign, organised through various websites, including 4chan and Reddit, and spurred on by anti-feminist activists on YouTube and Twitter. Women in gaming (and those who supported them) were besieged by abuse, threats and doxxing for years to follow.

The force Gamergate wielded online was unlike anything that had been seen before, and its strength came from a coalescence of various online subcultures. Many of these can be collectively termed the 'manosphere', a loose online network of websites, forums, podcasters and YouTubers. It was the manosphere that first popularised the use of the term 'red-pilling'. Those who are red-pilled within the manosphere are of the view that women play a dominant role in society and that men are being oppressed. They believe that feminism is a conspiracy to keep men subjugated, and that political correctness, the breakdown of traditional gender roles and SJWs are causing the destruction of the Western world. Feminists and their SJW allies are framed within these movements as perpetually offended 'snowflakes' who have been programmed through liberal society to hop onto the latest fashionable trend – be that caring about women's rights, the rights of refugees or the dangers of a disease.

It is important to say that men face many important issues that should not be dismissed. These include high male suicide rates, a lack of equality in custody disputes and few resources for male victims of domestic violence. It also needs to be said that there are elements within radical feminism that can take criticism of men to an extreme and refuse to acknowledge these issues. Many of the men who frequent the manosphere likely have very real grievances with society, but the answers that are given in these spaces feed an extremely toxic world view that can be particularly potent to those who feel rejected – whether romantically or, more generally, from society. Men are ranked as 'alphas' (charismatic, socially dominant men who have loads of sex), 'betas' (who are introverted and inept at relationships) or 'sigmas' (rare, lone-wolf types with alpha traits). Women are degraded, objectified and stereotyped as irrational and emotional beings who are 'hardwired to pair with alpha males' and seen as 'needing to be dominated.'[2] A common acronym in the manosphere is AWALT: 'all women are like that.'

Central to this thinking is a conspiracy theory known as cultural Marxism, which is in itself grounded in anti-Semitism. The theory claims that a small group of Marxist Jewish intellectuals from a school of social theory known as the Frankfurt School fled Nazi Germany in the 1930s and set up shop in the US. There they instigated a scheme to subvert Western thinking by promoting sexual liberation, multiculturalism and feminism.[3] Since the early 1990s, the theory has become popular among the right, where it has been used to decry anti-racist action, LGBTQ+ rights, feminism and generally anything that could be viewed as being under the umbrella of 'political correctness'. In 2011 Anders Breivik, a Norwegian neo-Nazi terrorist, killed 77 people in a bombing and shooting in Oslo and the nearby island of Utøya, motivated by what he thought was a cultural Marxist plot to corrupt European values. Cultural Marxism has since become a mainstay among various online movements, including the manosphere, Gamergate and the alt-right.

The manosphere evolved over time – from the men's rights movements in the late 1970s that refused to acknowledge male privilege and rejected feminism, to the rise of pickup artistry in the early 2000s, popularised by Neil Strauss's 2005 book *The*

Game, which gamified consent and gave men formulas to pick up women. As Dr Annie Kelly, who wrote her PhD thesis on digital anti-feminism, explained to me: 'If you look back on those spaces, you'll be surprised by how mild they seem compared to what we expect of [anti-feminist] spaces now.' Dr Kelly believes that today's manosphere, where rage, anger and the propensity to talk about women in the most toxic ways is par for the course, evolved out of 'a few canny entrepreneurs' who realised there was an appetite for hard-core misogyny within these spaces. In many ways, she says, 'pre-social media, they were responding to a function that we now understand, which is that abusive language, anger, punchy, shocking and controversial ideas rise to the top and get you lots of clicks and lots of advertising.'

The evolution of these disparate spaces into the collective manosphere and then into Gamergate, Dr Kelly reasons, was influenced by progressive movements like #BlackLivesMatter. They realised they could utilise social media and hashtags in the same way in order to get more eyeballs on their content, leading to more advertising and more donations. A few unsuccessful campaigns were attempted, but Gamergate was the one that broke through because they were able to tap into a huge digital community of gamers.

As Dr Kelly explained in her PhD thesis,[4] early gaming websites that promoted gaming news and events were often male-centric in nature and leant into a style of ironic misogyny. Gamers had their own history of sexist harassment campaigns, not just against Anita Sarkeesian, but many other women within gaming who called out misogyny or sexism. Women had also been speaking up for years about casual sexual harassment experienced while playing games, especially those where strangers play each other online and converse through voice chats. This culture, which often encouraged disrespecting women, made certain gamers more susceptible to the rhetoric of the manosphere.

Back at VidCon 2017, Anita Sarkeesian walked out on stage to find that the first three rows of the audience were filled with the exact people who had targeted her in the years-long abuse campaigns. Many were popular anti-feminist and men's rights YouTubers who had been key players in Gamergate and had made hundreds of videos attacking people like Sarkeesian and obsessively degrading her and her work. Their videos would receive tens – and sometimes hundreds – of thousands of views and were pivotal in galvanising the trolls who got a kick out of sending rape and death threats. They were in the audience to intimidate her and take their harassment into a real-life setting, and of course, they had their cameras out to record her reaction.

It didn't take long. A question was put to the panel on whether they had come up against obstacles in their career that they felt were linked to their gender or identity. Sarkeesian answered by talking about how her life completely changed following the targeted harassment of her. Then, gesturing towards the people in the first few rows, she said: 'If you Google my name on YouTube, you get shitheads, like this dude, who are making these dumb-assed videos. They just say the same shit over and over again. I hate to give you attention because you're a garbage human. These dudes just making endless videos that go after every feminist over and over again is a part of the issue of why we have to have these conversations.'

The 'garbage human' she was referring to was a British YouTuber named Carl Benjamin, who posts on YouTube under the name Sargon of Akkad. Benjamin was a hero to Gamergaters and made dozens of videos attacking Sarkeesian. In fact, he had essentially made a career out of it. In one particular video, Benjamin said that he didn't really think the harassment was affecting her because she didn't seem to be in 'extreme emotional distress'. If it was affecting her, he said, surely she would just leave Twitter. 'You are a charlatan. You're an imposter ... You do not care about gaming.' He then implied that Sarkeesian must issue the threats against herself, including bomb threats, in order to gain financially. 'Your threats sound made up, and they sound like they were made up by feminists ... who are pushing an agenda that you are profiting from.'

This is all the more ironic when you take into account that Benjamin at that time was bringing in almost $7,000 a month through his Patreon account and around $1.50 per 1,000 views on his YouTube channel (for context, Benjamin's YouTube channel currently has over 300 million views).

After VidCon, Benjamin appeared on *The Joe Rogan Experience* podcast where, when retelling what happened during the panel discussion, he accused Sarkeesian of harassing him. 'I did nothing to her,' he said with complete sincerity, despite stating in a video the evening before that they were planning to purposefully sit in the front row 'so she knows we're there'. His playing the victim after showing up at a discussion about harassment for the sole purpose of intimidating a woman whom he had spent many years harassing is the perfect analogy for the strategy of many in the manosphere, who think they are never to blame and seem incredulous to the idea that their actions bother people. A few minutes later, Benjamin looked directly into the camera and said: 'I've spoken to a lot of people who know you personally, Anita, and they say everyone hates you because you're a dick.' Charming. Benjamin has often been credited as the source of people's red-pilling into anti-feminism and on to further extremist movements.[5]

Sitting in the front row at VidCon beside Benjamin was Irishman Dave Cullen. Cullen had made a decent name for himself online in the early 2010s by critiquing tech products and reviewing games under the online moniker Computing Forever, amassing tens of thousands of subscribers on YouTube. He was so successful that he even wrote a book about how he was able to make a living off YouTube and earned himself a spot hosting a panel discussion at the tech conference Web Summit in 2015.

Cullen was a self-declared 'tech geek' and a review of his early videos showed that his knowledge in this area certainly warranted his success. Sometimes, Cullen strayed from his tech reviews and offered commentary on social issues that interested him, and mid-way through 2015, there was a clear indication that these thoughts were being influenced by the manosphere.

In a May 2015 video, Cullen said that efforts to attract more women to the tech industry were 'an attempt to make people question their natural inclinations', comparing this to trying to get men more interested in makeup tutorial videos. Cullen's main thesis, supported by cherry-picked scientific studies, was that differences between men and women are innate and driven by biology. He said feminism is 'trying to fuck with the natural order of things' by claiming that gender stereotypes are social constructs. 'Men and women are not designed to compete against each other in the workplace or the public sphere,' he said. Those who claim that women can do manual labour better than men are promoting 'populist rhetoric appealing to the "you go girl, bubblegum-brained Facebook generation"'. He called men who support feminists 'weak ass blue-pilled beta males' who are 'really just hoping … they might get laid.'

This video is quite typical of content produced by men's rights activists and anti-feminists in the manosphere, but one that is not supported by psychologists who research sex and gender. Writing in *The Conversation* in 2017,[6] Professor of Psychology Alice H. Eagly said that the science is complicated but agreed that 'neither nature-oriented nor nurture-oriented science can fully account for the underrepresentation of women in tech jobs'. She agreed that both biology and socially con-structed gender stereotypes play a role and warned against 'acting on the assumption of a gender binary', instead encour-aging people to 'treat individuals of both sexes as located somewhere on a continuum of masculine and feminine interests and abilities'. In other words, we're all different, and we're all different for different reasons.

Videos like this became more frequent on Cullen's channel throughout 2015. He described political correctness as 'a mind control mechanism that is designed to make people complicit in a lie'. Feminists and SJWs are 'cultural Marxists', he said, comparing them to communists and saying that they 'won't be happy until we all look the same and sound the same'. He viewed white heterosexual men as the real group being oppressed and blamed high male suicide rates on the 'feminisation' of mental health. In September 2015, he joined the Gamergate YouTube mob attacking Sarkeesian in a video where he called modern feminists like her 'annoying harpies, trying to control and brainwash women, particularly attractive ones that they're jealous of'. He reiterated the conspiracy theory floated by Benjamin about her using threats for financial gain, calling her a 'professional victim'.

By 2016, Cullen's tech reviews were becoming sporadic, and his channel descended into a hodgepodge of videos decrying the mainstream media, social justice campaigns, multiculturalism and the teaching of LGBTQ+ issues to children in schools. He supported Donald Trump's campaign for presidency and celebrated his win as a sign that 'a shit tonne of Americans have been red-pilled'. He also started collaborating with other YouTubers in the anti-feminist and men's rights activist scene.

In a December 2016 video, Cullen talked about the change of direction his channel took. He said he grew 'tired of the same old routine' reviewing tech products and became jaded by lazy innovation and the tech industry's reliance on planned obsolescence – that is, the deliberate manufacture of products that are designed to go out of date in order to keep people buying new products. Around 2013, he said he had a 'political awakening' and went from being a 'radical atheist with a contempt for religion and spirituality' to seeing 'the merit in the traditional Judeo-Christian values'. His belief that marriage is the 'fundamental building block of civilisation' and his 'respect for nationalism and traditional gender roles' made him realise that he had more in common with conservative Christians: 'We also seem to share common enemies in the globalists who wish to destroy the traditional Christian identity of their nations through multiculturalism and by using feminism to destroy the family unit.' Around this time, he 'discover[ed] things like Gamergate and Sargon of Akkad [Carl Benjamin] … and other anti-feminist content creators' and he began focusing more on politics in his videos. The friendship he sparked with Benjamin and others earned him a seat in the front row at VidCon alongside the main players in the anti-feminist and men's rights world who were there to intimidate Anita Sarkeesian.

Looking back on some of Cullen's earlier videos, there were signs that he was susceptible to the appeal of the red-pilled world. In a 2013 video, for example, he talked about his experience of depression and called antidepressants 'another marketing trick by Big Pharma to get people to part with their money and get them hooked on medication that is very, very bad for you'. It is clear in the video that he is passionate about good mental health services and seems frustrated by the pill-pushing approach of pharmaceutical companies.

There were also signs that he was wary of the potential effect the internet could have on the world. In a 2011 video, Cullen discussed whether the internet was contributing to lower critical thinking and shorter concentration spans. 'If humans become incapable of making insightful and well-informed decisions, will democracy suffer as a result?' he asked. In a number of other videos uploaded between 2011 and 2013, Cullen talked about social media addiction, the loss of privacy and the warped version of reality that the online world portrays.

In a 2014 video, Cullen spoke positively about the online world creating a 'global internet culture' that is beneficial when dealing with problems that 'we have to face together' such as environmental issues, terrorism or diseases. He even suggested that 'countries are an outdated model and we should have one global country'. By 2021, when Cullen was removed from YouTube for violating the platform's community guidelines, he was promoting white nationalist talking points, anti-globalist conspiracy theories about Agenda 21, Covid-19 conspiracy theories such as the Great Reset and climate change denial. Cullen did not respond to a request to comment on these claims.

Gamergate was a watershed moment in the evolution of toxic online subcultures. Its ability to bring together disparate groups and link communities that were not previously linked has had a profound impact on our social and political culture since. In order to fully understand the evolution of the manosphere and what it grew into after Gamergate, it's important to explore a website that has been critical in producing a very specific kind of toxicity online. It's time to talk about 4chan.

Memes, trolls & lulz

On 1 October 2003, a 15-year-old named Christopher Poole registered the domain 4chan.net and got to work coding his new website. It was inspired by a Japanese site called 2channel, a bulletin board where users could post anonymously without registering an account. 2channel was frequented by a mixture of Japanese subcultures – from the anime- and manga-obsessed *otaku*, to far-right xenophobes, or *netto-uyoku*. It quickly became one of the most visited and important websites in Japan. It was an anarchic place where rude and off-colour jokes were the norm, and anonymity was key to its success.[7]

Poole had come across 2channel while browsing another site called Something Awful (SA), which was founded in 1999 as a dark-humour site. SA attracted bored adolescents and gamers looking for shocking content, and the lax moderation on its forums meant that it spawned a particular type of culture. Dale Beran explains this in his book *It Came from Something Awful*: 'Rather than strip out all the bizarre aggression that inevitably accompanied forums, SA simply let it grow as a grotesque experiment, cultivated it, even. SA forums encouraged exactly what moderators elsewhere took great care to eradicate: bile, cynicism, cruelty, mockery and vulgarity.'

Poole's 4chan brought together the depravity of SA with the anonymity of 2channel. Unless you choose to give yourself a name (which most users don't), your post is automatically posted under the name 'anonymous', so 4chan users call themselves 'anons'. Critically, 4chan also took on the structure of 2channel, where discussion topics, or threads, would 'float' to the top of the page based on how many replies they had. Those with fewer replies would sink to the bottom of the page before being permanently deleted. This idea, of posts with the highest interaction floating to the top, would go on to be a feature of almost all social media networks.

Even though SA's moderation was lax, there were still rules. Poole's initial approach was much more laissez-faire (he was 15 years old, remember). If it was legal, it was allowed. That ruled out terrorism and child abuse imagery, although often these still slipped through the cracks. 4chan communities were divided into boards for different topics, and each board soon developed its own unique culture. The early days were full of anime, porn or anime porn. Soon came the furry community, people who felt a connection to cartoon animals with human traits, followed by the bronies, adults who were superfans of the kids' TV show *My Little Pony*.

4chan also cultivated new ideas and practices that would go on to shape the modern internet. Internet memes – ideas communicated through images, texts or videos – spread rapidly, both on 4chan and in mainstream culture. LOLcats (humorous images of cats with text overlaid) and Rickrolling (tricking people into clicking a link leading to Rick Astley's 1987 hit 'Never Gonna Give You Up') are both products of early 4chan culture. The site was providing laughs and entertainment to countless people who had never frequented the boards or even knew that it existed.

But there was also a darker side. Online trolls gathered on the /b/ board, or random board, and organised raids on unsuspecting online communities or individuals, also known as 'normies', mainly for the LOLs, or 'lulz', as they said. Their idea of a joke was often completely out of step with those living in the real world. One early example was the harassment of the parents of a young boy who had taken his own life in 2006, all because of a 'joke' spun by /b/ anons.

The power of 4chan soon became apparent. Shielded by a cloak of anonymity and bound by their desire to cause anarchy wherever they could, thousands of bored teenagers, hackers and trolls realised that they could do more than make memes and bully people online. Some of the denizens of /b/ came together in 2003 to form the anarchist hacker group Anonymous. In 2008, they began making a name for themselves by organising cyberattacks against the Church of Scientology. The same year, they hacked the email account of Republican vice presidential candidate Sarah Palin and shared her password on /b/.

Anonymous's reach extended across the world, with dozens of 'operations' linked to the group in the years following, including hacking the Tunisian government's website during the Arab Spring and a 2011 hack of the Fine Gael website. Although mainly known as an online vigilante group declaring cyberwar on organisations they saw as engaging in censorship and civil rights infringements, Anonymous was also involved in some of the nastier parts of 4chan's trolling, including a cyberbullying campaign against an 11-year-old girl. The damage they could do quickly became apparent and, soon, dozens of people were arrested all over the world for their involvement in the group.

Behind the lulz and the anarchic cyberbattles against evil forces, a darker and more twisted culture was forming. On the /r9k/ board, the jokes were becoming less funny and more filled with despair and self-loathing. For many, it became an entry point into involuntary celibate, or incel, culture. Incels sit at the most extreme end of the manosphere and are easily among the most disturbing subcultures on the internet. Incels believe they deserve sex but have been denied it by women. As a result, they hold overwhelming amounts of resentment and hatred towards women and wider society. As I write this, the latest post on a popular incel forum reads:

I boil with angery [sic] everyday, seeing everyone succeeding but me, even my friends are succeeding but me, I'm sick of failing in everything I do.

Girls, skills, socializing. I have no friends and shit so I don't care anymore. I will have my moment someday.

The not-so-very-thinly-veiled threat at the end of that post is not unusual for these forums, and a number of mass killers have been affiliated with the incel movement. Among them is Elliot Rodger, who killed seven people (including himself) in a murderous rampage in Isla Vista, California, in 2014. In 2018, Alek Minassian declared an 'incel rebellion' and praised 'Supreme Gentleman Elliot Rodger' in a Facebook post before killing 10 people in a van-ramming attack in Toronto, Canada.

The /r9k/ board had a similar culture and was frequented by many young men who felt isolated and angry that the world had denied them what they thought they deserved. Nihilism and misanthropy ruled, often cloaked in ironic humour about their perceived lack of status in life.

A post left on /r9k/ the day before a mass shooting at Umpqua Community College, Oregon, in 2015 is thought to have been left by the shooter, Christopher Harper-Mercer. The post read: 'Some of you guys are alright. Don't go to school tomorrow if you are in the northwest. Happening thread will be posted tomorrow.' Many replying to the thread wished the poster luck and encouraged him to target a girls' school. Harper-Mercer killed nine people that day and left a manifesto glorifying a number of mass killers, including Elliot Rodger.

A step to the left and a leap to the right

In what now seems like a predictable trajectory, by late 2011, neo-Nazis had started to flood the news board, /new/, with extreme content. In an effort to contain the problem, Christopher Poole created a new board called /pol/, which stood for 'politically incorrect'. It was designed to divert the white supremacists away from other parts of the site, but it soon became one of 4chan's most popular boards.

Users swarmed to /pol/ from other boards, and it quickly became a melting pot of racism, misogyny, anti-feminism, homophobia, transphobia, xenophobia … you get the picture. Ancient conspiracy theories mixed with new hatreds, like blaming all the world's ills on Jews, or women, or minorities, or social justice warriors or globalists. White supremacists calling for a white ethnostate promoted hate symbols like the number 1488, where '14' refers to a 14-word white nationalist slogan ('We must secure the existence of our people and a future for white children') and '88' is code for HH (Heil Hitler), H being the eighth letter of the alphabet. The trolls flooded /pol/ too, but they were now armed with swastikas for the lulz.

The /pol/ board was responsible for a significant shift in chan culture. Whereas 4chan was once associated with left libertarianism, reflected in groups like Anonymous, the addition of /pol/ swung 4chan to the far right. In 2013, another site joined the chan universe. 8chan was essentially a carbon copy of 4chan, but with the additional feature that users could set up their own boards for whatever topic they wanted. Its popularity soared after Christopher Poole banned conversations about

Gamergate from 4chan in 2014 (which indicates just how toxic Gamergate was). Gamergaters moved to 8chan and continued their coordination there. 8chan had one rule ('Do not post, request or link to any content illegal in the United States of America. Do not create boards with the sole purpose of posting or spreading such content.'), and it quickly became even more toxic than 4chan. It was aptly described in a 2018 *Politico* article as 'a sort of ISIS to 4chan's al-Qaeda'.[8]

This coalescence of movements and cultures on 4chan and 8chan was reflective of a wider shift taking place online, where the manosphere was becoming enmeshed with trolling chan culture and being influenced by older Nazi groups. A new, rebranded style of white nationalism was emerging in people like Richard Spencer, an anti-Semite and neo-Nazi who wore sharp suits and sported a haircut that was long on top and short on the sides, a style that would become associated with this emerging and extremely online movement. Spencer is often credited with naming this new movement the 'alt-right'. The alt-right worked by taking immature, disaffected young gamer types and trolls, and exposing them to white nationalism, misogyny and anti-Semitism in an ironic way (for the lulz). Quickly the jokes lost their humour, and followers became red-pilled into white nationalism.

Gamergate played a significant role in the alt-right's rise, especially through its promotion by the far-right site Breitbart News. At the time, Breitbart was run by Steve Bannon, a former investment banker turned political operative who took the reins of the site after the death of its founder Andrew Breitbart. Bannon didn't hide his love for fascism, often citing Julius

Evola, an Italian traditionalist philosopher and self-described 'superfascist' whose views influence global far-right movements to this day. Bannon would go on to become head of Donald Trump's 2016 presidential campaign and held the position of chief strategist within the Trump administration until August 2017.

At Breitbart in 2014, Bannon hired Milo Yiannopoulos, a British conservative tech journalist who was half-Jewish and gay (although in 2021 he declared himself an 'ex-gay' and advocated for conversion therapy). Yiannopoulos was the perfect poster boy for the alt-right. How could a gay half-Jew be accused of homophobia, racism and anti-Semitism? Yiannopoulos covered Gamergate relentlessly from the view that it was about 'protecting ethics in games journalism', calling people like Anita Sarkeesian and Zoë Quinn 'lying, greedy, promiscuous feminist bullies' and downplaying the death threats made against them. Yiannopoulos brought 4chan's trolling and hateful culture to *Breitbart*, and his slurs would often get picked up by mainstream media, which wrote about them with disgust. This ultimately spread his views even further – the ultimate goal of any troll.

In 2015, Yiannopoulos embarked on a university campus tour called 'The Dangerous Faggot Tour'. At this time, campuses were the battleground in culture-war topics related to race and identity, and his speeches would frequently be met with violent clashes with counterprotesters. When speaking in Milwaukee in 2016, he singled out a transgender student in the crowd, outing her and displaying her photo on a large screen. He deadnamed her (used her male name) and said she 'forced *his*

way into the women's locker rooms'. He also called her a
'tranny' and referred to her as an 'it', saying, 'It's just a man in a
dress, isn't it?' In 2016, in a scathing review of the new *Ghostbusters*
film, Yiannopoulos singled out actress Leslie Jones as 'a two-
dimensional racist stereotype'. The subsequent racist and
bigoted abuse directed towards the actress caused her to leave
Twitter for a period. After referring to Jones as a 'black dude',
Yiannopoulos himself was kicked off Twitter.

Emails uncovered by BuzzFeed in 2017 show that
Yiannopoulos was in contact with well-known neo-Nazi and
white supremacist figures, who consulted on (and essentially
edited) a key Breitbart piece on the rise of the alt-right. The
emails also showed how ruthless Bannon's editorial strategy
was. He had little cause to worry about the truthfulness of the
claims they were making, worrying more about 'sav[ing]
Western civilisation' in what he saw as a 'global existentialist
war'.[9] Yiannopoulos eventually fell from grace in 2017, when a
video emerged of him talking positively about teenagers having
sex with adults. Yiannopoulos put his remarks down to ironic
satire and explained that it was his way of dealing with his own
experience of child sexual abuse. He subsequently stepped
down from his position at Breitbart and was relegated to sporadic appearances on Alex Jones's InfoWars.

From the moment Donald Trump announced his candidacy
for president in the 2016 election, the alt-right embraced him –
here was a man who wasn't afraid to call out political correctness
or describe Mexican immigrants as 'rapists'. Trump would boast
about his sexual exploits, including sexual assault, and promote
conspiracy theories. The fact that Trump's opponent in the

election was Hillary Clinton, who was already a divisive figure in US politics, as well as being a woman and a feminist, solidified his support. Trump frequently referred to Clinton as 'Crooked Hillary', a criminal who needed to be 'locked up'. The alt-right hated Clinton and wanted to see her lose at any cost.

During the presidential campaign, the 4chan and 8chan segments of the alt-right engaged in what they termed the 'Great Meme War', a constant barrage of pro-Trump and anti-Clinton trolling and shitposting that used networks of fake Twitter accounts to spread their messages. Fake news websites (when 'fake news' still meant fake news) spread wild claims and conspiracy theories about Clinton to older and less tech-savvy generations of internet users on sites like Facebook. These were also bolstered by accounts and websites run outside of the US (most notably Russia), which were deliberately spreading disinformation in order to influence the election. Alt-right influencers, many of whom made a name for themselves during Gamergate, bolstered support for Trump even further. And Trump, in turn, leaned into the alt-right. On multiple occasions, he tweeted memes that originated on the chans. In November 2015, in what was in essence a hat tip to chan culture, Trump retweeted a meme of himself depicted as Pepe the Frog, a cartoon and meme co-opted by /pol/, which became a symbol of the alt-right during the presidential campaign. When Steve Bannon came on board Trump's campaign, his understanding of the alt-right and the online subcultures they came from upped the ante even more.

Hillary Clinton couldn't keep up. When she called out the alt-right in a speech two months before the election, chan users took it as a win. The moment was also co-opted by an audience member who shouted 'Pepe!' at the same moment she said 'alt-right'. The audience member was a 4chan anon, who was encouraged to shout it by users on /b/, where he was posting at the time. Just over a week later, Clinton's misjudged attempt to label half of Trump's fan base as a 'basket of deplorables' was also quickly reappropriated by the alt-right and worn as a badge of honour. It was made into a meme, when a poster for the film *The Expendables* was Photoshopped to become *The Deplorables*, featuring Trump, his sons, Alex Jones, Milo Yiannopoulos and, of course, Pepe the Frog among its 'cast'. Clinton's campaign then released a cringeworthy explanation and condemnation of the Pepe the Frog meme, which revealed how out of touch she was with the powerful online forces that were pushing for Trump to be president. She also had to put up with nonsense conspiracy theories about her apparent failing health, her support for ISIS and her supposed involvement in various murders and crimes.

When Trump was elected, many on 4chan were convinced it was down to their efforts: 'We actually elected a meme as president,' said one anon. That is certainly an exaggeration, as there were more elements at play than just the online antics of racists and trolls. However, there's no doubt that the tactics employed by the alt-right changed the rules of political campaigning – perhaps forever.

Alt-Éire

The Irish iteration of an alt-right had been brewing online for a number of years. The 2010s saw significant social changes in Ireland. The influence of the Catholic Church had been depleted after revelations of rampant child sexual abuse and the horrific treatment of women and children in church-run institutions. Same-sex marriage and abortion rights were legalised by popular vote and a country that was once ethnically homogenous was becoming more diverse. The Irish alt-right formed as a reaction to these changes, while also being influenced by the same online subcultures that spawned the alt-right in the US.

Throughout 2017, 2018 and 2019, Irish-themed threads were posted on 4chan on an almost daily basis, encouraging Irish users of /pol/ to join home-grown far-right groups and political parties, and directing attention to a small but growing group of Irish alt-right figures and media sites. Analysis I conducted in September 2019 while working with Storyful identified more than 22,400 posts made on /pol/ in the month previous from users who identified as Irish.

Like their US counterparts, Irish /pol/ anons organised abuse campaigns against their perceived enemies – journalists, feminists, liberals and anti-fascists – and in general, followed the culture that evolved with the US alt-right. Their misogyny was on full display when they were involved in collecting and sharing portfolios containing photos of Irish women. Some of the photos were of an intimate nature, and anons shared the women's personal details, while others bragged about stealing the photos directly from women's phones.

Irish 4chan users soon took their antics to the streets. In March 2018, in the run-up to Ireland's referendum on legalising abortion, marchers at a pro-choice rally in Dublin were deceived into carrying placards emblazoned with the symbol of the British Union of Fascists. A user on 4chan boasted that he and 'some mates' had printed the posters and handed them out and that 'the morons took the bait'. The user shared photos from the march and encouraged others to 'spread this shit'. The images went viral after campaigners such as John McGuirk, the communications director of the anti-abortion campaign and editor of the right-wing website Gript, called for condemnation of the rally-goers.

During the summer of 2018, Pantibar, a popular LGBTQ+ bar in Dublin city centre, had a brick thrown through its window during Pride weekend. The brick had *piteoga amach as Eireann* ('fairies out of Ireland') written on it. A teenager was arrested over the incident and my former Storyful colleagues discovered that he had been posting on 4chan at the time, writing, 'About to commit a hate crime lads it involves a stone and some piteoga wish me luck xxx'. He went on to say that there were 'a lot of faggots and bouncers' outside. When someone asked him what he was doing, he replied, 'I want to throw a brick through the window of this busy gay bar' and was egged on by other anons in the thread.

The daily Irish threads on /pol/ consistently urged users to join the National Party, an ethno-nationalist party that was formed in 2017 out of former members of the extreme anti-abortion group Youth Defence. The National Party's leader, Justin Barrett, has links to a number of European far-right movements, and in the early 2000s he spoke at events organised by neo-Nazis in Germany and Italy. In 1998, Barrett published his own manifesto called *The National Way Forward*, outlining his vision of a 'Catholic Republic' where immigration was restricted, and abortion and divorce were banned. He also campaigned against the legalisation of divorce – before proceeding to end his own marriage a number of years later and saying that he had changed his mind on the issue. Barrett's vision of a country where 'faith, family and nation' were at the fore, and in which a directly elected president would have the ultimate control, has echoes of the sentiments expressed by Ailtirí na hAiséirghe in the 1940s. Neither the National Party nor Barrett responded to a request to comment on these claims.

In 2018, a new far-right political party joined the ranks, also widely promoted on 4chan. Hermann Kelly, the press officer for former UKIP leader and leading Brexiteer Nigel Farage, formed Irexit, subsequently renamed the Irish Freedom Party. As the original name suggests, the party advocates for Ireland leaving the EU. It regularly promotes anti-immigrant and anti-LGBTQ+ rhetoric but rejects the far-right label, instead saying that it 'supports … the people of Ireland to make their own laws and determine their own future outside of the European Union'.

Kelly's relationship with Farage is not the only link between the Irish Freedom Party and the British right. Kelly has appeared in online live streams with Jim Dowson, a former member of the Orange Order and leading member of the British National Party. At the same time the first Irexit conference took place in Dublin's RDS Arena, anonymous accounts appeared online promoting Irexit, some gaining significant followings and reach. One such account, Muintir na hÉireann (People of Ireland), was linked to a website of the same name that promoted Irexit events, featured articles written by Irexit members and offered an Irexit newsletter. The content on the site propagated conspiracy theories about the dangers of globalism, migration and Ireland's membership of the EU.

An investigation into the website by an Irish anti-racism campaigner (which I independently verified) found that it was run by a former UKIP member named Dilip Sengupta, known as Jack Sen. Sen is an anti-Semite and neo-Nazi with links to David Duke, the former leader of the Ku Klux Klan. Sen stood as a candidate for UKIP in 2015 but was kicked out of the party just days before the election for an anti-Semitic tweet he directed at Labour candidate Luciana Berger. Sen subsequently accused UKIP of being 'in the pockets of Jewish special interest groups'.

Sen's email address was listed on the Muintir na hÉireann website, along with his physical UK address. Further investigation into the website found that it had previously been called the European Knights Project and dated back to 2014. This site contained blatant white supremacist, neo-Nazi and anti-Semitic content, including pictures of Sen himself, and records of bank payments he had made to known white supremacists. The site also contained white supremacist memes created for an Irish audience.

Just days before the first Irexit conference, the European Knights Project website was rebranded as Muintir na hÉireann and began promoting Irexit. Although the Irish Freedom Party denied having any knowledge of or contact with Jack Sen, and said that it had no connection to the Muintir na hÉireann website and social media accounts (which closed down shortly after this information was made public), there are multiple instances of Hermann Kelly and other members interacting with the account in a personal capacity. This includes tweets congratulating the person running the accounts on the birth of their child. Sen told *Byline Times* that his involvement extended to hosting the website only. He subsequently moved to Donegal, where he was arrested in October 2018 (and released without charge) when Gardaí found ammunition in his house.

Questionable online antics associated with the Irish Freedom Party didn't end there. During the local elections in 2019, an email was sent to a number of media organisations in County Kerry informing them of a candidate running for the Irish Freedom Party named Mairead Donovan. The email said that Donovan, a retired nurse, made the decision to run after attending an Irexit conference, and that she would be opposing the closing of rural post offices and fighting for more money for carers and ambulance services. It continued by saying that Donovan 'has seen her beloved Ireland change to something she [could] no longer recognise'.

There was a major problem, however. Mairead Donovan did not exist. She was a fiction, and the image used in both the email and on a profile for her listed on the Irish Freedom Party website was a stock photo. When questioned about the non-existent candidate, Hermann Kelly denied the party had sent the email, accused the local Kerry media of fake news and said the image and detail about Donovan on the website was a 'place filler'.

Through 2018 and 2019, the new, emerging Irish alt-right was growing and coalescing in a similar way to the US, where anonymous online trolls mixed with known members of far-right groups who were then interviewed and promoted by a growing number of YouTubers. These, in turn, were bolstered by right-wing media sites such as the paradoxically named The Liberal and Gript, which both regularly host content sympathetic to the far right.

Joining YouTubers like Dave Cullen, who had started promoting Irish far-right figures on his channel from around 2017, were people like former journalist Gemma O'Doherty. O'Doherty attempted to stand for presidential election in 2018 but failed to secure enough votes for nomination. Her campaign was plagued with controversy after she claimed there was state collusion in the murder of journalist Veronica Guerin. This was a sign of the direction her political interests would take her. O'Doherty was descending into conspiratorial and far-right narratives for a while, but the years following her failed presidential bid would see her rise to the top ranks of the Irish far-right movement by broadcasting various bizarre conspiracy theories on YouTube (before she was removed in 2019) and launching a conspiracy-laden political party called Anti-Corruption Ireland.

Representing the ultra-conservative Catholic side of the alt-right is a Donegal man named Niall McConnell and his tiny ethno-nationalist and anti-Muslim group Síol na hÉireann. McConnell also began streaming on YouTube, interviewing British far-right nationalists including Jim Dowson and BNP president Nick Griffin. In July 2020, Síol na hÉireann was one of the organisers of a protest staged outside Croke Park football stadium in Dublin, after Muslim worshippers used the grounds to celebrate Eid. The Eid celebrations were a target for disinformation at the time, with The Liberal spreading the false claim that the stadium would be used to 'host a Muslim large blood sacrifice ritual' involving the slaughter of animals. A month later, McConnell posted a video online of himself and other members of Síol na hÉireann protesting outside a church in Ballyhaunis, County Mayo, after the priest had allowed Muslims to pray in the chapel. McConnell confronted the priest, calling him a 'heretic' and accusing him of bringing 'foreign, Satanic cultists' into the church.

Between mid-2018 and the end of 2019, the growing Irish far right found a focus for their attention: direct provision centres. The system Ireland uses to house asylum seekers, direct provision had long been widely criticised for being inhumane and poorly managed, with people often living in centres for years before their applications were processed. It was condemned as expensive, with private companies making millions of euros through the cruel system in the 20 years it had been in place.

In 2018, in order to deal with increasing pressure, the government began seeking contracts for direct provision centres in empty hotels and B&Bs in rural areas of the country. In many instances, locals were not properly informed about the plans to house sometimes hundreds of asylum seekers in tiny towns where services were already few and far between. Understandably, people had concerns, and these concerns and the lack of consultation were quickly seized upon and exploited by far-right actors.[10]

The first signs of trouble came in late November 2018, when a hotel in Moville, County Donegal, which was planned as a direct provision centre, was targeted in an arson attack. Following that, in the space of less than three months, two more similar attacks targeted a hotel in Rooskey, County Roscommon, spurring anti-racism demonstrations in the town. The centres planned in both Moville and Rooskey were subsequently abandoned. The arson attacks coincided with a visit to Ireland by Lauren Southern, a Canadian far-right activist working for the Breitbart-esque Rebel News. Southern met with Irish far-right activists to propagate conspiracy theories about the refugees coming to Ireland.

In March 2019, a meeting about the launch of a community pilot programme to welcome one Syrian family to Lismore, County Waterford, was disrupted by far-right activists shouting about whether there were members of ISIS in direct provision. In this case, their tactics were wholly rejected by locals, who happily welcomed the Syrian family.

Later in 2019, plans were made to open a direct provision centre in the small town of Oughterard, County Galway – again, with little public consultation. The town has a population of 1,300, and there were plans to house 250 asylum seekers in a centre there. Increasing the population of a small, rural town with limited services by 20 per cent understandably came with frustration and concern, which were quickly seized upon by far-right figureheads.

Gary 'Gearóid' Murphy is a leading figure within the Irish far right. Murphy had visited Moville, Rooskey and a number of other towns where direct provision centres were planned, but he was particularly influential in Oughterard. As well as speaking to people on the ground and handing out flyers, Murphy was using social media to steer the conversation. He had recorded a two-hour video using legitimate flaws about direct provision to claim there was a left-wing conspiracy at play to 'subvert, undermine and intimidate people who oppose the opening of ... direct provision centres in their local communities'. He falsely claimed that most asylum seekers were not legitimate and that the Syrian war had 'ended for some time'.

Murphy said that welcome groups set up to help asylum seekers when they move to rural areas were part of a sinister totalitarian government plot and reasoned that the arson attacks in Rooskey were 'false flags'. The endgame of this conspiracy, he said, was to make it illegal to oppose direct provision. He encouraged people in local communities to 'identify and marginalise' people working for NGOs and 'engage in Machiavellian thinking'. The video was viewed over 14,000 times before being removed from YouTube for copyright infringement.

Meanwhile, Conor 'McZorba' Rafferty, a former Irish Freedom Party member and administrator of a group for Gemma O'Doherty supporters, joined Facebook groups used by locals to discuss proposed direct provision centres and shared Murphy's video with the aim of influencing their opinion on the subject. 'Very detailed and meticulous fact-based investigation into the refugee industry in Ireland,' he wrote in a Connemara group. 'A DIY kit for targeted communities,' he said in another. Links to far-right media sites such as Breitbart were also shared in these groups as an effort to influence the opinions of locals.

Local residents discussed the video in an Oughterard Facebook group set up to organise protests against the centre. One key organiser called it 'extremely factual and well put together … it explains the whole thing.' Another called it an 'eye-opener to the reality of what's going on'.

The situation in Oughterard was promoted widely by national and international far-right figures. Many locals who felt like they had legitimate concerns about the impacts of a direct provision centre on their town were angered by the involvement of the far right, because it meant they were being branded as racist. The plans in Oughterard were eventually abandoned after continued local opposition.

Many locals were not against housing asylum seekers but took issue with the lack of public consultation, the lack of planning to increase services and the inhumane treatment asylum seekers received in direct provision centres. 'I am not alone in this community in wanting to welcome families who need help, but don't put them in a prison, which is what a direct provision centre is,' a local teacher told the *Sunday Times*.[11]

It's difficult to assess the impact Murphy's video and the wider far-right campaign had – and Murphy did not respond to a request to comment – but it's clear that they were attempting to take control of local debates about immigration, both on the ground and online, and to spread fear and conspiracy theories.

Murphy mentioned his involvement in Oughterard in a live stream on which he appeared with a British far-right figure in September 2020. In response to a comment made by the host, who said there was 'nothing of substance to be gained from having racially and culturally foreign people imposed upon you', Murphy discussed his engagement with locals in Oughterard: 'I had liaised with them [the locals] and kind of red-pilled them a bit. Not to toot my own horn, but I gave them the language and the wherewithal [to push back].'

Those watching Murphy's video likely didn't see themselves as racist, but they were engaging with far-right talking points and using them to form opposition.

Oughterard was a turning point, however, and further campaigns attempted by members of the National Party, the Irish Freedom Party and other far-right individuals in towns like Borrisokane, Carrickmacross and Ballinamore were rejected by locals. There's no doubt that the wholly flawed direct provision system and the government's lack of consultation with the public were the initial sources of a lot of anger. In February 2021, plans were announced to end direct provision by 2024 and replace it with a not-for-profit system.

From the tweets to the streets

Trump's election in 2016 brought with it a wave of violent protests in the United States between a galvanised far right and the emergence of a loosely connected anti-fascist force, often collectively known as antifa. The Proud Boys, a self-described group of 'Western chauvinists' whose members also hold far-right beliefs and think women belong at home raising children, were prominent within these clashes (easily identified by their Fred Perry polo shirts), as were members of more blatant neo-Nazi groups such as Identity Evropa. This violence was spurred on after a video of Richard Spencer getting punched in the face went viral, along with the question, 'Is it okay to punch a Nazi?'

In August 2017, the alt-right show of force was put on display for the world to see when they descended on Charlottesville, Virginia for a rally called 'Unite the Right'. Two years earlier, then-21-year-old Dylann Roof had gunned down nine African Americans who were attending a Bible study in Charleston, South Carolina. This mass shooting had caused many cities to remove Confederate statues and flags from their public spaces. Charlottesville also decided to remove a statue of the Confederate general Robert E. Lee, a decision that was seen as an attack on white history by many far-right movements and supporters of the Confederacy.

Various groups were protesting the statue's removal through-out the summer, which resulted in clashes with police and counterprotesters, and arrests. The August rally was organised by Spencer along with white supremacist and blogger Jason Kessler. The event was planned for Saturday the 12th, but on Friday evening, Spencer and Kessler led a group of about 250 people, mainly white men, through an area on the campus of the University of Virginia. The group carried tiki torches and chanted 'Jews will not replace us', 'You will not replace us' and the Nazi slogan 'Blood and soil'. They met a group of counterprotesters, and violent clashes broke out. Eventually, the police arrived to break up the groups. The next day, it would get even worse.

The crowds gathered early. Various white nationalist and neo-Nazi groups, holding anti-Semitic banners, Confederate flags and swastikas, were joined by militia groups in full military fatigues. Many had come armed with guns, shields and sticks. Counterprotesters gathered too, and some of them were also armed. At first, those who gathered sang hymns, prayed and linked arms before the scenes took a violent turn. Police struggled to contain the situation, and dozens of people were injured. A state of emergency was declared, and the gathering was deemed unlawful.

A couple of hours later, a man named James Alex Fields Jr deliberately drove his car at high speed into a group of counter-protesters, before reversing back through the crowd and driving off. One person, 32-year-old Heather Heyer, was killed, and dozens more were injured in an attack that was described as an act of domestic terrorism. A fan of Hitler, Fields was seen earlier in the day holding a shield with the logo of neo-fascist group Vanguard America, although they denied he was a member. He was found guilty of first-degree murder and is serving two life sentences.

Trump's initial response to the events in Charlottesville was to say that there 'were very fine people on both sides', which prompted outrage from both Republicans and Democrats. Eventually, he found the right words, declaring that 'racism is evil, and those who cause the violence in its name are criminals and thugs', while calling out the KKK, neo-Nazis and white supremacists as 'repugnant'. Steve Bannon's position in the Trump administration also came under scrutiny in the days that followed, and less than a week later, he left his position as Trump's chief strategist. Bannon's exit had been coming for a while, apparently, but his pandering to the alt-right and the events of Charlottesville had all but caused the door to slam behind him.

Although meant to be a display of force and power and a way to show the country that they weren't just an internet meme, the Charlottesville rally ended up poisoning the name of the alt-right and fractured the movement. Richard Spencer retreated from public life, as did many of the other Unite the Right leaders and speakers. Spencer, Kessler and a number of other prominent organisers on that day were subsequently found guilty of conspiracy and race-based harassment in a lawsuit brought by nine Charlottesville residents. In its online bubble, the alt-right was still trolling, harassing and bending reality, but its effort to be seen as a united force on the ground had failed.

Only whites need apply

Vice reporter Tess Owen reported from the Unite the Right rally on the day and embedded herself with a number of the event's main speakers. At one point, she met David Duke, the former Grand Wizard of the Ku Klux Klan. He complained that they were not allowed to set up their speakers and said this was because they were telling the truth: 'We're talking about the ethnic cleansing of America and the destruction of the American way of life, and a new Bolshevik-style society with no freedom, no freedom of speech, in this country.'

The protesters' chants on the Friday evening ('Jews will not replace us' and 'You will not replace us') and Duke's mention of an 'ethnic cleansing' are rooted in variations of the white geno-cide conspiracy theory, which is inherently associated with white nationalism and supremacy. The white genocide conspiracy theory was popularised in the mid-1990s by David Lane, a white supremacist and member of the terror organisation The Order. Lane died in prison in 2007 while serving a 190-year sentence for his role in the 1984 murder of Jewish talk radio host Alan Berg. Lane also came up with the '14 words' mentioned earlier. The chants about replacement are references to the Great Replacement, a term coined by French philosopher Renaud Camus in his 2011 book *Le Grand Remplacement*, which is essentially a less offensive term for white genocide.

Both white genocide and the Great Replacement theories are cut from the same cloth. They claim that there is a deliberate elitist plot at play to eradicate the native/white populations in Western countries and replace them with ethnic and cultural minorities. Those who subscribe to these baseless theories claim that mass immigration is to blame, along with low birth rates among white people because of the promotion of interracial marriage, abortion, same-sex relationships and feminism. They claim that the alleged effort to destroy native populations and their culture is being orchestrated by politicians, the media, 'globalists', the Jews or a mixture of all of the above. Similar theories are seen in the Kalergi Plan, which alleges a deliberate plan by elites to undermine the white European population through mass immigration. Another version of this is the concept of Eurabia, which claims there is a plan to 'Islamise' Europe. Oslo terrorist Anders Breivik subscribed to this version.

These claims are simply not rooted in reality. To begin with, a genocide involves committing acts of violence or harm against a particular ethnic, religious, racial or national group with the intention of destroying them. The Holocaust was genocide. The killing of thousands of Bosnian Muslims in the mid-1990s was genocide. In Cambodia, the organised mass killing of ethnic minorities by Pol Pot's Khmer Rouge was genocide. The slaughter of Rohingya Muslims in Myanmar is genocide. What white supremacists describe as 'genocide' or 'ethnic cleansing' or 'replacement' is simply people of different ethnicities or religions moving to predominantly white countries and living there. The use of the word 'genocide' to describe the presence of people trying to make a better life for themselves is not just deeply disrespectful to those who have survived conditions of genocide, but it implies that immigrants are somehow 'impure' and an existential threat to the native populations, which they are not.

People emigrate for various reasons – war, persecution, natural disasters or in search of better economic opportunities. The decision to emigrate is not an easy one. As Bryan Fanning, professor of migration and social policy at University College Dublin and author of *Diverse Republic*, pointed out: '[Immigrants] make decisions (or are forced) to uproot themselves and their families and stake their futures on their ability to build new lives for themselves in new places that, for many, lack the comforting familiarity of the places they left.'[12] Professor Fanning also points out that many immigrants share the same problems as natives but often have additional financial burdens and may face discrimination in their everyday lives. Those who feel like the presence of immigrant populations somehow impacts upon their own rights and privileges see themselves as victims who are under attack, and white genocide and Great Replacement theories bolster those beliefs.

It is true that birth and fertility rates are declining in developed countries, but this is down to higher standards of living. Improved access to education and more career opportunities, especially for women, as well as access to birth control and better health services, have contributed to declining birth rates since the middle of the last century. So yes, demographics are changing, but it is certainly not the result of some sinister conspiracy to wipe out white or native populations.

The fear of native populations being 'replaced' by immigrants is nothing new. Nativism forms the backbone of many far-right groups, and it has been defined by political scientist Cas Mudde as 'an ideology that holds that states should be inhabited exclusively by members of the native group ... and that non-native elements ... are fundamentally threatening to the homogeneous nation state'.[13] Nativists have always feared that the arrival of immigrant groups to a country would somehow destroy the lives of the native population. When Jews first started to become a visible minority in Ireland, Cumann na nGaedheal deputy Denis Gorey furiously tried to alert the Dáil that Irish people were going to be 'replaced absolutely by the Jews' and 'driven out to starve and leave the country and allow it to become a Jewish colony'. Irish Catholics who emigrated to the United States in the 1800s were routinely the victims of mob violence at the hands of nativists, who saw their presence as an 'invasion'.

In recent years, the European Identitarian movement has been among the loudest proponents of replacement conspiracy theories. Identitarian groups are inherently nativist and believe that closing the borders to immigrants and 'remigration' – that is, the repatriation of immigrants back to their country of origin – are the only ways to deal with so-called 'replacement'.

Generation Identity (GI) is a popular pan-European Identitarian youth movement. As my colleague Julia Ebner noted in her book *Going Dark,* GI is the European equivalent of the American alt-right. GI has successfully utilised social media to recruit people to the movement and has made efforts to appear sleek and stylish, making Identitarianism appealing to its young, and mostly male, base. In 2019, analysis by Ebner and Jacob Davey found that GI had a combined following of over a quarter of a million people across Twitter, Facebook, YouTube and Telegram,[14] although many of these accounts and groups were subsequently banned by mainstream social media platforms. In Germany, GI was classified as an extremist right-wing group in 2019, while in France, the movement was banned in 2021.

Davey and Ebner's analysis found 1.48 million posts online mentioning the Great Replacement between 2012 and 2019, showing how the online world has acted as a vehicle for the theory to spread. Proponents of the Great Replacement have on multiple occasions been linked to acts of terrorism. Most horrifically, in March 2019, Brenton Tarrant, a 28-year-old Australian, strapped a GoPro to his head, grabbed a rifle and a semi-automatic shotgun from his car and entered the packed Al Noor Mosque in Christchurch, New Zealand, during Friday prayer. While live-streaming on Facebook, Tarrant shot incessantly at worshippers in scenes that emulated those of a first-person shooter video game, only it most certainly wasn't a game. After five minutes of shooting people inside and outside the mosque, Tarrant got back into his car and drove 5 km to the Linwood Islamic Centre, where he repeated his actions before being apprehended by police.

Fifty-one people, aged between three and 77 years old, were killed that day; dozens more sustained life-altering injuries. Prior to the shooting, Tarrant wrote a 74-page manifesto in which he outlined his reasons for the killings. The manifesto was titled 'The Great Replacement'. It opened with the line, 'It's the birth rates. It's the birth rates. It's the birth rates.' He said the attacks were to show 'the invaders that our lands will never be their lands, our homelands are our own and that, as long as a white man still lives, they will NEVER conquer our lands and they will never replace our people'.

Tarrant was a white supremacist terrorist who believed so strongly in white genocide and replacement conspiracy theories that he murdered 51 innocent people in cold blood in their place of worship. He murdered them because of their religion, their ethnicity and because they had chosen New Zealand as the place to live their lives. He murdered them because he had been radicalised to believe their existence somehow threatened his.

Tarrant's actions were fuelled by the far-right media eco-system he frequented. The Christchurch Attack Commission found that Tarrant had spent time on 4chan, 8chan and other similar sites where extreme right-wing topics were discussed, and also that he spent 'much time accessing broadly similar material on YouTube'. In fact, Tarrant's entire rampage was a hat tip to those online cultures. He graffitied his guns with white supremacist slogans and memes. His manifesto was littered with trolling and shitposting, some designed to trick credulous journalists. He blasted anti-Muslim songs from a speaker he had attached to his vest as he killed people. Before the shooting, he left a post on 8chan linking to his manifesto and the Facebook live stream, and instructing users there to spread his message. They complied, dubbing him 'Saint Tarrant', copying the video and his manifesto and spreading them widely as propaganda. On top of that, it was revealed that Tarrant had donated almost AU$6,600 to two different branches of Generation Identity.

Just over a month after the Christchurch attacks, a 19-year-old gunman opened fire in a synagogue in California, killing one person and injuring three. According to a post he left online, he targeted Jews because he believed they were responsible for the 'genocide of the European race'. Just three months after that, a 21-year-old shot and killed 23 people in a Walmart in El Paso, Texas. Like Tarrant, he also left a manifesto on 8chan that cited the Great Replacement, a 'Hispanic invasion' and the Christchurch attack as inspiration. In May 2022 in Buffalo, New York, an 18-year-old entered a supermarket in a predominantly Black neighbourhood and shot dead ten people. Like Tarrant, the Buffalo shooter live-streamed his attack online and left a manifesto outlining his motive – his belief that white people were being replaced by Black people as part of the Great Replacement.

Right-wing politicians and media pundits around the world have endorsed the Great Replacement, including 2022 French presidential candidate Marine Le Pen, Hungary's Viktor Orbán and a number of members of Germany's Alternative für Deutschland. In the US, Fox News' *Tucker Carlson Tonight*, the most watched show on cable news, has mentioned the Great

Replacement theory 400 times, according to *New York Times* analysis. Carlson's version claims that Democrats are bringing migrants into the country to vote for them. Anti-immigrant fears played a big role in the UK public's decision to vote to leave the EU, and research found that a third of Brexit voters believed that Muslim immigration to the UK was part of a plan to make Muslims a majority in the country.

In 2019, Gemma O'Doherty tweeted a photo of an advertisement for the supermarket chain Lidl that featured an interracial couple and their young child, saying, 'German dump Lidl gaslighting the Irish people with their multicultural version of "The Ryans". Kidding no one! Resist the Great Replacement wherever you can by giving this kip a wide berth. #ShopIrish #BuyIrish'.

The couple from the advert, Fiona Ryan and her partner Jonathan Mathis, were the subject of racist and abusive posts online as a result. Speaking to the *Irish Times*, Ryan said, 'I got so upset and angry at the same time. These people are looking at my child and saying all this hurtful stuff. He's a completely innocent child.' The couple expressed frustration at the lack of action from the Gardaí to take their fears seriously, and after a death threat was issued targeting both the couple and their child, the family decided to leave the country.

Other Irish figures talk about replacement by invoking sentiments that play on historic atrocities inflicted on the Irish people, often referring to replacement as a 'plantation'. Columnist John Waters, who in recent years became somewhat of a sidekick of Gemma O'Doherty, was speaking about asylum seekers to an audience in 2019 when he said, 'Your village has been taken … and you can go to Hell or to Connaught', a reference to Oliver Cromwell's ultimatum to Irish Catholics in 1653. In 2020, Waters tweeted a list of books on European nationalism, including Renaud Camus' *You Will Not Replace Us!*

In 2018, the Irish government unveiled a new capital expenditure plan called Project Ireland 2040. The plan detailed an ambitious strategy to provide housing, jobs and infrastructure for a population that was projected to grow by one million people in two decades. The predicted population growth was based on estimates for immigration and emigrants returning home, but it was easily twisted into a conspiratorial narrative that claimed the government was planning to import a million migrants into the country.

This narrative spread across the international far-right news circuit, from Alex Jones's InfoWars (which called it 'ethnic cleansing') to Breitbart and the Athlone-born men's rights activist and white supremacist YouTuber Stefan Molyneux (who said it was a 'population replacement plan'). The conspiracy theory was bolstered when *The Times Ireland* reported that the Irish government had initiated an advertising campaign that placed sponsored content in regional newspapers that were made to look like independent news stories to present the plan in a positive light, a manoeuvre that should anger anyone who is interested in a normal functioning democracy, and one that provided an open goal for the conspiracy theorists.

The Irish Freedom Party's Hermann Kelly has on multiple occasions evoked Great Replacement-type tropes. In a video interview discussing abortion and immigration along with Britain First's Jim Dowson, Kelly said that Irish political parties want 'to kill Irish kids and replace them with every other nationality'. In June 2020, Kelly shared a video of teenagers engaging in anti-social behaviour and claimed that a 'multicultural society is a recipe for endless aggro and trouble'. In response to accusations of promoting the Great Replacement and supporting white nationalism, Kelly said that 'there is one human race and ideas of separate or superior races is [sic] absurd', but that the Irish Freedom Party will 'continue to highlight the demographic crisis' and 'reject the policy of mass immigration as a solution'.

In November 2021, Kelly published a video on the back of the news that Ireland's fertility rate that year had dropped to 1.5 children per woman. He called this news 'seismic' and a sign of Ireland heading into a 'demographic winter'. He blamed the low fertility rate on a 'culture saturated by the influence of childless feminists and also homosexuals [who] have all the sex but no children'. 'No country can have a future without children,' he said, before saying that the Irish Freedom Party is 'encouraging and helping young couples to get married, have children and raise them up in their own Irish culture.'

Now is a good time to think back to the 14-word chant – the one coined by a white supremacist who was a member of a terrorist organisation and who was sent to prison for 190 years for his part in the murder of a Jewish radio host. The words that are spoken and repeated by white nationalists around the world. They are: 'We must secure the existence of our people and a future for white children.'

Is there an echo in here? I swear I can hear an echo …

* * * *

Most people see Gamergate as something that happened in the past. Sure, the hashtag use dissipated, but the online mob lives on. Many of the women who were harassed are still targeted to this day, and the kind of abuse that shocked the public in 2014 is now just part of the lives of many people, especially women and minorities, who dare to have an opinion on the internet.

In July 2021, Brianna Wu, another game developer targeted in the same way as Sarkeesian and Quinn, tweeted: 'Back in 2014, I genuinely believed standing up to Gamergate would wake the game industry up and lead to a better workplace for women. Nothing substantive changed. We keep having the same scandal like it's Groundhog Day. It breaks my heart that nothing I went through mattered.'

Gamergate swallowed disaffected gamers who were afraid of feminism destroying their hobby, fed them the ironic racist memes of the alt-right and spat them out spouting white supremacist talking points. Liam Porter is a film-maker who has made a number of documentaries about YouTubers of the far right, including Gamergate. He has kept a keen eye on many in the community for years, and described this to me. 'You see it again and again. Young lads who start off as happy little gamers fall into this historical pattern. They come across anti-feminist stuff, make videos about it, and start to generalise their gripes with feminism and liberalism, and eventually they become white nationalists.' He talked about the YouTube algorithm, which has been known to power this radicalisation: 'YouTube has a way of rewarding your consistent viewing of one genre with more stuff from the same pool of creators that they've grouped together. If you watch one video, YouTube recommends another.'

Misogyny and anti-feminism feed into the far right through the belief that the traditional heterosexual family is the backbone of the nation. They often see women solely as mothers, or as mothers-to-be. Because feminism supports abortion rights and encourages women to work, it should be rejected at all costs, as should LGBTQ+ rights, immigration and interracial marriage. In the eyes of the far right, and especially to white nationalists, all of these things lead to fewer white babies.

At times, the far right will attempt to claim pseudo-support for women, but this is often interwoven with xenophobia or claims that migrant men threaten the lives of women. In Ireland, this reaction was seen most clearly after the horrific killing of Ashling Murphy in January 2022. The alleged killer was a Slovakian national, which the National Party took as an opportunity to launch a campaign claiming, 'Irish women are not safe in multicultural Ireland' and calling for Irish men to 'man up'.

Similarly, they will claim pseudo-support for the LGBTQ+ community, often coupled with opposition to Islam. This was prevalent following the 2016 mass shooting by an Islamic extremist in an LGBTQ+ nightclub in Orlando, Florida, in which 49 people were killed. This was seized upon by figures on the right to spread anti-Muslim rhetoric within LGBTQ+ circles.

The xenophobia and racism of the Irish far right are experienced on a daily basis by those who do not fit with their ethno-nationalist ideal, especially those with a public image. There are groups set up online for the sole purpose of targeting abuse and harassment at artists, musicians, academics, journalists, politicians and anyone else who is seen as representing the diversity of Ireland.

The internet has changed our world. Although it has brought some people together, it has also torn many others apart. For some, it has fed the very worst parts of their consciousness and warped reality by providing toxic answers to their problems. It has made people deride being kind, compassionate and empathetic as a liberal 'woke' conspiracy, and instead led them to embrace hatred that comes at the expense of others. The tool that should have allowed the world to see different perspectives and learn from them has instead highlighted our differences and said, 'Be afraid!'

Chapter 4

The Children

HRC [Hillary Rodham Clinton] *extradition already in motion effective yesterday with several countries in case of cross border run. Passport approved to be flagged effective 10/30 @ 12:01am. Expect massive riots organized in defiance and others fleeing the US to occur. US M's* [Marines] *will conduct the operation while NG* [National Guard] *activated. Proof check: Locate a NG member and ask if activated for duty 10/30 across most major cities.*

RESEARCHERS NOW AGREE THAT THE ABOVE POST (left on 4chan's /pol/) is the first post attributable to the movement that would become known as QAnon. The post was made on 28 October 2017, and there was nothing extraordinary about it. As well as trolling, nihilism, memes, white supremacy and conspiracy theories, 4chan was full of LARPing, or live action role playing. LARPing is essentially when someone pretends to be someone they aren't. 4chan anons would regularly pretend to be members of the CIA, or federal agents, or government insiders with some sort of secret knowledge. Most 4chan anons would see through the LARP and reply for kicks, and a small number would reply hoping that the person was real, but the general feeling was that these kinds of posts were nonsense.

The first Q drop (Q posts are known as drops) was no different. It was actually posted as a response to another LARPer, who had said, 'Hillary Clinton will be arrested between 7:45 AM – 8:30 AM EST on Monday – the morning on Oct 30, 2017.' The Q drop was correcting this LARPer with another LARP by saying that, actually, Clinton's arrest was already in motion. These posts didn't cause a stir because they were run-of-the-mill on the boards at the time. One user even responded, 'Oh God, not another one.'

In the days after, the drops kept coming. They were often long, tantalising posts, many posing vague, open-ended questions with strange acronyms and code words, like:

SCI[F] Military Intelligence. What is "State Secrets" and how upheld in the SC?
What must be completed to engage MI over other (3) letter agencies?
What must occur to allow for civilian trials? Why is this relevant?

On 2 November 2017, the anon started signing the posts as 'Q', a nod to their supposed top-secret Q-level clearance in the

Department of Energy. On 9 November, Q added a tripcode to their posts. A tripcode is a method that some (but not many) users on 4chan and 8chan employ to identify themselves. Tripcodes have an extremely weak security system where users input a password with their post, which then appears as a scrambled series of letters and numbers in the spot where it would normally just say 'anonymous'. Q used this to identify themselves and to let anons keep track of the posts that were coming from them.

At this stage, Q was telling anons that they were close to Donald Trump, that there was a plan in place and that the drops were 'breadcrumbs' leading to something huge. 'Patriots are in control. Sit back and enjoy the show,' said Q. Some anons were intrigued and began following the drops, trying to 'decode' them. Soon, some small-time YouTubers got on board and started covering the drops in their videos. By December, the small, dedicated group of followers had set up a board on Reddit, and Q had moved the operation from 4chan to 8chan.

Before I go on, I should get a big question out of the way: who is Q?

I, and most other researchers in this field, believe that Q was more than one person, but for the most part, the person controlling it was likely a guy called Ron Watkins. Ron is the son of Jim Watkins, the owner of 8chan. 8chan, remember, is an even more toxic version of 4chan, and multiple mass shooters, including the Christchurch shooter Brenton Tarrant, used the platform to post their manifestos before going on killing sprees. Jim and Ron Watkins found little wrong with this, as they are free-speech absolutists.

Jim is in his late 50s and was once a recruiter for the US army. In the early 2000s, he moved to the Philippines after making a lot of money hosting Japanese pornography sites from servers based in the US, circumventing Japanese censorship laws. In 2004, he started using his servers to host 2channel, the Japanese site that inspired Christopher Poole to make 4chan. Shortly after, and in questionable circumstances, he seized control of 2channel completely. In 2013, Jim also took control of 8chan from the site's founder, Fredrick Brennan, and installed his son Ron as the site administrator. As well as hosting and owning some of the worst websites in the world, Jim also ran a junk news website called The Goldwater, which published right-wing conspiracy theories.

Ron is suspected of being linked to Q due to a sequence of events that took place in December 2017 and January 2018. The first 8chan board on which Q posted was controlled by Paul Furber, a South African tech journalist and avid 4chan user. Furber has described in multiple interviews how he dedicated long and relentless hours to maintaining the Q board in the initial few months of the movement. In December 2017, Q's tripcode was cracked. What was the tripcode that a supposed high-level government insider used to disseminate some of the world's most highly classified information? It was 'Matlock'. When the tripcode was cracked, imposters started posting as Q. After this, Q claimed that the board was compromised and moved to a new board, created and controlled by Ron Watkins. Q even communicated with Ron through Q drops to 'confirm' his identity.

Paul Furber was not happy. He said that the new Q was an imposter and soon left the movement. Many (myself included) suspect that Furber was the one initially posting as Q. He has always denied this, but his absolute certainty that the new Q was an imposter raises suspicions. Researchers and journalists who cover Q agree that what likely happened was that Ron co-opted the Q account from Furber and started running it himself. After this, Q was forever tied to 8chan and the Watkinses, and they never posted on another site, even when 8chan was kicked offline for a number of months following the Christchurch and El Paso mass shootings.

Another key piece of evidence linking both Ron and Jim to Q is Q's use of a pen and watch in the drops. A number of times over the years, Q would post a photo of the same pen and the same watch to confirm their identity. It just so happens that Ron is an avid watch collector and Jim has a strange obsession with pens, which to me is as good as a nod and a wink.

The 'takeover' of the Q account came directly after QAnon had its first big break. Paul Furber and another avid QAnon follower named Coleman Rogers were invited on to InfoWars to discuss the movement. This exposed QAnon to a much larger audience. Thousands of people joined the subreddit overnight and began visiting 8chan, many of them of an older and less tech-savvy generation. This moment was key in QAnon's evolution. Suddenly, a LARP that had started on 4chan was worming its way into the minds of a susceptible generation of Alex Jones fans, who began waiting with bated breath to decode the next drops. The 8chan Twitter account (likely controlled by Ron) even exclaimed, 'We joked about it for years, but #QAnon is making it a reality: Boomers! On your imageboard.' This is yet another reason why it would have been in Ron and Jim's interests to control Q. QAnon was making 8chan more popular than ever.

Ron and Jim have always denied being Q, except for a semi-admission by Ron in Cullen Hoback's HBO document-ary *Q: Into the Storm*. Although there is no smoking gun and much of the evidence linking Ron and Jim to Q is circumstan-tial, it has been enough to convince me and many others that the Watkinses are intrinsically tied to Q.

The identity of Q rarely mattered to those following the drops. All that mattered to QAnon followers was that Q was spreading the *truth* and helping to red-pill the public. Even when information about Jim and Ron's ties to Q was publicly revealed, it didn't make a difference. Q was telling people what they wanted to hear: that Trump was the good guy and that the Democrats were evil. Cognitive dissonance also likely played a role here. If someone had dedicated a significant amount of time to QAnon only to find that Q was a fraud, they would attempt to rationalise this in whatever way possible to keep believing.

From January 2018, the movement hit a new stride. The catchphrases and slogans that bonded the movement – like 'Where We Go One, We Go All', or #WWG1WGA – were introduced. Jerome Corsi, a veteran conspiracy theorist who worked with InfoWars, began reporting on QAnon regularly and became part of the inner circle of Q drop decoders. QAnon also gained some celebrity support, most notably from actress Roseanne Barr, and Q followers started becoming a visible presence at Trump rallies. In 2018 the potential for QAnon to lead people to take extreme action or turn to violence also became apparent.

On 15 June 2018, Matthew Philip Wright grabbed multiple guns and hundreds of rounds of ammunition and used an armoured vehicle to block the Hoover Dam bridge. He put a sign up to the window of the truck that said 'Release the OIG report'. The OIG (Office of the Inspector General) report into the handling of the FBI investigation into Hillary Clinton's leaked emails in 2016 had been released the day before, but Q had told their followers that Trump had an unredacted version that would reveal the *truth*. This is the report Wright was demanding be released. After 90 minutes, police managed to apprehend him. No one was hurt, but Wright was sentenced to seven years in prison on charges of terrorism.

This was the first of many incidents and crimes where QAnon belief was a motive, and they would get much, much worse as time went on. In the years that followed, multiple murders and kidnappings would be linked to QAnon, including the horrific killing in California of two young children by their father, who had been 'enlightened by QAnon and Illuminati conspiracy theories and was receiving visions and signs revealing that his wife ... possessed serpent DNA and had passed it on to his children'.

What can drive people to take such extreme action? What motivates them? What do QAnon followers actually believe?

The conspiracy theory soup

The power of QAnon lies in its ability to ingest all other conspiracy theories into its mix. Think of it like a conspiracy theory soup. You can drop in whatever conspiracy theory you want, and it will ultimately become part of QAnon. Conspiracy theories about Bill and Hillary Clinton being involved in murders and cover-ups (the so-called 'Clinton body count') had been floating around in fringe right-wing communities for decades. This was spurred on by Donald Trump's claim that he would 'lock her up'. The idea that Hillary, along with Obama and other people involved in her campaign, was a criminal was widely accepted among both fringe and mainstream Trump supporters, so it was an easy ingredient to add to the QAnon soup.

So too were conspiracy theories about the Hungarian-born philanthropist George Soros. Soros was born into a non-observant Jewish family and fled Nazi-occupied Hungary as a teenager to live in the UK. He made billions working as an investment banker, becoming one of the richest men in the world, before setting up a philanthropic organisation called Open Society Foundations (OSF), which donates money to various progressive and liberal causes supporting education, public health and justice (including, for the sake of transparency, ISD).

According to *Forbes*, Soros has donated 65 per cent of his original fortune through OSF. This has turned him into a bogeyman of right-wingers, who see him as the globalist, Jewish, puppet-master financier behind a worldwide liberal conspiracy. These claims, plus the frequent mentions of the Rothschild banking dynasty in Q drops, clearly echo those from the *Protocols of the Elders of Zion*.

One particular QAnon influencer called GhostEzra embraced the anti-Semitic elements of QAnon and pushed one of the most extreme brands of the movement to his 300,000+ followers. GhostEzra became one of the most popular QAnon channels on the messaging app Telegram during 2021, sharing content ranging from bizarre flat earth theories to blatant anti-Semitism, Holocaust denial and neo-Nazi propaganda. In 2021, investigative unit Logically.ai identified the man behind the GhostEzra account as Robert Smart, an evangelical Christian from Florida.

Q also flirted with conspiracy theories about the Freemasons, 9/11, the JFK assassination, creeping communism and time travel. They could all be worked into the story of a government insider divulging secrets. To add a grain of truth to the claims, Q would also mention real conspiracies – things that did happen. These included a number of covert CIA operations from the Cold War era such as MKUltra, an illegal mind-control experiment, and Operation Mockingbird, a supposed deal between journalists and intelligence services to spread propaganda through the news media.[1] All Q had to do was allude to any of these in a drop, and their conspiratorially minded followers would do the rest.

The key ingredient – the stock, if you like – that brings the conspiracy theory soup together into QAnon lies in the belief that Donald Trump's presidency was actually part of a years-long plan in a secret war being fought against the forces of evil. These forces, collectively referred to as the 'deep state', consist of Democrats, the intelligence community, philanthropists, bankers, liberal Hollywood celebrities, the mainstream media, Big Tech, Big Pharma … anyone who could be seen as an enemy of Trump. According to Q's mythology, members of the deep state are unimaginably evil for many, many reasons. Not only are they working to destroy Trump, but many of them are also accused of being engaged in the most heinous of crimes: child trafficking, paedophilia and the Satanic ritual abuse of children. According to Q, *this* is what Trump is fighting against, and *this* is what many QAnon followers believe they are fighting to reveal.

QAnon is rooted in a quasi-apocalyptic promise of a day of retribution, known as the Storm, when the deep state would be brought to justice (either executed or sent to Guantanamo Bay) and the world would finally see what was really going on. Evil would be forever cast to the shadows, and a new utopian golden age would be born from the ashes, with Trump as the leader of the new Free World. From the very beginning of the drops, Q was leading their followers along, telling them that the Storm was imminent, that the truth was *just* about to come out and that their beliefs would soon be vindicated. Everyone would see that Donald Trump was a hero and that Hillary, Obama and the rest of the dirty Democrats, who had fooled millions into thinking that *they* were the moral ones, were in fact more evil than anyone could imagine.

At the beginning, the predictions were specific – such as the imminent arrest of Hillary Clinton, which didn't happen. Then Q said the Storm would happen on 3 November 2017, when John Podesta would be arrested, followed by Huma Abedin, who worked on Clinton's campaign team. None of this happened. The predictions kept coming but became increasingly vague, with indistinct claims of 'false flags', 'resignations' and 'sealed indictments' leaving loads of room for decoders to interpret different meanings from the drops. No matter how many of these predictions didn't come true, QAnon followers would find reasons to keep believing.

Over three years, Q left almost 5,000 drops. Some were short – just a word or two; others were long strings of nonsense. To many Q followers, decoding became a vocation. They would wait impatiently for the next drops, then gather on 8chan or Reddit, or in Facebook groups, and decode what they meant. Q told anons that they were 'digital soldiers' fighting the battle alongside them, and encouraged the followers to 'Research for yourself. Think for yourself. Trust yourself.'

Claims of child trafficking, Satanism, paedophile rings and rituals involving children made by Q were tapping into a specific part of the human psyche. As already discussed, many of these claims were taken wholesale from ancient anti-Semitic claims of blood libel. Instead of blood, QAnon followers claim that adrenochrome is extracted from tortured children during these rituals. Adrenochrome is a real substance found naturally in the body that has, through its inclusion in some cult classic tales of fiction, developed a mythology of its own as either a mind-altering drug or an anti-ageing substance. In reality, it does neither of these things, and even if it did, you can buy it online quite easily, so no need for the kidnap, torture and murder of children.

In recent decades, countries around the world have had to face up to the realities of rampant child sexual abuse within institutions and organisations that were meant to protect children. Crimes against children are the most evil of crimes, and they understandably evoke visceral feelings of horror. QAnon not only blames innocent people for these crimes, it also clouds the realities around how they occur, creating panic and hysteria. This is not the first time it's happened.

Satan is coming for your children

In the United States in the 1980s and '90s, elements of blood libel and claims of ritualistic abuse became rampant. The fear wasn't attributed to Jews but to Satanism, and this era became known as the 'Satanic panic'. Widely agreed upon to be a moral panic – that is, an exaggerated and irrational fear over something that wasn't even happening – the frenzy was traced back to a number of things.

In the 1970s and '80s, evangelical Christianity, led by people such as Billy Graham and Jerry Falwell's political organisation the Moral Majority, had become a dominant force in the US. The threat of Satanism was widely promoted in their writings and sermons at the time.[2]

Incidents like the Manson Family murders and the Jonestown Massacre prompted an anti-cult movement (ACM) in the 1960s and '70s to warn people against joining new religious groups, which were seen as child-stealing cults working to brainwash their recruits through mind control. Satanism was easily incorporated into the broader ACM framework and working to counter the rise of Satanic cults became part of their mission.

The fear of Satanism was reinforced by the rise of actual Satanist groups, such as Anton LaVey's Church of Satan. The Church of Satan was tiny (2,000–5,000 members), but it was given considerable media attention due to its use of staged events such as Satanic baptisms and weddings. Contrary to popular belief, the Church of Satan did not believe in or worship Satan. Its members were mainly atheists who believed in a secular and scientific worldview, and Satan was a symbol of nonconformity. They expressed a belief in 'magic' (but not of a supernatural kind), and they engaged in rituals and ceremonies that would generally be viewed as strange but that certainly did not involve sacrifices or harm to animals or children.

At this time, there was a heightened public awareness about the realities of child sexual abuse, the horrors of which were only just being revealed. There were campaigns centred around the need to protect children from neglect, abuse and sexual exploitation and to believe the accusations made by victims. The fear of strangers abducting children, so-called 'stranger danger', was also widely promoted. Hugely exaggerated claims of over 400,000 children being kidnapped every year were unquestioningly accepted by politicians, the media and the public, despite the true numbers being a tiny fraction of this. Photos of missing children were printed on milk cartons during this time, making it seem like an immense, widespread issue, but the photos were of the same 106 kids.

This was the climate of fear that produced the Satanic panic, which began in 1980 with the publication of a book called *Michelle Remembers*, written by Michelle Smith and her husband, psychiatrist Lawrence Pazder. Smith was a long-time patient of Pazder, and the book outlined how his use of hypnosis had helped Smith to recover memories of horrendous abuse at the hands of her mother and a Satanic cult when she was five years old. The details were graphic, including descriptions of being raped and tortured with candles and crucifixes, being locked in a cage full of snakes, witnessing babies being killed and having devil's horns surgically attached to parts of her body. Smith coined the term 'ritual abuse' to describe her ordeal.[3]

The book has since been largely discredited after claims were refuted by Smith's family and none of the details could be substantiated. No evidence could be found of an alleged car crash that Smith said she was in, or of long absences from school during which time the abuse was alleged to have occurred. There was also no evidence of hospitalisations as a result of the injuries she sustained, or scars from the supposed torture. Pazder, who was a devout Catholic, was found to have studied witchcraft rituals in Western Africa, details of which were echoed in some of the descriptions made by Smith. All in all, it is well agreed that the abuse she recounted never took place.

Despite the fact that the book's claims were questioned shortly after its publication, *Michelle Remembers* received widespread attention and became a bestseller. Pazder became known as an expert on Satanic ritual abuse and spoke frequently in news reports about it, igniting fears that the practice was commonplace. The book's popularity spurred on the use of 'recovered memory therapy', the idea that hidden memories could be uncovered through things like hypnosis or guided visualisations. This practice has been widely discredited since and is now seen as unethical and pseudoscientific, but in the 1980s and '90s, it was highly regarded. The suspicion of Satanic ritual abuse, mixed with the discredited practice of recovered memory therapy, led to therapists across the US 'discovering' thousands of repressed memories of ritual abuse.

In 1983, accusations of Satanic ritual abuse were made against the McMartin family, who owned a preschool in Manhattan Beach, California. One parent filed a report with the Los Angeles Police Department, alleging that her two-year-old son had been abused by his teacher, Ray Buckey, the grandson of the school's founder, Virginia McMartin. The detail she provided was horrific and included claims that the young boy was probed anally, that rituals had been performed with animals and that 'Ray flew in the air'. The LAPD arrested Buckey and, in an effort to collect evidence, sent a letter to the parents of the children in the school asking them to come forward with anything they thought may be suspicious about him. An excerpt of the letter said:

> Our investigation indicates that possible criminal acts include: oral sex, fondling of genitals, buttock or chest area, and sodomy, possibly committed under the pretense of "taking the child's temperature". Also photos may have been taken of children without their clothing. Any information from your child regarding having ever observed Ray Buckey to leave a classroom alone with a child during any nap period, or if they have ever observed Ray Buckey tie up a child, is important.

This letter sparked mass hysteria in Manhattan Beach. Parents began questioning their offspring (most aged between three and five), who initially denied that anything had happened. Fearful parents who thought their children had been scared into silence continued to ask them questions, often using leading statements and planting ideas in their heads. Soon, over a dozen youngsters, who had initially denied that anything untoward had taken place, were changing their stories and accusing Ray Buckey and other teachers of sexual crimes.

Hundreds of kids were then sent for interviews to an organisation providing therapy and services for abused children. Using a technique that had not been tested, interviewers used puppets and 'anatomically correct dolls', complete with breasts, penises, vaginas, anuses and pubic hair, to encourage children to talk about the abuse. Recordings of the interviews showed that the youngsters were often coaxed to say certain things, with interviewers repeatedly asking them the same questions and leading them to answers. One account of the interviews noted how little talking the children did and the fact that none of them spontaneously disclosed allegations.

Out of this process, over 300 children in the McMartin preschool said they were abused in ritualistic circumstances by seven teachers: 79-year-old Virgina McMartin, her daughter Peggy McMartin Buckey, Peggy's children Ray and Peggy Ann Buckey, and three other female teachers. Again, the accusations were startling and often grotesque, with some kids claiming that they had witnessed animals being butchered, or that they had been forced to drink blood. Other claims were just bizarre and obviously untrue: one boy said he was taken to a cemetery where they had unearthed coffins and watched teachers cut up dead bodies. No corroborating physical evidence was ever found to back up the claims made by the children.

Despite this, the case proceeded. An advocacy group called Believe the Children was set up to support the parents, and Lawrence Pazder and Michelle Smith even visited the town to speak to the parents and children involved in the case. To much of the community, the McMartins and Buckeys were already guilty. They were frequently targeted with death threats and attacks, while the preschool was set on fire and graffitied with the words 'Ray must die'.

The pre-trial hearing, which began in June 1984, lasted for 18 months and led to the charges against five of the defendants being dropped citing 'incredibly weak' evidence. Ray's and Peggy's cases proceeded to trial. By this time, the mother who filed the very first complaint against Ray had been diagnosed with paranoid schizophrenia. Among the increasingly absurd things she said about her son's abuse (she was speaking on his behalf because he was so young) were claims that one of the teachers had put scissors in his eyes and that he was hurt by a lion and an elephant. She died in 1987 from severe liver disease brought on by alcoholism.

Despite the mother's death and clear indications that her initial accusations were made up, the case proceeded. The trial opened in July 1987 and lasted for three years, after which Peggy was acquitted of all charges. Ray was acquitted of the majority of his, with the jury failing to reach a verdict on 13 other counts. But it didn't end there. The prosecution soon announced that they would retry Ray over eight of the counts that hadn't been decided on by the first jury. This resulted in a hung jury and a mistrial being declared. The prosecution dropped the case after this. Seven years after the first accusations were made, and after five years in jail, Ray Buckey was free. It was the longest-running, and most costly, criminal case in US history.

The reporting around the McMartin case and other Satanic panic tales shone a light on the worst parts of the media. The stories of Satanism were sensationalised, often went unchallenged and stoked people's fears, feeding into the mass hysteria. Oprah Winfrey, for example, interviewed a number of people making claims of Satanic ritual abuse, including Michelle Smith, but she never questioned the claims they were making, no matter how ludicrous. A 1988 two-hour TV special by Geraldo Rivera became one of the most watched TV shows of that time and propagated the widely untrue claim that interest in heavy metal music could be a pathway to Satanism. Specific reports on the McMartin case lacked the fairness and scepticism that should form the backbone of journalism, with the Buckeys and McMartins generally assumed guilty. This, no doubt, tainted the jury's perception of the case.

But the McMartin case is just one of many. Across the US and beyond, throughout the 1980s and '90s, hundreds of other cases followed the same pattern. Prompted by their parents' fears, children were coerced into making false allegations in dubious therapy settings, and people were arrested and imprisoned for years for crimes they didn't commit. In cases like that of the West Memphis Three, dressing like a goth and listening to Metallica were seen as signs of Satanism, and also led to wrongful imprisonment. In other cases, playing the fantasy board game Dungeons and Dragons was seen as an indication of Satanism. Some people are still in prison to this day. Not one instance of Satanic ritual abuse has ever been corroborated, and it is now widely agreed that the practice is a myth.

Myths like blood libel and Satanic ritual abuse can wreak havoc and horror. It should come as no surprise to learn that, when this particular fear was coupled with the power of the internet and attached itself to a political movement, the damage would be absolutely devastating.

Democrats are coming for your children

In October 2015, James Alefantis, a Washington, DC-based chef and restaurateur, agreed to guest-chef a Hillary Clinton fundraiser being held in the home of Tony Podesta, a Democratic lobbyist and the brother of Clinton's campaign manager, John Podesta. Alefantis had a good reputation in DC. He owned two popular restaurants in the city: Buck's Fishing and Camping, which served contemporary American cuisine, and a family-friendly pizza place called Comet Ping Pong. He was passionate about art, previously owning a gallery of his own before taking a seat on the board of a non-profit art gallery in DC. As a gay man, Alefantis supported and celebrated the LGBTQ+ community, often putting on shows featuring queer artists and bands. His success and reputation had earned him a spot on *GQ's* '50 most powerful people in Washington' list in 2012. He was a supporter of liberal politics and had become friendly with some powerful people, leading to his guest-chef appearance at the Clinton fundraiser.

A year later, in October 2016, John Podesta's hacked emails were released by WikiLeaks. The emails included correspondence between the Podesta brothers about the aforementioned fundraiser, as well as some other innocuous exchanges between

John Podesta and Alefantis. Alefantis told *Inc. Magazine* in 2017 that his initial reaction was, 'Oh, this is so funny. I'm in WikiLeaks', but he could never have foreseen what would come from it.

In the dark recesses of the internet, thousands of people were poring through the leaked emails, obsessively trying to find *something* to pin on Hillary Clinton before the election. On 4chan, a user claimed that mentions of 'pizza' found in the emails were actually references to paedophilia. 4chan users ate this up. For years, anons had been using the term 'cheese pizza' as a euphemism and meme for 'child pornography', along with other phrases using the initials 'CP'. This was bolstered by another anon, who gave them more code words to look for: hot dog = boy; pizza = girl; cheese = little girl; pasta = little boy; ice cream = male prostitute; walnut = person of colour; map = semen; sauce = orgy.

Although these were complete works of fiction, they were exactly what the trolls, LARPers, racists, conspiracy theorists and nihilists of 4chan were looking for. In 2017, a 4chan user who claimed to be in the original Pizzagate threads told *Politico*: 'It was absolutely a joke and a guy just made it up on the spot … I was on the thread and people thought it was hilarious and halfway through they were like, "How can we get people to take this seriously?"'

It wouldn't take much. By tapping into the conspiratorial mindset that finds meaning in connections that don't exist, the joke soon caught on. Take this email, for example, sent to John Podesta:

Hey John,

We know you're a true master of cuisine and we have appreciated that for years …

But walnut sauce for the pasta? Mary, plz tell us the straight story, was the sauce actually very tasty?

John Podesta, as it turns out, is a skilled chef and is very passionate about food, but with the made-up code words, a light-hearted email about a recipe became something much more malevolent. To conspiracy theorists willing to ignore John Podesta's passion for cooking, this was gold dust.

Further conspiratorial gold dust was found in an email between Tony Podesta and Marina Abramović, the world-famous conceptual and performance artist. In the email, she said she was 'looking forward to the Spirit Cooking dinner at my place'. 'Spirit Cooking' is a reference to a 1990s performance piece by Abramović, described by the Museum of Modern Art as 'a series of "aphrodisiac recipes" that serve as evocative instructions for actions or thoughts'. Some recipes contain things like '13,000 grams of jealousy' or instruct you to 'try to eat all the questions of the day'. Others say to 'mix fresh breast milk with sperm'. These are clearly not recipes in the literal sense of the word. They are a piece of art. Abramović has described that particular work as poetry, and her work, in general, is meant to be shocking and lurid – that's part of her artistic style.

In 2013, Abramović had launched a Kickstarter campaign to fund her art institute, and those who pledged over $10,000 were offered a 'Spirit Cooking dinner' with the artist in return. She named it this as a joke, and the description clearly said that it was a 'dinner night with Marina, during which she will teach you and other backers at this level how to cook a series of traditional soups'. An avid art collector, Tony Podesta was both a fan and a friend of Abramović, and he was invited to the dinner in return for his donation. These details, once again, were ignored in favour of taking the reference to Spirit Cooking as a sure sign of the Podestas engaging in Satanic rituals. Suddenly headlines from junk news sites were bouncing around the internet accusing them of such.

False and lurid allegations of paedophilia related to those in Hillary Clinton's inner circle were compounded by a number of real-life situations. First, the investigation into the paedophile, child-trafficker and powerful financier Jeffrey Epstein was starting to ramp up, and Bill Clinton's association with him was understandably causing problems for Hillary's campaign. Epstein's horrendous crimes and his links to powerful people would also become an important element of the QAnon mythology, lending the ultimate kernel of truth to the theory that well-connected, powerful people were engaging in crimes against children.

Second, Congressman Anthony Weiner, the husband of Clinton's long-time aide Huma Abedin, was caught sending sexually explicit messages to teenagers, and his laptop was seized. The discovery of emails from Clinton's private server on the laptop caused the FBI to reopen their investigation into her use of the server, just days before the 2016 election. Rumours started flying around about content on Weiner's laptop, and a broadcast on InfoWars on 2 November took this story to new heights when they claimed – without evidence – that the laptop confirmed that Hillary had also taken part in Epstein's horrendous sex crimes.[4] This story was picked up by Breitbart and the wider right-wing and conspiracy ecosystem, which went into overdrive to push the story as far as possible.

The last piece of the puzzle came with the discovery of the emails mentioning James Alefantis and Comet Ping Pong. Online sleuths found out that Alefantis's ex-boyfriend was David Brock, a Clinton supporter and the founder of the conservative-media watchdog Media Matters for America. In a virulent display of homophobia that's typical of these online groups and that taps into long-standing hate narratives around the gay community, 4chan anons decided, without evidence, that Brock and Alefantis were paedophiles. They started looking into Comet Ping Pong, finding images and videos of art displays and queer music performances, and once again linking these to paedophilia. They claimed that logos found in Comet Ping Pong were paedophile logos and evidence of Satanism. After trawling through Alefantis's personal Instagram account, they did more of the same, finding photos he posted of his godchildren and claiming that the sarcastic captions used by Alefantis proved that they were children being trafficked and abused. A large walk-in fridge in one photo was taken to be a 'kill room' in the basement of the restaurant. Comet Ping Pong, they decided, was the centre of the Clinton's and Podesta's child-trafficking ring.

And so, the meaningless mentions of pizza and other foods in Podesta's emails, the tongue-in-cheek reference to Spirit Cooking in the email to Tony Podesta, the completely unsubstantiated claims of Hillary Clinton's involvement with Jeffrey Epstein's sex crimes, and the fact that James Alefantis ran an LGBTQ+ friendly pizza restaurant all came together to form Pizzagate.

In a lot of ways, that would seem like the end of the story, but it was only getting started. In the days and weeks following the election, the entire right-wing and conspiracy-laden ecosystem came together to push Pizzagate as far as it could go. Alex Jones consistently told his audience of millions that 'We're in the hands of pure evil … Pizzagate is real' and encouraged his audience to investigate the matter for themselves. Alt-right influencers with hundreds of thousands of followers did the same.

Alefantis and his staff faced constant harassment, receiving a barrage of phone calls that accused them of raping children, or violent messages threatening to kill them. Even the artists whose work was displayed in the restaurant were harassed and abused with the same. The whole affair was taken to new heights when alt-right provocateur and conspiracy theorist Jack Posobiec live-streamed himself from inside Comet Ping Pong, where he had gone to 'investigate' the claims that Satanic rituals were taking place there.

In North Carolina, Alex Jones fan Edgar Maddison Welch decided to take matters into his own hands. On 4 December 2016, he grabbed an AR-15 rifle and a handgun, left his wife and two daughters, and drove 350 miles to Washington, DC. He was convinced, like most Pizzagate followers, that the basement of Comet Ping Pong was housing dozens of children who had been trafficked to the Clintons and Podestas for Satanic and paedophilic acts. He entered the packed restaurant with his weapons and fired a number of times at a locked door, convinced it led to the secret basement (Comet Ping Pong doesn't have a basement). After aiming his gun at staff, he ran out of the restaurant, where he was arrested. Thankfully, no one was hurt.

Because of a few trolls on 4chan who thought it would be funny to link the word 'pizza' to paedophilia, Welch decided to arm himself and start shooting in a packed restaurant that was, ironically, full of kids. Text messages show he believed he was 'standing up against a corrupt system that kidnaps, tortures and rapes babies and children in our own backyard'. In reality, he had been radicalised into violent extremism.

One would think the lack of a basement in Comet Ping Pong, let alone the complete absence of any evidence besides the wild speculation of online conspiracy theorists, would make people realise that perhaps they had been fooled. But that is wishful thinking. The seeds were firmly planted and couldn't be uprooted. A poll conducted by *The Economist* and YouGov at the end of 2016 found that 46 per cent of Trump voters believed 'somewhat' in the core tenets of Pizzagate. Less than a year later, when Q came along and 'confirmed' all the information that Pizzagate supporters had been consuming, while also saying they would soon be vindicated and that paedophiles and Satanists were going to be arrested, it was too good a story for many to resist.

Q hits the mainstream

Throughout 2018 and 2019, QAnon became more visible offline as the number of Q followers at Trump rallies continued to grow. Online, the movement was also growing. QAnon merchandise and books were flooding sites like Amazon and Etsy, making some savvy entrepreneurs thousands of dollars. But the movement was also fragmenting. Hundreds of different QAnon influencers emerged, each interpreting the drops in their own way, like disciples preaching different interpretations of sacred scripture.

There were those who brought an evangelical twist, where the Storm was recast as the End Times. Q had quoted Bible verses multiple times in the drops, making the movement prime fodder for devout Christians, and pastors began preaching QAnon-like prophecies in their sermons. There was the MAGA (Make America Great Again) crowd, the typical Trump supporters whose minds were already open to various conspiracy theories. There were the New Agers, who folded their beliefs in cosmic battles and extraterrestrial forces into QAnon. These factions, analysed by QAnon researcher Dapper Gander, took different views on QAnon's mythology, but they were still bound by the central tenet of the movement – namely, Trump's war with the deep state.

The most significant evolution of QAnon came during 2020, as the Covid pandemic turned the entire world upside down. Until then, most would still have called QAnon a fringe movement – it was mainly confined to the US and attracted middle-aged white Trump voters. However, in the space of six months in 2020, QAnon became one of the most important, and dangerous, political movements in the US and internationally.

In the first few months of the pandemic, conspiracy communities online that were once dedicated to specific movements – anti-5G, anti-vaccine, conspirituality and so on – all turned their attention to Covid-19, and QAnon was no different. Although largely quiet on all things Covid for the first few months of the year, from April 2020, Q shifted to posting about the pandemic. The drops echoed Trump's claims that it was a 'China virus', downplayed the severity of the disease and touted unproven cures like hydroxychloroquine. Q's followers were more than willing to lap up Covid-19 conspiracy theories. The foundations had been laid over the years with Big Pharma-related claims and Q even dabbled in anti-vaccine theories back in 2018. QAnon followers had been primed to think the pandemic was a hoax.

The increased time people were spending indoors and online, plus the understandable desire to find answers to the situation the world found itself in, meant that people were more exposed than ever to conspiratorial narratives. Because almost all conspiratorial communities started talking about the same subject, the algorithms powering platforms like Facebook and YouTube recommended this kind of content to its users. This was especially evident with Facebook groups. Analysis by *The Guardian*[5] found that Facebook's algorithms were recommending QAnon groups when people joined pro-Trump, anti-vaccine or anti-lockdown groups. Analysis conducted by myself and my ISD colleagues Jacob Davey and Mackenzie Hart in June 2020 found that membership of QAnon Facebook groups increased by 120 per cent in March 2020, just as lockdowns were being rolled out around the world.[6] Engagement rates in these groups grew by 91 per cent, meaning that people were not just joining the groups – they were taking part in conversations at a rate we hadn't seen before. QAnon, the conspiracy theory of everything, was quickly becoming the conspiracy theory of Covid-19.

Another reason for QAnon's rise to the top of the conspiracy world during 2020 was down to QAnon-linked claims involving celebrities, which broke into the mainstream. Various celebrities had been targeted by QAnon over the years, many because of their inclusion on a fake Jeffrey Epstein flight log, or because they dared mention Pizzagate code words online. Chrissy Teigen had to block over one million Twitter accounts on the back of the abuse she received. In 2018, QAnon had levelled a baseless accusation of paedophilia against Tom Hanks. Hanks also happened to be one of the first celebrities to catch Covid-19. Almost immediately, QAnon-style rumours started circulating claiming that the actor had actually been arrested on child-trafficking charges in Australia, or that he didn't have Covid-19 – he was actually suffering from a shortage of adrenochrome. Similar claims were made about Oprah Winfrey and Ellen DeGeneres, alleging they were under house arrest on sex-trafficking charges, prompting fact checks debunking the rumours and even provoking Oprah to address the claims directly on Twitter.

Pizzagate also made a return to the headlines when a new generation was exposed to the conspiracy theory, prompted by an alleged sign Justin Bieber gave during an Instagram live video (he touched his hat). A documentary film that laid out many of the claims of Satanism and paedophilia from Pizzagate and QAnon (without mentioning either of those words) also went viral during the summer of 2020, as did the bizarre Wayfair conspiracy theory, which alleged the furniture company was trafficking children in large cabinets for sale on their website.[7] Although these claims were popular across all platforms, there was a worrying spread of them on TikTok, a site associated with younger users.

All of these ludicrous claims were easily traced back to QAnon, and the social media platforms were under increasing pressure to do something. In the summer of 2020, they started cracking down on QAnon-related hashtags, blocking usage of some of the favourites, including #WWG1WGA. QAnon changed tack. They hijacked the hashtag #SaveTheChildren, which was already used by a legitimate anti-child-trafficking organisation of the same name. This move would change QAnon forever. Interestingly, it wasn't instigated by Q, but by the wider movement, which had grown into a life form of its own.

#SaveTheChildren allowed QAnon to spread a 'lite' version of its theories – less Hillary Clinton torturing babies, more child trafficking – to a much wider audience. A hashtag like #SaveTheChildren is hard to ignore because who doesn't want to save children? It worked, and analysis by PhD researcher and QAnon tracker Marc-André Argentino found that hundreds of thousands of people on Facebook were joining anti-child-trafficking groups that in reality were full of QAnon propaganda.

QAnon took over Instagram too, moulding itself into the world of inspirational quotes and soft-coloured, easily digestible slide shows shared by lifestyle, alternative healing, spirituality and wellness influencers. Argentino dubbed this version 'pastel QAnon'. It was very different from the memes generated on 8chan in the years previous, showing Hillary Clinton with devil horns surrounded by screaming children. As Kaitlyn Tiffany wrote in *The Atlantic*,[8] 'We're used to conspiracy theories appearing on the internet's strange and ugly spaces, laid out with blurry photos and eyesore annotations. But those visual cues are missing this time. There's no warning – just a warm, glamorous facade, and then the rabbit hole.'

You may be asking what exactly is wrong with joining a movement that is against child trafficking? Surely any movement that wants to raise this kind of awareness shouldn't be criticised? The issue is that the claims spread by #SaveTheChildren put forward a completely unrealistic idea of what child trafficking actually involves, undoing the work of real organisations dedicated to protecting children, and creating a moral panic akin to the stranger-danger environment that bred the Satanic witch hunts in the 1980s and '90s.

One of the most prominent claims that spread within #SaveTheChildren circles was that 800,000 children go missing every year in the US. Shocking statistics like this, posted in meme form with no other context, spread fear that strangers were kidnapping children off the streets at an unprecedented rate. This number, based on stats from a 2002 survey, leaves out the very important point that 99 per cent of these children return home shortly after being reported missing. The majority of kidnapping cases are related to custody disputes and involve the parents of the children in question. Many of the rest are runaways. In the US, statistics from 2011 showed that there were just 65 kidnappings committed by strangers in the year previous, and again, most of these victims were found alive.[9] They were still, of course, tragic and horrific instances, but they were just not happening at the scale, or in the way, #SaveTheChildren followers thought they were.

Like kidnappings and missing children cases, the realities of child sex trafficking are also very different to what people picture in their heads, which is often something akin to the situation portrayed in films like *Taken*. Again, that is not to deny that this happens, but it doesn't happen as often as the memes of QAnon make out. As Michael Hobbes pointed out in his *HuffPost* piece looking at this exact issue,[10] child sex trafficking by definition includes anyone under the age of 18 who exchanges sex for anything of value: money, food, drugs, a place to sleep. The vast majority of minors who fall into sex trafficking come from the most vulnerable segments of society, and they do so out of desperation. Many are homeless, or victims of abuse or LGBTQ+ kids who have been excluded by their families. Those who are forced into sex trafficking have often been brought up in vulnerable situations. As Hobbes concluded in his piece, the way to solve this problem is to improve social services and figure out how to stop these children from seeing sex trafficking as their only choice.

Legitimate child welfare groups spoke out about the damage that QAnon was causing – from being targeted by online mobs who accused them of being part of the deep state, to constantly having to debunk false claims about child trafficking. All of them agreed that QAnon's promotion of child-trafficking myths and the exploitation of hashtags like #SaveTheChildren were doing a lot more harm than good. There is no doubt that QAnon has made a difficult job a lot harder for those working at these organisations and has pulled time and resources away from dealing with actual victims. Rebecca Bender, an activist working with sex-trafficking survivors, told *HuffPost*, 'I've heard people say, "Oh well, at least [QAnon] is raising awareness." But you know, we don't go telling everyone cancer is contagious in the name of awareness.'

As well as creating hysteria about child trafficking, #SaveTheChildren was leading people right into QAnon. The influencers who started sharing #SaveTheChildren content suddenly saw their engagement and follower rates increase as QAnon followers flocked to their pages to support them. Many of them continued down the QAnon path because that was what their audience wanted. Concerned mothers who came across #SaveTheChildren content started doing their own research. The mainstream media wasn't reporting on child trafficking (because it wasn't happening in the way it was being portrayed online), so they researched on social media. Following hashtags and pages sharing #SaveTheChildren content would inevitably lead them to claims that the deep state was running a child-trafficking ring, that the media was covering it up and that the only person paying attention to it was Donald Trump.

They didn't need to find the Q drops to find QAnon – the content was ready and waiting, and it had been building up for almost three years. Many people were not even aware that what they were consuming was QAnon content, and many of those who did didn't see it as a problem. Fake child-trafficking scandals had been their red pill. They had been sucked down the rabbit hole, and they were okay with it, because they believed they were fighting to help the children.

The Storm[ing] arrives

Outside of retweeting dozens of QAnon-linked Twitter accounts, both Trump and the US Republican Party had kept QAnon at arm's length for the years leading up to 2020, but as the year rolled on, the two began drifting closer and closer together. Ninety-seven candidates who had endorsed QAnon in some way ran for office, and the 2020 election saw two of them – Marjorie Taylor Greene and Lauren Boebert – elected to Congress. Trump also acknowledged the movement for the first time and essentially endorsed them as people who 'love our country', while churning out the old 'what's wrong with being against paedophiles?' line. QAnon followers were over the moon with this reaction. It was a moment they had waited on for a long time.

Throughout 2020, and beforehand, Trump was setting the scene for how he would react if he lost the election: there was no way he could lose, and if he did, it would be because the election was rigged. Voter fraud had been a mainstay of Q drops since the beginning, and during 2020, marching in lockstep with Trump, Q was posting about mail-in ballot fraud and ballot harvesting, while also claiming that Joe Biden was mentally and physically unfit to run for office.

The election took place on 3 November, and by 7 November, Biden was declared the winner by a clear margin of seven million votes. Sure enough, the right-wing media ecosystem was awash with claims of voter fraud. By far, the most prolific group creating and spreading post-election conspiracy theories was QAnon. Even though social media platforms had cracked down on QAnon in the months leading up to the election, the movement still yielded vast power online. Most of the key influencers were still active on Twitter, where they spread their claims to networks of millions of people.

A notable addition to the world of QAnon Twitter influencers in the days and weeks after the election was Ron Watkins of 8kun (as 8chan had rebranded itself in 2019). In a strange (and coincidental?) turn of events, Ron resigned his position as administrator of 8kun on the day of the election. Before this, he had kept a low profile, using his Twitter account mostly to respond to issues related to 8kun. However, following his resignation, Ron burst on to the scene and presented himself as an 'expert' in voting machines (which he was not). He became a dominant voice promoting one of the most pervasive conspiracy theories related to election fraud: claims that Dominion Voting Systems, a company that supplied voting machines and software to 28 states to use during the election, was involved in rigging the election for Biden.

As Ron was becoming the public face of a conspiracy theory created and spread by QAnon followers, another major figure in the QAnon world was notably absent: Q. Q had posted just four times since the election; at the time of writing, there hadn't been a drop posted since 11 December 2020. Ron went on to gain over 450,000 followers on Twitter in the two months following the election, where his tweets were often suspiciously similar in tone and style to Q drops. He obtained the ultimate approval when he was retweeted four times by Trump himself. Ron's relentless touting of false claims related to Dominion resulted in low-level election workers being doxxed and threatened. In one case, a noose was left outside the front door of a 20-year-old contractor working with Dominion.

Trump's base in the 2020 election was a mixture of regular people who still believed in his promise to Make America Great Again. They were joined by the alt-right and white nationalist movements, which had regrouped after Charlottesville, and by ever-expanding militia groups. The cherry on top was QAnon, a movement that had radicalised countless regular people.

The vast majority of them simply could not accept that Trump had lost. The conspiracy theories created and spread by people like Ron were being pushed directly to Trump's base through a new movement that encapsulated all those groups: Stop the Steal. The sheer volume of false claims and conspiracy theories gave them more and more reason to believe they had to fight to keep Trump in power. Voter fraud, or the Big Lie, as it is now known, was the conspiracy theory that brought all the disparate groups of Trump supporters together. On 6 January 2021, in Washington, DC, a Stop the Steal protest organised to coincide with the certification of the electoral votes would show the world how much damage such a lie could cause.

To anyone who had been keeping an eye on the pro-Trump media ecosystem in the months and years before 6 January 2021, what happened on that day did not come as a surprise. Many in Trump's base had spent years engulfed in a different version of reality, devoid of logic and common sense, and consumed by conspiratorial narratives that cast Trump as the saviour of the Free World. They were never going to take his defeat lying down. Even still, from my flat in Dublin, I sat glued to multiple live streams and couldn't believe what I was seeing. Thousands of protesters tearing down barriers, beating cops and security guards, breaking windows and scaling the walls of Congress in order to take back an election that they were convinced, through conspiracy theories they had read online, had been stolen.

Q goes global

As QAnon was causing democracy to crumble in the US, it was also becoming a force within the growing international Covid-sceptic community, who during 2020 protested everything from masks and lockdowns, to social distancing and vaccines. QAnon promoted a blanket distrust of the mainstream media, of most politicians (besides Trump and his allies) and in global institutions, such as the World Health Organization (WHO). This fit nicely into the Covid-19 conspiracy theories that claimed the pandemic was a hoax orchestrated by global elites for sinister reasons. Placards saying 'Child trafficking is the real pandemic' became a mainstay at protests across the world, as different elements of QAnon began winding themselves around regional narratives outside of the US. By September 2020, Marc-André Argentino had found online QAnon communities in 75 countries.

In the UK, a group called Freedom for the Children held regular marches across the country against child trafficking, paedophilia and Satanic rituals, as well as decrying the pandemic as a scam. This offshoot of QAnon seized on real past incidents of horrendous child abuse involving powerful individuals and cover-ups. The crimes of BBC children's TV presenter Jimmy

Savile were often mentioned, for example, as were historic child abuse allegations made against UK members of parliament. The Paedophile Information Exchange, a pro-paedophilia movement that was active in the UK in the 1970s and '80s, and Prince Andrew's ties to Jeffrey Epstein also provided British QAnon adherents with plenty of truth kernels to pull people in.

In February 2021, *Sunday Times* journalist Mark Tighe spoke to two protesters attending an anti-lockdown protest in Dublin who were wearing matching hoodies emblazoned with the words 'RTE sold there [sic] souls' and 'Save our children from the reptilians'. When asked to explain this, they said that 9,000 people go missing in Ireland every year, that babies were being killed and their adrenochrome was being used by celebrities at RTÉ (Ireland's national broadcaster) to keep them looking young. The bodies, they said, were buried under a new children's hospital being built in the city. They also said that the politicians in government were 'basically paedophiles'.

This fully formed Irish version of QAnon was quite unbelievable to see, even for someone who looks at these communities every day. It was an indication of the movement's ability to mould itself to an international audience. For many, it was the first realisation that QAnon had made it to Ireland's shores – but it had actually been here for years. One man in particular was responsible for spreading QAnon in Ireland: Rowan Croft, who goes by the online moniker Grand Torino.

In June 2021, Croft spoke as a guest on an Irish anti-lockdown Telegram voice chat and explained that in 2015 he had become disillusioned with mainstream media. He had been using YouTube to build up his carpentry skills. 'I would go from one video to the next, and I came across a couple of videos that kind of sparked my curiosity.' He didn't mention what these were, but in May 2018, he claimed that 'the number-one influence on me throughout that YouTube experience was Alex Jones. Without Alex Jones, I would not be in this position.' By October 2016, Croft had joined Gab, a far-right 'free speech' Twitter equivalent. His second post on Gab was content from InfoWars. His third post was from an Islamophobic troll and his fifth post was about Pizzagate.

Throughout 2017, Croft shared a mixture of far-right conspiracy content: more InfoWars, some Stefan Molyneux, more Islamophobia. Then, at the end of 2017, he started his own YouTube channel, where he became one of the earliest QAnon decoders outside of the US. In one of his first decoding videos from January 2018, Croft explained that he had spent the few days previous down the Q rabbit hole, and he was 'horrified' by what he had been exposed to. He put out the video, he said, because he thinks the world will be shocked when they find out what is happening, and he wants to 'ease out' the information. Then, in a display of mental gymnastics quite typical of QAnon decoders, he said that the following day #TheStorm and #TheGreatAwakening would start trending on Twitter in a meme war that would 'deprogram us and confront us with some horrific truths' relating to the Clintons. He said that Julian Assange was also involved, and that 10,000 indictments would be unsealed to reveal everything. 'It's martial law and Armageddon for these people [the Clintons, etc.] that will soon come to light and soon be exposed for their graphic crimes.' Croft takes a breath. 'Ho-ly fuck.'

It's clear in this video that he has invested in what Q is saying. He's wound up and seems to fully believe that everything will soon be revealed. The Storm is coming. Needless to say, the Storm didn't come. None of the above happened, but Croft continued down the QAnon path. He became a regular contributor to one of the biggest QAnon YouTube channels of the time, Patriots Soapbox. This was a 24/7 channel run by Coleman Rogers, one of the original 4chan anons who appeared on InfoWars at the end of 2017 and helped catapult QAnon from a 4chan LARP to a unified conspiratorial movement. From there, Croft became a contributor to other YouTube QAnon decoder channels, including that of Jerome Corsi, InfoWars's QAnon correspondent. Croft also ran chat servers on the platform Discord for Irish and European QAnon followers.

He talked about his experience of finding QAnon on the Telegram voice chat. 'It was a real eye-opening experience … The more I went down that rabbit hole, the more I came to understand the reality of how dark our existence really is … I came across more and more dark stuff that really shocked me and actually upset me.'

Croft was heavily invested in the US political aspects of QAnon. Styling himself as a 'citizen journalist', he would promote claims about the Clintons, George Soros and the Rothschilds while using the language and slogans of QAnon and attempting to link it all to Ireland. In an example of this Irish-tinged QAnon, Croft and Gemma O'Doherty joined forces in March 2020 in a series of videos that implied a bizarre Pizzagate-type conspiracy taking place at a house in County Wicklow, which they claimed was owned by an associate of Hillary Clinton.

Croft said that his journey into QAnon made him realise how open borders facilitated human trafficking, which is indicative of the direction his QAnon belief took him. Similar to Dave Cullen, Croft began interviewing the who's who of the Irish far right, including Hermann Kelly from the Irish Freedom Party, Niall McConnell from Síol na hÉireann and the National Party's Justin Barrett, to name a few. He also forged explicit ties to European far-right activists, including members of Italy's Lega Nord[11] and British far-right figures Anne Marie Waters and Jim Dowson. Croft was also central in organising protests in towns around Ireland where direct provision centres were planned, activism that he claimed was based around the protection of children and fighting human trafficking.

'I was always an advocate for the rights for the protection of children ... When I started talking about direct provision centres ... my main concern was human trafficking.' In a 2019 video, Croft said that people in direct provision were being 'ferried in' as part of 'a human-trafficking Ponzi scheme'. This is a common conspiracy theory trope within the far right. It allows them to shield their racist ideology as pseudo-humanitarian, while also casting genuine humanitarian organisations offering aid to refugees as part of a human-trafficking scheme. It also fits nicely into the rhetoric around the Great Replacement. Refugees, they claim, are being trafficked to Europe by NGOs to replace white native populations. Croft did not respond to my request to comment on his promotion of QAnon in Ireland, but it is clear that he brought a specific brand of the cult-like movement to Irish shores while utilising the child-trafficking conspiracy theories enshrined in QAnon to push white nationalist talking points.

Croft and O'Doherty weren't the only people promoting QAnon in Ireland, but they were the most prominent ones. Members of Yellow Vest Ireland, which was formed in 2018 during the international evolution of the populist, anti-government Yellow Vest movement, regularly touted QAnon's narratives about paedophile cabals. During 2020, QAnon protests organised by Gemma O'Doherty's former sidekick Dee Wall were regularly held outside the GPO in Dublin.

No reasonable person would disagree with the fact that pandemic restrictions were hard for children, but Covid-sceptic communities latched on to cries to 'save the children' from masks and vaccines, even protesting outside school gates in some parts of the country. Parents and teachers, who were understandably upset with children being targeted in this manner, were routinely harassed and intimidated by protesters. In one instance, the principal of a Cork school was accused of being a child abuser.

Just like it did all over the world during the pandemic, QAnon became enshrined in the wider Irish conspiratorial movement and stuck to it.

The LGBTQ+ agenda is coming for your children

Following the 6 January events, as the heads of many QAnon followers were still spinning from Trump's loss, the movement in the US changed tack and began promoting a new strategy: infiltrate school boards. In the US, public schools are governed by boards of elected officials who manage things like budgets and resources, as well as school policies. QAnon followers were instructed to protest school-board meetings, make their voices heard and put themselves forward for election to positions on the boards. Across the US in 2021, these meetings often erupted in pandemonium, sometimes turning threatening and violent, as radicalised parents battled over masks, vaccines and, most notably, the teaching of issues related to race and sexuality.

At the behest of QAnon influencers and the wider right-wing media ecosystem, parents were up in arms about the teaching of critical race theory (CRT). This is an academic concept that analyses systemic racism in legal and public con-texts. Though related concepts, such as the impact of slavery, are taught in schools, there is little to no evidence that CRT itself is taught to students. Despite this, it morphed into a catch-all term to describe teaching anything related to diversity and racial equality, with education about LGBTQ+ issues receiving similar attention. The teaching of these subjects was seen as 'indoctrination' and 'grooming' within conspiratorial commun-ities, and videos began to go viral of parents accusing schools with LGBTQ+ books in their libraries of promoting paedophilia.

Since the earliest days of LGBTQ+ activism, opposition forces have claimed that LGBTQ+ rights are a 'slippery slope' to normalising paedophilia and have attempted to frame queer people as 'perverts'. One of the first anti-gay rights move-ments in the US was a coalition called Save Our Children, fronted by singer Anita Bryant, who explicitly attempted to conflate homosexuality with paedophilia. This is one of the most damaging and long-lasting hateful tropes directed at, mostly men within, the queer community.

John Waters, when speaking to Rowan Croft about the child abuse perpetrated by the Catholic Church, said that the media were wrong to describe the crimes as paedophilia, claiming that most of the abusers were 'predatory homosexuals'. This is the same position regularly taken by members of the Catholic Church regarding the abuse scandals, and one that has been widely criticised as the Church's attempt to rewrite the history of its crimes and blame them on the gay community. Research undertaken on this subject has concluded that there is no link between LGBTQ+ sexual orientations and child abuse, and that the majority of child abusers are heterosexual men. Yet old hatreds die hard, and QAnon's obsession with paedophilia has helped to bring these tropes to the fore.

In one of the most public and blatant attempts to forge a link between homosexuality and paedophilia in Ireland, in 2020 a smear campaign was launched against Roderic O'Gorman, the Minister for Children and a gay man. Abuse against O'Gorman began immediately after the announcement of his ministerial position but went into overdrive when a photo that he had posted on Twitter in 2018, in which he posed with veteran UK LGBTQ+ rights campaigner Peter Tatchell at Dublin Pride, was circulated. Tatchell was criticised for comments he made in the past regarding age of consent laws, which he has repeatedly clarified were taken out of context.

Members of the Irish far right used the photo of O'Gorman and Tatchell together to claim that O'Gorman was a paedophile apologist. O'Gorman responded to these claims, rightfully saying the campaign was 'rooted in homophobia'. He said he was unaware of Tatchell's controversial statements, and that he found a number of quotes 'completely abhorrent', while adding that Tatchell had indeed clarified his views, 'I would have seen him primarily as an advocate for LGBT rights in the UK in the 1990s and 2000s, but more recently particularly vocal on treatment of LGBT people in Russia and Chechnya,' O'Gorman said.

In rhetoric and tactics lifted straight from QAnon and Pizzagate, O'Gorman was also accused of being a Satanist after he shared a tweet of a person in a Halloween costume depicting Cronus, who, according to Greek mythology, ate his children for fear of being overthrown by them. 'It's a painting of a famous Greek legend and I like a well put together Halloween costume. But now it's being cited as an example that I support Satanism. It's gone to the ridiculous,' O'Gorman said in response to the claims.

The campaign against O'Gorman was promoted by practically every far-right activist and group in Ireland. This included the National Party, the Irish Freedom Party, Rowan Croft, Gemma O'Doherty and John Waters. It was spurred on by right-wing news sites Gript, The Burkean and The Liberal, as well as anonymous far-right accounts across social media[12] that harassed and abused Minister O'Gorman with vile homophobic comments.

In July 2020, the campaign culminated in two protests – one dubbed the 'March for Innocence' and the other 'Hands Off Our Kids' – organised by the National Party and Irish Freedom Party in Dublin city centre. Protesters called for the minister's resignation and shouted 'paedo scum off our streets' at counterprotesters. They carried placards with nooses or 'P9' on them, the latter a reference to the National Party's ninth principle to bring back the death penalty for 'particularly heinous crimes'.

Across the US at the time of writing, 15 anti-LGBTQ+ education bills were being proposed in multiple states that would put restrictions on the teaching of LGBTQ+ issues and about LGBTQ+ people in schools. This includes Florida's Parental Rights in Education bill, which Florida Governor Ron DeSantis signed into law in March 2022. Critics have referred to this as the 'Don't Say Gay' bill, with supporters dubbing it the 'Anti-Grooming' bill. The legislation prohibits the discussion of topics related to gender and sexuality between kindergarten and third grade, and limits these discussions with older children to 'age-appropriate or developmentally appropriate' topics. Parents are allowed to sue the school district if they believe there are violations, and schools will have to pay the legal costs.[13]

Opponents criticised the use of vague language such as 'age-appropriate' as being subjective and open to interpretation. Could it even prohibit LGBTQ+ teachers talking about their partners? Could it mean the children of LGBTQ+ couples would have to refrain from discussing their parents? Supporters of the bill pushed back against these claims and said the bill simply allowed parents to have more of a say over the topics taught to their children – but there is no doubt it will have a detrimental impact on LGBTQ+ youths in the state.

In Ireland in recent years, the far right has been particularly vocal and vicious about pushing back against any efforts to introduce LGBTQ+ inclusive education in schools, claiming that doing so promotes 'degeneracy' and 'paedophilia'. In January 2022, Gemma O'Doherty shared a video titled 'The War on Children: How The Key Purpose Of The LGBT+ Agenda Is To Normalise Paedophilia'. In December 2021, Philip Dwyer, a former member of the National Party, recorded himself walking around schools in Dublin that displayed Pride flags, calling them 'absolutely disgusting' and accusing the schools of 'pushing paedophilic material on children'.

At the moment, primary school curriculums in Ireland do not oblige schools to be LGBTQ+ inclusive in their teaching. Anti-bullying procedures introduced in 2013 do require teachers to engage in education to prevent LGBTQ+ based bullying, however. There are objectives that teachers can choose to meet within certain subjects to make them LGBTQ+ inclusive. The choice over whether to do this lies with the individual schools and there is currently no robust data available on how many schools are doing so.

The far-right and conspiratorial campaigns against the teaching of LGBTQ+ issues propagate the myth that children are being shown sexualised content at a young age in an attempt to 'groom' or 'indoctrinate' them. In reality, this kind of teaching is about promoting inclusion and acceptance. For example, social, personal and health education (SPHE) can be made LGBTQ+ inclusive by discussing the diversity of families. This involves talking about all different family types, including families with opposite sex, same-sex or trans parents, or those with disabilities or one-parent families.

A spokesperson from the Irish National Teachers Organisation (INTO) explained to me that this kind of education is rooted in efforts to prevent bullying by building lessons around what it means to be a good friend and have empathy for others: 'Our approach is that if same-sex couples and same-sex families are included in these discussions from Junior Infants, then children will become familiar with them, develop more empathy and [the LGBTQ+ community] are then less likely to be an object of ridicule.' As a gay woman who grew up in rural Ireland in the 1990s, I can testify to the fact that hearing something as simple as 'Gay people exist, and that is perfectly normal' when I was a child or teenager would have made a monumental difference in my life.

Clearly, this kind of education is critical. A 2019 survey of LGBTQ+ students in Irish secondary schools conducted by BelongTo, an organisation supporting LGBTQ+ young people in Ireland, found that 73 per cent of LGBTQ+ students felt unsafe at school and 77 per cent had been verbally harassed because of their gender identity or sexual orientation.

Despite the positive nature of this kind of inclusive education, teachers working to promote these efforts, and teachers who are themselves LGBTQ+, are regularly subjected to allegations of grooming and paedophilia from far-right activists, both online and in real life. As the INTO spokesperson told me, 'As teachers who work with children all day, this is particularly upsetting.'

In recent years the debate around trans rights has resurfaced many of the old and discredited tropes that were directed at the gay community in the past. Transphobia is not just confined to 4chan trolls, the far right or conspiratorial communities, however. It is also propagated by prominent celebrities, used by certain comedians as the butt of jokes and discussed in the pages of seemingly respectable national newspapers. Much of this stems from the 'gender critical' movement, whose followers are often referred to as 'trans-exclusionary radical feminists', or TERFs. This movement has been successful at spreading the myths that trans women are a threat to women's safety, or that trans-inclusive language is an effort to 'erase' women. The result is a new moral panic, targeting one of the most vulnerable groups of people on the planet, as well as an effort to create a schism within the LGBTQ+ community.

Just like anti-gay rights groups before them, the anti-trans rights movement has co-opted fears around children's safety, with claims including that the internet is 'turning children trans', that huge numbers of people regret transitioning and end up detransitioning, and that there is an agenda in place to coach children into changing their gender.

None of these claims are true. The research commonly cited that claimed the internet was 'turning children trans' was based on a survey of the parents of trans children who had visited websites promoting that exact claim, so of course they were likely to agree with it.[14] No trans children or clinicians were included in the survey.

Although research on detransitioning is sparse, information that does exist has shown that the numbers are a lot lower than detractors allege, and that the reasons for these decisions are complex and not simply down to people coming to the realisation that they are not trans. A 2021 meta-analysis looking at results from 27 different studies (just under 8,000 people) found that less than one per cent regretted their decision to transition.[15] Another 2021 analysis (17,151 participants) put detransition rates higher, at 13.1 per cent.[16] But over 80 per cent of these said that external factors were of impact in detransitioning, including pressure from family members, difficulties securing employment and social stigma. In other words, a lack of acceptance among society was the driving force. As Lilith Ferreyra-Carroll from the Transgender Equality Network Ireland (TENI) told me, 'The majority of those who detransition do so because it's just too fucking hard.'

No one is denying that detransitioning happens, but the small number of people who detransition because they no longer identify as trans gets undue media attention[17] and feeds into the idea that children are being coached into transitioning as part of a 'trans agenda'.

In Texas in 2022, the Department of Family and Protective Services began investigating the parents of trans children, claiming that allowing them to have access to gender-affirming health care constituted 'child abuse'. This is a particularly worrying escalation, considering research has found that 52 per cent of transgender or non-binary youths in the US have attempted suicide.[18] As Hannah Solley from TENI told me, 'A lot of the time, parents are just trying to keep their children alive … we're talking life and death.' She made the point that the decision to give trans children access to the healthcare they need is a hard one and that parents 'don't do it on a whim'.

In Ireland, the services available for trans children and adolescents are essentially non-existent, and waiting lists for services for adults are up to five years long. Instead of denying trans people access to the care they need, it's quite clear that better investment and resources dedicated to understanding trans issues are necessary in order to provide the appropriate services to the people who need them.

Anti-LGBTQ+ conspiracy theories that try to claim that there is some sort of insidious agenda in place to turn children queer is an effort to frame LGBTQ+ people as being inappropriate and a danger to children. In doing this, they make the lives of LGBTQ+ people – especially youths, who are already at high risk of bullying, self-harm and suicide – much more difficult. The real 'LGBTQ+ agenda', it turns out, is simply the promotion of acceptance, tolerance and empathy – things that are terrifying to those who refuse to understand and accept the complexities of sexuality, and view gender non-conformity as an existential threat to their existence.

* * * *

Children represent the future and are always innocent. It is not surprising that their safety has often been the source for moral panics, false accusations and conspiratorial movements. People will understandably do everything in their power to protect children, but it's clear that this urge can be easily manipulated.

Through Pizzagate and QAnon, the instinct to protect children has been weaponised into a political conspiracy theory that benefits Trump and his allies, but the effects ripple into anti-immigrant and anti-LGBTQ narratives, spreading hatred and bigotry under the guise of protecting children, when in fact they do the opposite.

Chapter 5

The Science

WHERE WOULD WE BE WITHOUT OUR ABILITY to understand science? Probably still living in caves. Or perhaps we would be extinct. As Dr David Robert Grimes aptly puts it in his book *The Irrational Ape*, in our natural state, compared to other species, 'we are confined to the earth, incapable of flight, unable to survive long in open water … but our greatest endowment is just over a kilogram of fleshy matter with the consistency of gelatine, encased in the protective fortress of our skull'.[1] That is, of course, our brain. And our ability to use our brain to manipulate the world around us has allowed us to get to where we are today. Each generation learns a little bit more, passes it on to the next generation and hopes that the knowledge will be used to further our survival.

Science is absolutely central to our survival. It's easy to be complacent about science. We're surrounded by it every day

– in the structure of our buildings, in our cars, in our food, in our home appliances. We don't need to know the exact details of how the car works in order to drive it, or how the oven functions so the chicken comes out perfectly cooked. We just need to know how to use them: turn the key, press the accelerator, turn the knob to the correct temperature. Easy. But the ease of our existence is only possible because of the many, many people who *do* know how the car works or how to build a functioning oven. We trust that their knowledge is accurate, and we benefit immensely from this knowledge without ever having to understand it.

But over the years, certain scientific advancements have contributed to complacency, and many people now take these achievements for granted. A prime example is vaccines, which in many ways have become the victims of their own success. We no longer see the crippled and paralysed bodies of people affected by polio, because polio has largely been eliminated through vaccination. Before the roll-out of the smallpox vaccine (which eradicated the disease), three out of ten people infected with smallpox died. It killed hundreds of millions of people around the world, devastating families and leaving those who survived with deep scars, a constant reminder of the disease. In the 1960s, a rubella epidemic swept across the United States, resulting in 20,000 babies being born deaf, blind or intellectually disabled.[2] Diphtheria, also known as 'the strangling angel of children', was once the third leading cause of death among children, killing about one in every five infected with it.

I could list numerous other examples, but the point is that, thanks to the success of vaccinations, for the most part we no longer have to deal with these horrific diseases. Because we no longer see the diseases, many no longer see them as a problem and therefore they decide not to vaccinate their children. 'Why would I vaccinate against a disease that isn't a threat?' is a regular refrain. But the truth is that for every parent who decides not to vaccinate their children, we are sending the world backwards one step at a time. Vaccine hesitancy is different from being anti-vaccine. The vast majority of parents who don't get their child vaccinated are not militant anti-vaxxers – they are simply scared of making the wrong choice for their child. But vaccine hesitancy is driven by the anti-vaccine community, and if the numbers of vaccine-hesitant parents continue to increase, we run the risk of diseases that were once largely eliminated resurging and devastating the world again.

Complacency is also a factor when it comes to our grasp of the realities of climate change. The scientific consensus on whether humans are causing climate change is overwhelming. Numerous studies have found that upwards of 97 per cent of climate scientists agree that climate change is caused by human activities.[3] As John Cook, a psychologist and climate change communicator from Monash University, summarised: it is definitely real, we're definitely causing it and it's bad, but there is hope.[4]

Although in the grand scheme of the history of the world climate change is happening quickly, to the average person who is not affected by it directly, it is an abstract occurrence, happening slowly over time and not easily noticed. Similar to with vaccines, if we can't see the problem, we question whether there really is a problem. This is changing in places like Australia and other regions that are regularly seeing the impact of climate change. In places that don't suffer visible consequences, climate change denial and scepticism (summed up by John Cook as 'it's not real, it's not us, it's not bad, climate solutions won't work and the experts are unreliable') are more difficult to counter.

When the Covid-19 pandemic brought the world to a standstill, no one knew what to expect. The videos out of China, Italy and other countries like Ecuador were terrifying, showing overwhelmed hospitals and bodies on the streets, but many countries, including Ireland, escaped such scenes. To those who weren't working on the front lines treating the patients, the virus was an invisible threat. Poor communication at the beginning of the pandemic compared Covid-19 to the flu, and the idea of asymptomatic spread (the fact that you could have the virus and not realise it) became confusing for many.

This all led to – you guessed it – complacency. For sceptics, the idea that Covid-19 wasn't as dangerous as it was being made out to be became a stake in the ground that was then easy to exploit. If Covid-19 was no more dangerous than the flu, then there was no need for lockdowns, masks, social distancing or vaccines. For the record, the flu and pneumonia killed 49,783 people in the US in 2019. The following year, Covid-19 killed 345,323.

The lack of visible consequences over very real threats has been weaponised by science deniers. Contrary to the name, science deniers do not deny that science exists; they deny the scientific consensus on topics. They do this in a very specific way, by using science badly and choosing to believe only in certain parts of science to rationalise their rejection of agreed-upon facts.

All this science I don't understand

Science is complicated, and scientists often speak using language that is confusing to the layperson. For that reason, communicating science can be very challenging. Jonathan Jarry, a science communicator with the McGill Office for Science and Society, Montreal, Canada, told me, 'Scientists need to develop a self-awareness that some of our expert terminology may be misinterpreted by a non-expert public.' For example, the word 'theory' to a scientist means that something has been repeatedly tested using the scientific method and has therefore been substantiated. To the public, the word 'theory' means that something is speculative. So, a creationist will claim that Darwin's theory of evolution is 'just a theory', but Darwin's theory is backed up by 150 years of scientific evidence. 'Uncertainty' is another word that has two distinct meanings. Scientists use it to refer to an estimated range of values, whereas the average person uses the word to talk about something that they're not sure about.

Misunderstandings might also arise when the public perceives words as being scary – radiation, for example. A long-running misunderstanding of radiation has led to unfounded fears around everything from radio broadcasts and microwaves to Wi-Fi and mobile technology. The anti-5G movement is the latest iteration of an old, recycled fear.

Everything around us, including humans ourselves, emits radiation or, more precisely, emits electromagnetic (EM) radiation. All EM radiation has a frequency and is part of the electromagnetic spectrum. Visible light – that is, EM radiation that can be seen by the human eye – is just a tiny part of that spectrum.

The EM radiation frequencies below visible light include infrared (such as heat from radiators), microwaves (used in microwave ovens) and radio waves (used in radio and TV broadcasting). This is also the part of the spectrum used by mobile phone and Wi-Fi networks. Critically, the radiation at these lower frequencies, which is known as non-ionising radiation, does not cause harm to human health. It simply doesn't have enough energy to do so. The most it can do is emit heat, like when your phone runs hot or your microwave oven heats up your food.

EM radiation of higher frequencies (and higher energy) include ultraviolet (from the sun or tanning beds), X-rays and gamma rays (used in nuclear reactors). Prolonged exposure to these frequencies, known as ionising radiation, can damage DNA and cause cancer. Gamma rays can also be used in radiation therapy to kill cancer cells by damaging their DNA to stop them dividing and growing. *This* is the radiation that people most often think about when they hear the word. Although it is true that 5G operates on a higher frequency than 4G, it is still well inside the safe zone of non-ionising radiation.

A similar lack of understanding is also exploited by the anti-vaccine movement, which uses scare stories about 'toxins' in vaccines to frighten vulnerable and vaccine-hesitant parents into not vaccinating their children, despite the fact that the so-called toxins are nothing of the sort. This relates to the fallacious appeal to nature, or the idea that everything natural is good for you while 'unnatural' is bad. Anti-vaccine advocates often list the ingredients in a vaccine and claim that they are toxic poisons that will cause grave damage to your child. One common example is formaldehyde.

To the average person, formaldehyde immediately triggers thoughts of embalming agents or dangerous chemicals. Without the correct context, you can see how this could induce fear. Are you really going to shoot formaldehyde into your child's body? But in reality, formaldehyde is a naturally occurring substance. We produce it in our bodies, and the amount of formaldehyde in vaccines is tiny (I mean *minuscule*) and much less than the amount we produce naturally. Formaldehyde is also present in many fruits and vegetables, and we regularly ingest much larger quantities every time we eat an apple, a pear or a potato.

Another contentious topic in the anti-vaccine world is thimerosal, a mercury compound. The mere mention of mercury is enough to scare the average person who has any knowledge of the history of mercury poisoning. Thimerosal, however, is broken down into ethylmercury in the body and has been found to be safe (the only side effect being redness at the injection site). *Methyl*mercury is the toxic variety of mercury. Ethylmercury is only present in tiny amounts in vaccines (the few that contain it) and is quickly excreted by the body. In fact, you ingest greater amounts of harmful mercury when you eat a can of tuna.[5]

In the US in 1999, before there was a proper understanding of the differences in toxicity between methylmercury and ethylmercury, the Food and Drug Administration (FDA) carried out a review of thimerosal in vaccines. This led to a directive being issued to vaccine manufacturers to remove the ingredient for fear that children were being exposed to it in dangerous doses. Critically, the review found that the only reaction caused by thimerosal was a slight skin reaction at the site of the injection. However, because the doses in some vaccine combinations could end up exceeding a safe level (working on the assumption that ethylmercury could be as dangerous as methylmercury, although we now know it is not), they decided out of an abundance of caution that it was best to remove it.[6]

The growing anti-vaccine movement at the time interpreted the removal of thimerosal from vaccines as an admission that the substance was dangerous. It also used this in order to claim that mercury poisoning was the reason behind increasing autism diagnoses. The thimerosal/autism link found a willing advocate in Robert F. Kennedy Jr, who used his previous work as an environmental lawyer and his celebrity status as the son of slain US Senator Robert F. Kennedy to claim that there was a government conspiracy at play to conceal thimerosal's dangers.

There is overwhelming, large-scale scientific research[7] that thoroughly debunks the claim that thimerosal causes autism, or even that it is harmful, yet the anti-vaccine movement still touts this theory. Robert F. Kennedy Jr has since become one of the world's leading anti-vaxxers, blaming vaccines for a range of conditions from ADHD and cancer, to autoimmune diseases and diabetes. He continues to claim that there is a large-scale cover-up between the media, governments and pharmaceutical companies to conceal their dangers.

Great expectations

As Lee McIntyre stated in his book *How to Talk to a Science Denier,* 'the only people who insist that science must be perfect are those who have never done any science'. That's not to say that there are no branches of science that can determine things with absolute precision, but these are based around mathematical sciences, such as physics and astronomy and are not the kind of science being discussed here. Empirical science, on the other hand, is based on evidence that contributes to a fuller understanding of a certain topic, leading to degrees of certainty, but never absolute certainty. This is why the scientific consensus on a topic is based on a reading of the entire body of evidence and not just single pieces of research.

Jonathan Jarry explained this to me: 'An individual study can be flawed in myriad ways. So the reason we arrive at the scientific consensus on certain issues is because we have so many different studies, done by different groups, using different methodologies.' If these all triangulate towards one result, then that is how scientists reach a consensus. This is often done by performing a meta-analysis – that is, a statistical review of all the available research on a topic. Jarry used the research linking smoking to lung cancer as an example, explaining that eventually there was a massive body of evidence to show clear causation.

The anti-vaccine community, however, will ignore the scientific consensus on the safety of vaccines, the certainty of which increases all the time as more research is added to the body of evidence. Instead, they will use a small number of research papers (which to the untrained eye can be convincing) that confirm their belief that vaccines are dangerous. This is known as cherry picking, and it is a very common tactic that involves selecting data that confirms a position on a topic, while ignoring data that contradicts it. Climate change deniers, flat-earthers and many other movements that deny the scientific consensus on a topic use this strategy regularly.

John Cook says that global warming is particularly susceptible to cherry picking because the earth's surface temperature fluctuates year on year. It's therefore possible to choose a small period of time that shows that temperatures aren't increasing, even though the data over 40 years clearly shows that it is.

Anti-vaccine campaigners will regularly say a version of, 'I'm not anti-vaccine, I'm pro safe vaccines, so I'll take a vaccine when you can prove it is 100 per cent safe.' What they are demanding is an expectation that can never be met. Like any drug or medical treatment, there is always a possibility of side effects. (Have you ever read the list of possible side effects on the insert in a pack of paracetamol?) The demand that science must always be perfect undermines the nature of science itself, which is based on degrees of certainty.

This is also exploited by anti-5G campaigners, who will often bring up the fact that the World Health Organization categorises radiofrequency (RF) electromagnetic fields as 'possibly carcinogenic' as proof that 5G is unsafe. This is yet another example of science not translating well to the layperson. 'Possibly carcinogenic' sounds scary. In fact, the word 'possibly' is likely to be ignored, but it's included for a very important reason.

As it stands, there is an absence of evidence that proves RF fields cause harm, but this is not enough for the WHO to unequivocally say that they *don't* cause harm, hence the 'possibly'. (The next level up is 'probably' and the level down is 'unclassifiable'.) Any studies that have been performed to date have not found a causal relationship between cancer and RF fields. (One such study followed 350,000 people for 27 years to examine this.[8])

Scientists looking at this issue do not believe that harm is possible due to the nature of non-ionising radiation. Also, if there were a link between RF fields and cancer, the huge increase in usage of mobile phones, Wi-Fi and other RF technologies in the past 30 years would provide proof, as presumably, there would be huge increases in cancer rates. This is simply not the case.[9]

During the Covid-19 pandemic, the demand on science to get things perfect all the time was immense, but the public was demanding something that wasn't possible. Because the situation was ever evolving and changing so rapidly, science was also changing. Unfortunately, the changing science was often taken to mean that the science was failing or, worse, that scientists were lying and that a narrative was being manufactured.

A clear example of this was seen in the roll-out of the vaccines. When the first vaccines were developed, the results were extremely positive, with some vaccines up to 90 per cent effective against the disease. When the new Delta variant of Covid-19 appeared, the effectiveness of the vaccines was reduced. Towards the end of 2021, the Omicron variant changed this effectiveness again, and booster shots were needed.

Science can do marvellous things, but it cannot tell what the future will bring. This ever-evolving situation was used – especially by those opposed to Covid-19 vaccines – as proof that the vaccines weren't working, despite clear evidence that they were.

As Jonathan Jarry explained, scientists will use language like 'we have found no evidence' or 'we reject a causal relationship' because they know that they can never be 100 per cent certain. (If you find a scientist telling you that something is 100 per cent certain, you should probably be sceptical.) To people unfamiliar with science, this can be misinterpreted as an attempt to hide something. 'If vaccines are definitely safe, why don't they tell us with absolute certainty?' This is just not how science works and not how it should work. When it comes to understanding science, consensus is always best.

Let me tell you a story

'You can never convince a chimpanzee to give you a banana by promising that after he dies, he will go to Chimpanzee Heaven and there receive countless bananas for his good deeds ... Only humans believe such stories.' This reasoning, from Yuval Noah Harari's book *Sapiens*, has always stuck with me. We are a story-telling species. It's one of the things that sets us apart from all other creatures on the planet.

Stories are the most powerful means of communication we have. We tend to trust personal stories, especially those that elicit an emotional reaction. Personal stories, told well, stick in our heads. Science, however, is not built on storytelling, and that is a problem. Graphs, data, ratios and probability do not make for interesting stories. For this reason, practices that don't have the backing of scientific evidence will rely on stories – testimonials and anecdotes – to sway people to their products or beliefs.

Homeopathy is a good example of this. Homeopathy was invented in the late 1700s by Samuel Hahnemann and is based on the flawed doctrine of 'like cures like'. Homeopaths therefore treat their clients' symptoms with a substance that causes symptoms in a healthy person (for example, onion causes your nose to run, so onion will cure a cold). Key to homeopathy is also the (again, flawed) idea that 'less is more', so the substance thought to cure the condition is diluted repeatedly to the point that none of the original material exists and clients are essentially being treated with water or sugar pills.

Homeopathic products are diluted according to the centesimal scale (C), created by Hahnemann, with higher numbers denoting higher dilutions. 1C means that the product (the onion, for example) is diluted by one part onion in 100 parts distilled water. 30C is a typical homeopathic dilution, which means that this initial dilution is repeated 30 times. The result is that the amount of onion in your homeopathic cold cure is one in 1,000, 000,000,000,000,000,000,000,000,000,000,000,000,000,000, 000,000,000,000,000 (that's 60 zeros).

Both of these ideas – 'like cures like' and 'less is more' – fly in the face of all logic and science, and there is no evidence proving that homeopathy cures anything. It has rightfully been described as 'placebo therapy at best and quackery at worst'.[10]

Because there is no data or science-based evidence that homeopathy works,[11] homeopaths rely on testimonials as a marketing tool. On one Irish homeopathy site, there are dozens of testimonials from people claiming that homeopathic treatment helped to cure a range of ailments including hormone issues, irritable bowel syndrome, flu, eczema, depression, heartburn, urinary tract infections and stress. How do you explain these stories if homeopathy is nonsense?

There are a few possibilities, the first of which is the aforementioned placebo effect. This very real effect is a function of the brain. As explained by Professor Ted Kaptchuk, who researches the phenomenon, 'Placebos may make you feel better, but they will not cure you.' The placebo effect has been found to be most effective for conditions associated with pain, stress, fatigue and nausea, and it is a likely reason for many homeopathic testimonials.

Another explanation is known as 'regression to the mean'. If someone first visited a homeopath when their pain or illness was at its worst, the severity of their pain is likely to decrease even without intervention. This is true of any self-limiting illnesses like a cold or the flu, from which you will eventually recover after a given amount of time, even if you don't treat it.

I hear you say, 'So, where's the harm? If it makes people feel better, who cares if it's nonsense?' I understand that reasoning if it is being used to relieve things like stress or insomnia. But, as with all alternative treatments, the harm comes when homeopathy claims to cure diseases and encourages people to dismiss or refuse real medical treatments, as in the cases of Jacqueline Alderslade and Paul Howie detailed in Chapter 1.

Also, these therapies can be extremely expensive (considering that all you're getting is sugar and water), and they tend to appeal to people who are feeling extremely vulnerable and willing to part with whatever amount of money it will take to help them.

The issue with testimonials is that you never hear about the countless people who sought treatments and felt nothing, or whose condition worsened. All you hear are the positive stories. This is simply not reflective of reality, but it works well as a marketing tool.

If testimonials within alternative health completely omit the negative side of the story, they do the opposite within the anti-vaccine movement, highlighting *only* negative stories. Worried parents who want nothing more than to make the right choices for their children can be easily swayed by heartbreaking stories of parents who blame vaccines for changes in their child's development (or, in more devastating cases, the sudden death of their child). These stories get millions of shares online, driven by a determined, well-funded and well-organised anti-vaccine movement.

These heart-wrenching stories are difficult, if not impossible, to counter, because the distress of parents is clearly very real. But more often than not, vaccines are the misplaced targets of their anger. The tragic death of six-month-old Evee Clobes is an example of how grieving, vulnerable parents can easily get swept into linking their despair to vaccines. Evee's beautiful face featured on billboards in Minneapolis throughout 2019, along with the words 'Healthy babies don't just die' and the web address of a local anti-vaccine website.[12]

Evee's mother, Catelin, says that her daughter died 36 hours after a check-up with their paediatrician, who told her Evee was in 'perfect health' and administered her vaccines according to the standard childhood vaccination schedule. Two nights later, Catelin said she put Evee to sleep in her bed, checked on her throughout the night and woke up to find Evee still and lifeless at 7 a.m. the next morning. Catelin has since been battling for justice for Evee, who she is convinced died due to vaccine injury.

However, Catelin's story goes against the police investigation, medical examiner and autopsy reports, which noted that the marks on Evee's body, and fluid found on the bed sheets, were consistent with positional asphyxia. Evee had been sleeping in the bed with Catelin and had accidentally suffocated.

Catelin's grief following Evee's death is unimaginable. The day after (before the autopsy or medical examiner reports), she posted a video of Evee on Facebook and shared her pain and confusion. 'The unanswered questions of how or why make it worse,' she wrote in the post. Her post caught the attention of strangers, who offered their sympathy. Among the comments were those directing Catelin to look into vaccine injury as a cause of death. Other comments linked to stories from parents who also blamed their children's deaths on vaccines.

To Catelin, searching for an explanation for her loss, this seemed more than plausible, and the stories she heard were convincing. She joined anti-vaccine communities online and soon Evee's story was being shared by hundreds of thousands of people, and a fundraiser was set up to raise money for a private autopsy. The pathologist hired to conduct the autopsy told *NBC News* that he didn't find any evidence linking vaccines to Evee's death, but Catelin claimed online that he had.

When contacted by *NBC News* in 2019, Catelin rejected the medical examiner's findings and said that co-sleeping had 'nothing to do with [Evee's] death'. Despite all the evidence against her claims, Catelin continues to share her story and has said that there was a 'cover-up' to hide Evee's real cause of death.

Evee's story isn't the only case of a baby's sudden death being falsely linked to vaccines. The same *NBC News* piece that detailed Evee and Catelin's story also contained two further stories of sudden infant deaths being falsely linked to vaccines and used to promote anti-vaccine causes.

This reminds me of my conversation with Lydia Greene, who talked to me about her journey into and out of the anti-vaccine movement in Chapter 1. 'There were probably hundreds of parents reading my own anecdote about my daughter crying after the vaccine,' she said. 'But it turns out I was wrong about it.'

The despair of the parents who have to deal with the sudden deaths of their young babies, or changes in their child's development, is something that I cannot even comprehend. But members of the anti-vaccine community feed on this grief. They have a one-track mind. If *anything* happens to a child within days or weeks of receiving vaccines, then vaccines are to blame. They have extremely powerful and coercive ways to recruit people at times of intense vulnerability, giving them something to blame and a support network of people who will believe them no matter what.

Between 2006 and 2019, there were more than four billion doses of vaccines administered in the US. In the same time period, 6,252 people were compensated for injuries.[13] In 70 per cent of those cases, a settlement was reached without clear determination that vaccines had caused the injury. Many claims were made related to shoulder injuries sustained from poor administration of a vaccine as opposed to the contents of the vaccine itself.[14] Every injury is tragic, but the rate of injuries pales in comparison to the risks that come with *not* getting vaccinated.

In Ireland, one brave young woman's story caught national attention and laid bare those risks. Laura Brennan was only 25 when she was diagnosed with terminal cervical cancer in 2017. Seven years earlier, the human papillomavirus (HPV) vaccine had been rolled out to teenage girls in Ireland, but Laura was too old to get it at the time.

HPV is a sexually transmitted virus that is carried by the vast majority of sexually active adults. There are more than 100 different types, and for the most part they do not cause significant harm to those who carry it; however, a small number of variants can cause genital warts and a number of different cancers. In fact, HPV is responsible for upwards of 90 per cent of cervical cancers, a disease that kills hundreds of thousands of people every year.

So when a vaccine against the main HPV strains leading to cancer was developed, it was seen as a miracle treatment that would save countless lives and prevent the misery of diagnosis and treatment for many more. Safety and efficacy rates for the vaccines were found to be high following repeated trials and studies.

But at the time of Laura's diagnosis, the HPV vaccine uptake rate in Ireland had plummeted from a high of 87 per cent to 50 per cent.[15] Anti-vaccine movements around the world, including a determined Irish contingent backed by Gemma O'Doherty, had done what they do best: spread fear and hesitancy. They had launched campaigns cemented in emotional stories of parents and young girls who blamed the vaccine for a range of conditions including chronic fatigue, migraines, insomnia and muscle pain. The media in some instances promoted their causes, despite a lack of evidence that the conditions were linked to the vaccine, including through a documentary broadcast on TV3 in 2015.

Speaking to the *Irish Times* in 2017, a number of paediatricians pointed out that they had been treating children and teenagers for conditions with the same symptoms as those described by the anti-vaccine groups for years before the HPV vaccine was introduced. If the conditions were linked to the HPV vaccine, they would have seen a massive surge in cases, which they didn't.

'These symptoms are the commonest cause of prolonged absence from secondary school in Ireland, yet we don't truly understand them. It's a complex condition requiring a complex response,' said Professor Alf Nicholson of Temple Street Children's University Hospital. He also pointed out that he had plenty of boys under his care with the same conditions, and the vaccine had not yet been rolled out to boys.

Upon receiving her terminal diagnosis, Laura Brennan contacted the Health Service Executive (HSE) in Ireland to tell her story. She had been frustrated at the pushback against the vaccine and was determined that her suffering would not be in vain. She became the face and voice of both a national and international campaign, based on science and evidence, to show people what refusing a life-saving vaccine could lead to.

You couldn't help but be moved by Laura's story. Her remarkable bravery and kind, funny and caring spirit in the face of a fate that most can't even imagine were something to behold. Her determination to spend the last of her time alive making sure that others who were in a position to get the vaccine would do so no doubt saved countless lives. Laura died on 20 March 2019, aged 26, and the whole country mourned her death. By that time, the HPV vaccine uptake in Ireland had increased again to almost 80 per cent, showing that when the right stories are heard, they can have an amazing impact.

I do my own research

Doing your own research has become a badge of honour within various conspiratorial communities, whose faith in sources like governments, media and health institutions has been annihilated, leaving only themselves to trust. When it comes to researching science and healthcare, the stakes are arguably higher.

As already discussed, science is decided by looking at the strength of the entire body of evidence available on a certain topic. However, many who do their own research online will read Facebook posts, watch YouTube videos or find articles published on sketchy websites. They will also pad out their research with seemingly legitimate science, cherry picking published studies that seem to fit with the conclusion they are looking for. But individual studies can be flawed in countless ways and often do not represent the agreed scientific understanding of a topic.

Not only that: scientific papers are incredibly hard to understand if you don't have the relevant expertise.

Online amateur researchers will often turn to a website called PubMed, which Jonathan Jarry defined as essentially a 'Google search engine of the life sciences'.[16] It is widely used by students and researchers to find published papers or dig into the track record of a researcher. It contains more than 33 million citations. In other words, it is an extremely useful resource.

However, among those 33 million citations, there are a high number of flawed research papers based on dodgy methodologies and poor data. Jarry pointed out that there are thousands of studies referring to homeopathy, for example. It also features articles published in a journal called *Medical Hypotheses* that previously promoted AIDS denial and that was founded by a man named David Horrobin, who was referred to by the *British Medical Journal* as the 'greatest snake oil salesman of his age'. One paper published on PubMed from *Medical Hypotheses* is titled 'Ejaculation as a Potential Treatment of Nasal Congestion in Mature Males'.

Jarry also pointed out that PubMed hosts what he calls 'predatory journals', which are 'set up for the sole purpose of making money' and will 'pretty much publish anything'.

Without knowing these limitations and driven by a desire to prove the truth about their version of reality, online amateur researchers will point to articles on PubMed, claiming that, because they are published papers, they must be reliable.

To demonstrate how flawed the research can be within these online communities, take one of the most contentious issues throughout the pandemic: mask wearing. In the early stages of the pandemic, questions like whether or not asymptomatic people could spread the virus or if it spread in the air had not yet been answered. Many countries were also dealing with issues around the supply of personal protective equipment (PPE) for healthcare workers, and there was a fear that telling everyone to wear masks would result in even further shortages.

As the science developed and understanding of the virus grew, it became apparent that face masks should be worn by everyone, and guidance was changed, also including instructions to use cloth masks if nothing else was available.

At the time of writing, the scientific consensus on face masks was clear: mask wearing reduces the spread of the virus.[17] Respirator masks (commonly called FFP2 or N95 masks) are the best, followed by surgical masks and, lastly, cloth masks. Yet masks alone could not completely halt the spread, so they were used along with other interventions, like hand washing, social distancing and vaccines, when they were made available.

The mixed messaging made masks a flashpoint for the entire pandemic and provided ammunition to those who were against any and all restrictions. Anti-mask activists claimed masks were a violation of civil liberties, that they actually damaged people's health and that making children wear them amounted to child abuse. Conspiratorial communities reasoned that masks were a muzzle, a way of showing governments that people were complying with the 'plandemic'. The change in messaging around masks was taken as proof that scientists were lying, instead of what it was: the understanding of the science changing.

Those who believed the above were doing their own research to prove that they were right. One example of this research was circulated widely within online Covid-sceptic and conspiratorial communities throughout 2021 (including by Ireland's own Jim Corr) and consisted of '30 links to use from published studies and resources that show the risks from masks and that they offer NO protection'. People were told to share the list with parents, teachers and politicians as proof that masks were useless at best and dangerous at worst. Let's take a look at these 30 links to see if this claim stands up.

First, two links lead to videos: one where an alternative health doctor tells a spiritualist that wearing a mask is akin to 'killing yourself', the other with an acupuncturist claiming that there is no evidence that mask wearing is beneficial, and anything that tells you it is beneficial is propaganda. Neither can be considered a reliable source, so can be discounted.

Another link leads to an article written in 1967 on the history of surgical face masks, which is a frankly gushing review of how successful they have been at stopping the spread of disease. I have no idea why this is included. Since it isn't a scientific study (and since it actually advocates for mask wearing), it's also removed.

Two of the linked studies don't mention masks at all. Another leads to notes about a clinical trial design, but not an actual study. Ten links lead to the same four studies, so we can discount six as repeated. Three more are about methods to decontaminate dirty masks so that they can be reused when there are mask shortages, like pandemics. These are discounted, leaving 15 links, half of what we started with.

Three are about the physiological effects of mask wearing. One of these looks at the effect of mask wearing on 39 patients with end-stage renal disease when receiving dialysis and did show a drop in oxygen levels, but as the sample is not representative of the wider public, it is also disregarded. Another shows that oxygen saturation levels of surgeons wearing masks while operating decreased slightly but were still within a normal range. The study could not conclude whether the decrease was caused by the mask or the stress of the job. Another looked at the effects of wearing N95 masks covered with a surgical mask, which found an increase in carbon dioxide levels, but a 'minimal effect on physical work performance'. None of these shows that masks are either useless or dangerous, so they are also dismissed.

Twelve studies remain that look at the efficacy of face masks in different ways. It's surprising to find that what they show is pretty much in line with the scientific consensus on mask wearing. They show that masks do reduce the spread of viruses, but that masks alone cannot stop infection and should be used alongside other personal protection practices such as hand washing. They even reflect the consensus when it comes to the efficacy of different mask types.

There is a single study on the list that claims face mask use had no benefit in curbing the spread of the common cold. But the data set is tiny (it only looked at mask wearing on 32 health workers), and the conclusion even states that the study wasn't large enough.

So, there you have it: one (flawed) study out of 30. At a glance, the list looks reputable, because 18 links lead to PubMed and others link to reputable journals like the *British Medical Journal* and *Nature*. But it's quite clear that whoever put the list together had no medical or scientific experience and likely just typed certain search words into a resource like PubMed. Some of the study titles may give the impression that they were critical of masks, but a closer look at their contents shows that this 'evidence' falls apart with even a cursory glance.

At the time of writing, the list still featured as a pinned message in a popular Irish Covid-19 conspiracy Telegram group as apparent solid proof against wearing masks.

The little drug that couldn't

If there is one story that epitomises the need for due diligence and rigour when it comes to scientific research, it is the story of ivermectin and the Covid-19 pandemic. Let's get a few things straight about ivermectin, which is an anti-parasitic drug. First, it's a wonder drug. It is thought that, along with aspirin and penicillin, ivermectin is one of the drug discoveries that changed the world. It was discovered in the late 1970s by William Campbell, a parasitologist born and raised in Ramelton, County Donegal, and Japanese microbiologist Satoshi Ōmura, who both received the Nobel Prize in Physiology or Medicine in 2015 for their work.

Ivermectin has relieved suffering and saved the lives of millions around the world affected by parasitic diseases such as river blindness. It is also widely used in veterinary medicine to treat and prevent infections of parasitic worms. During the pandemic, desperate people who believed that ivermectin could treat Covid-19 began buying the (cheaper and more widely available) veterinary version of it, leading to many in the media dubbing the drug 'horse paste' and mocking those who were using it – one of the many low points in pandemic media coverage.

In many ways, the pandemic changed the way science was conducted. The situation called for rapid research to answer a mountain of questions about the virus and the best way to deal with it. The usual course of action is for research to be submitted to a journal and put through the peer-review process, an integral part of scientific research in which a study is examined by independent researchers to catch flaws before its official publication.

Peer reviewing is time consuming and has the potential to delay the dissemination of vital research; therefore, during the pandemic, peer reviewing was conducted in record time. In many cases, instead of waiting for the peer-review process to be complete, researchers released their studies as a preprint, so that they could be shared quickly, if needed. Both the speedy peer-reviewing process and the high number of preprints were bound to lead to the promotion of some bad studies.

Early in the pandemic, it was discovered that ivermectin had antiviral effects on Covid-19 in vitro – that is, in a Petri dish. But the concentrations used were huge, much higher than what would be considered safe for human use, and killing Covid-19 in a Petri dish is of course a lot different from treating a living, breathing human.

Even so, the idea that a cheap and widely available drug could be the way out the pandemic took hold, and in April 2020, a preprint observational study was published that seemed to breathe some life into these wishes. It claimed that ivermectin was associated with lower mortality and shorter hospital stays, but that the results would need confirmation in a randomised control trial (RCT), the gold standard for clinical trials.

Because ivermectin was widely available and already known to be a safe drug, some countries in Latin America, namely Peru and Bolivia and some parts of Brazil, decided to recommend ivermectin as a treatment for Covid-19. It was a scary time, with infections rising worldwide, so it's understandable that they would take a chance on the drug, although many researchers expressed concern that they were moving too quickly and there was not enough evidence. Soon after, the drug received its first setback in its fraught relationship with Covid-19.

Concerns raised by researchers and an investigation by *The Guardian*[18] found that the preprint paper that showed ivermectin was associated with lower mortality was based on highly flawed data from a questionable company called Surgisphere. The company had also provided the data for a paper published in the prestigious journal *The Lancet* that claimed patients taking hydroxychloroquine were more likely to die in hospital. Hydroxychloroquine was another drug that was briefly considered to be a possible treatment for Covid-19 and was widely touted by Donald Trump at the time. *The Lancet* paper had prompted the World Health Organization to halt its clinical trials of hydroxychloroquine. (They were resumed following these revelations, but the drug was found to be ineffective.)

Surgisphere claimed to be collecting patient data from 1,200 hospitals around the world, but when hospitals were contacted, they had never heard of the company. Other major discrepancies were also found in the data, around case numbers and mortality rates, data that didn't make any sense to researchers who looked into it. *The Guardian* found that Surgisphere had been a textbook publisher that seemed to branch into the world of scientific analytics out of nowhere. The company had only a small number of employees, many of whom didn't seem to have experience in scientific research (one was a science fiction writer, another a model), and its chief executive (who was also a co-author on the flawed papers) was a vascular surgeon who had been named in three malpractice suits in the United States.

The company denied wrongdoing when challenged by *The Guardian* and defended its data, but it also failed to account for the major discrepancies and issues highlighted in the investigation. Surgisphere's research was soon retracted by the journals that had published it, and *The Scientist* called the whole debacle 'the first big research scandal of the Covid-19 era'. For ivermectin it was, unfortunately, only a taste of what was in store.

In December 2020, a critical care specialist named Dr Pierre Kory testified at a Senate Committee hearing about the use of ivermectin to treat Covid-19 patients. Dr Kory was a member of a group called the Front Line Covid-19 Critical Care Alliance, or FLCCC, and he was working on the front lines treating Covid-19 patients at the time. He spoke in no uncertain terms (take note): ivermectin works.

'There is a drug that is proving to be of miraculous impact, and when I say "miracle", I do not use that term lightly … ivermectin basically obliterates transmission of this virus.' He also said it could even prevent people from getting sick at all if taken as a prophylaxis. 'If you take it, you will not get sick,' he said.

Dr Kory's certainty was something to behold. He wasn't speaking like a cautious scientist, who might say things such as 'There is some evidence that ivermectin may work as a Covid treatment.' He was absolutely sure about what he was saying, and he cited data and research to back it up.

Dr Kory's testimony went viral, and suddenly people were asking why health authorities and governments weren't listening to him. Then, in a move that raised suspicions even further, YouTube removed the video of his testimony from the platform. Now the question being asked was, 'Why is a tech platform suppressing information about a life-saving drug that could end the pandemic?'

But there was no consensus within the scientific community on whether ivermectin was a wonder drug against Covid-19. A preprint meta-analysis published online in January 2021 that looked at the results of 18 RCTs showed use of ivermectin resulted in a 75 per cent reduction in mortality. Great news – although the article also said that 'many studies included were not peer reviewed and meta-analyses are prone to confounding issues', and it recommended larger RCTs be conducted to confirm the results.

At the same time, other trials were showing the drug did not have an effect. Neither the US National Institutes of Health nor the European Medicines Agency recommended ivermectin as a Covid-19 treatment outside of its use in clinical trials, but neither ruled it out as a potential future treatment if the evidence became available. Other countries around the world – including Slovakia, Czechia, Mexico and India – felt like there was enough evidence and began adding ivermectin to its list of treatments. The drug started to thrive on the black market around the world, and people began to seek out the veterinary version of it to take as a preventative. Reports began to surface of people being hospitalised for self-medicating with the drug.

At this point, the conspiracy theories about ivermectin were billowing online. Some research showed the drug had a huge effect, so it became easy to cherry pick these studies as proof that health authorities were seemingly 'ignoring' the evidence. According to many, ivermectin was *the* Covid-19 cure, but it was being suppressed because Big Pharma couldn't make money from it; instead, they wanted to inject people with vaccines. Often, these claims were tied in with vaccines being unsafe, or being some form of a depopulation tool or biotech weapon.

The claims of Big Pharma suppression and Big Tech censorship found willing audiences in the right-wing media ecosystem and in the followers of those associated with the so-called Intellectual Dark Web. This is a loosely defined group of media commentators and podcasters who rail against topics like cancel culture, political correctness and social justice while claiming freedom of speech is being suppressed. Many of those in this collective became promoters of false information about Covid-19 and vaccines, with two particular podcasts – Bret Weinstein's *DarkHorse Podcast* and *The Joe Rogan Experience* – becoming almost like a rite of passage for those spreading false information about Covid-19.

In June 2021, Dr Kory was interviewed on the *DarkHorse Podcast* and subsequently appeared with Weinstein on Joe Rogan's podcast for an 'emergency' episode, where they claimed, among a litany of untruths, that ivermectin was being

suppressed by Big Pharma for profit. Bret Weinstein took ivermectin live while recording a podcast, and Joe Rogan took it
(as part of what he called the 'kitchen sink' drug cocktail) when
he got infected with Covid-19 in September 2021.

Dr Kory was soon joined in his ivermectin quest by
UK-based Dr Tess Lawrie, who set up an FLCCC UK equivalent called the British Ivermectin Recommendation
Development Group (BIRD). Lawrie had co-authored a
meta-analysis published in June 2021 that found that 'large
reductions in Covid-19 deaths are possible using ivermectin',
and she also began to appear on the podcast circuit.

But in mid-July 2021, the suggestion that ivermectin was a
miracle drug against Covid-19 would take one of its biggest
hits. In the UK, Jack Lawrence, a master's student in biomedical
science, was given an assignment by his professor to critically
review a preprint study out of Egypt that showed that ivermectin cut the risk of death for Covid-19 patients by an
amazing 90 per cent. The paper had held significant weight in
the various meta-analysis results and had been widely cited as
proof of the drug's effectiveness. Lawrence had no idea what he
was about to uncover.

On first reading the paper, he noted that the English used
was relatively poor, although he put this down to English not
being the authors' native language. But every now and then,
sentences stood out to him as very well written, which he
thought was odd. He Googled these sentences and quickly
found that they had been plagiarised. In fact, he found that the
entire introduction, bar one sentence, had been plagiarised,
often done in a patchwork fashion by making minor edits,

including changing 'severe acute respiratory syndrome' (SARS) to 'extreme intense respiratory syndrome'.

From there, Lawrence found that the numbers listed as deaths within the data didn't match those that were listed in the actual paper. He found that they had taken away deaths in the ivermectin groups and added deaths to the control groups – a pretty big red flag. As Lawrence explained to me, 'There really isn't much room for error when it comes to death. Either someone died or they haven't.' At this point he enlisted help from science fraud expert Nick Brown, who found errors everywhere in the data, including evidence that lines of data had been copied between patients. In a blog post detailing these errors, Brown said that he believed the data 'does not faithfully represent the results of the study, and indeed has probably been extensively manipulated by hand'.

Further flaws included at least a dozen instances where the data of patients who died had been duplicated and instances where patients seemed to have passed away before the study had even begun. The study was awful at best and fraudulent at worst, and it was quickly withdrawn from the preprint server that published it.[19] The authors of the paper did not reply to the points of concern raised by Lawrence and others.

From there, things got worse. In September 2021, an Argentinian study (published the previous November) that had shown ivermectin was 100 per cent effective (take note) at preventing Covid-19 infection was found likely not to have taken place at all, or at least not in the way it was described. The study had been published in a little-known predatory journal – one that publishes studies in exchange for a fee and does few checks or reviews on the research – and had also been widely cited as proof of ivermectin's miraculous nature.

Gideon Meyerowitz-Katz, an epidemiologist at the University of Wollongong in Australia, noted in a blog post that the results of the study alone were a red flag: 'There aren't any medications ever that have 100 per cent benefit for anything – this would make ivermectin more effective than antibiotics for tuberculosis or AZT for HIV.'

Meyerowitz-Katz also noted how implausible the practicalities of the study were. The paper said that three doctors recruited 1,400 medical staff in one month, across four different hospitals that were at least an hour away from each other. Each participant then allegedly took the drugs as instructed and reported back once a week. No participants dropped out. All of this seemed quite unbelievable to Meyerowitz-Katz. 'Recruiting people into a clinical trial takes ages,' he said. There are consent forms, biological measurements to take (this study claimed each participant had five physical exams); you need to instruct them clearly on how to use the drug you're testing, and you have to follow up with each one. Three doctors doing that in one month is 'extraordinarily unlikely', he said.

Meyerowitz-Katz also said that the timelines didn't match and that there was no funding noted for the study, which he estimated would cost somewhere in the region of US$400,000. Further investigation by BuzzFeed News found that the hospital where the main study was meant to have taken place had no record of it even happening.[20] The study's main author stood by the results when challenged about it by BuzzFeed, even when it was clear that the data he provided to them did not match the results of the study.

Because these two studies had claimed to show such astonishing results for ivermectin's performance against Covid-19, they had formed the basis for a lot of the positive coverage of the drug. Both studies were referenced in Dr Kory's viral Senate testimony from December 2020. In fact, he specifically mentioned the '100 per cent' Argentinian study as part of his assertion that 'If you take it, you will not get sick.' Both studies also played a significant role in the results of Dr Lawrie's meta-analysis from June 2021 and the meta-analysis from January 2021. When the flawed studies were removed, the efficacy of ivermectin in reducing Covid-19 deaths was found to be insignificant.

Following these grave revelations, Jack Lawrence and Gideon Meyerowitz-Katz teamed up with three more independent researchers to comb through other ivermectin studies. Looking at 26 studies in total, the group found that 10 of them contained significant errors, some of which looked very much like fraud. This included a study out of Lebanon where patient data was copied 11 times (the study's authors said a training file was mistakenly included in the analysis, and the study has since been retracted) and one from Iran that also had significant inconsistencies.

Dr Kyle Sheldrick, one of the independent researchers, told the BBC that they had not found one clinical trial showing positive results for ivermectin that didn't contain signs of errors or fraud. In an article in *Nature*, the group of researchers called for changes in the way meta-analyses are conducted, and said transparency in data is key: 'Any study for which authors are not able or not willing to provide suitably anonymised [data] should be considered at high risk of bias for incomplete reporting and/or excluded entirely from meta-syntheses.'[21]

As it stands, there is very little solid evidence that ivermectin is an effective treatment for Covid-19. The largest trial to date, published on 30 March 2022, found that patients treated with ivermectin did not show any significant benefits compared to those who received a placebo.[22] Although there is still a small chance that it will be found to have some modest results in certain situations, it is certainly not the 'miracle' drug that 'obliterates transmission' of the virus; nor does it prevent people getting sick. In fact, Dr Kory contracted Covid-19 when on the protocol that he alleged would prevent sickness.

Both Dr Kory and Dr Lawrie have doubled down on their assertions about ivermectin, continuing to claim that there are cover-ups preventing the drug from being widely used. Both have become woven into the alternative health and anti-vaccine influencer circuit, with Dr Lawrie even co-founding a group called the World Council for Health, which has called for an immediate halt to Covid-19 vaccines, continues to promote ivermectin and also encourages the use of homeopathy and other alternative treatments.

As Meyerowitz-Katz has said, the story of how so many people became convinced that ivermectin was a miracle cure for Covid-19 will be written about for years to come. We'll likely never know the effect it had or how many people died as a result of believing in it. Even the scientists who put together some of the earliest meta-analyses were fooled by it. Andrew

Hill, whose January 2021 meta-analysis showed the supposed 75 per cent reduction in mortality, told *MedPage Today*, 'I've been working in this field for 30 years, and I have not seen anything like this. I've never seen people make data up. People dying before the study even started. Databases duplicated and cut and pasted.'

Hill has since been accused of being involved in a vast conspiracy by Dr Lawrie, Dr Kory and others, and he has had death threats issued against him and his family, simply for adjusting his meta-analysis following the data fraud revelations.

The desire to find a cheap, effective and widely available treatment for Covid-19 is understandable, and when seemingly sound scientific evidence is presented that shows just that, of course people will want to shout it from the rooftops. But what this episode shows is that, especially in times of crisis, caution is best. The story of ivermectin is a clear example of why rigorous, transparent, scientific research is so important and why cutting corners – even in the middle of a global emergency, when it seems like the right thing to do – can have deadly consequences.

When good experts go bad

A question I'm often asked is how and why there are so many supposedly well-educated experts at the centre of campaigns around conspiracy theories, false information and science denial. One of the pillars of science denial is the presence of 'bad experts', a term I use to describe people with qualifications who use their expertise to support movements like anti-vaccination, climate change denial, the anti-5G movement and Covid-scepticism. They will often incorporate a lot of the strategies already discussed – cherry picking, unrealistic demands of certainty, anecdotes – but will wrap them in a white coat or a PhD, giving them much more credibility.

First, it's important to point out that a string of letters after someone's name doesn't make them immune to conspiracy theorising or corruption; nor does it necessarily mean they are good at what they do. So many Nobel Prize winners have fallen headfirst into pseudoscience that the term 'Nobel disease' was coined to describe it. Among them is Luc Montagnier, who won the Nobel Prize in Physiology or Medicine in 2008 and went on to support the basic tenets of homeopathy and claims that vaccines cause autism.

Knowledge and qualifications in one area of science do not translate to others, but, at times, bad experts can convince people of their supposed knowledge on subjects outside their expertise by falling back on unrelated qualifications. The online world has created the perfect environment for confident individuals to persuade people that they have expertise in areas they do not.

Dublin man Ivor Cummins, who posts online as the Fat Emperor, has a degree in biochemical engineering but made a name for himself as a diet and nutrition influencer before speaking on issues related to Covid-19 during the pandemic. In an interview from 2018, Cummins said that he started down the road of health and nutrition after he received some high readings on blood tests. He wasn't satisfied with the answers his doctor gave him about the implications or causes of the readings, so he decided to start doing his own research: 'I went to ResearchGate [a website academics use to share research], to PubMed … and I studied deeply all of the biochemistry and metabolic science around them. Within a matter of weeks of obsessive study, I essentially had my answer: that excessive carbohydrate in my diet was a primary root cause.' Cummins then started posting videos on YouTube and co-wrote a book on the benefits of a low-carb ketogenic diet.

During the summer of 2020, Cummins's videos pivoted towards criticising lockdowns and other pandemic responses. His stake in the ground at this time was his repeated assertion that Covid-19 was no more dangerous than the flu and that measures such as lockdowns and masks were doing little to stop the spread of the virus. On multiple occasions over the summer months of 2020, Cummins tweeted that the pandemic had largely ended after the first wave, saying there would be 'no second wave without a second virus' and that any winter resurgence would be 'much, much smaller than April 2020'.

In September 2020, he gathered these thoughts in a video that promised to explain the trajectory of Covid-19 using 'science, logic and data' – a phrase he often repeats throughout his videos, seemingly in an effort to reassure his audience that he is suitably placed to speak on the issues. With unwavering confidence, Cummins explained that when Covid-19 started to spread in countries such as Ireland and the UK, only about 20 per cent of the population was susceptible to the disease. Around 80 per cent of the population, he said, was already 'de facto immune through cross immunity [and] T-cell mucosal immunity from prior coronaviruses'. This, he reasoned, meant that the 'epidemic largely ended around May or early June' in Europe after the first wave had subsided.

He explained increasing case numbers after June as being a 'casedemic' – a result of increased PCR testing detecting the virus in previously infected people, and high rates of false positive results that created the illusion of mass infection. 'They're calling them cases when they get PCR positive. They are not.'

Dr Dominic Pimenta is an ICU doctor who spent considerable time challenging the claims Cummins made in this video. 'This isn't really science,' said Dr Pimenta. 'This is sort of gobbledygook that's been mixed up together to look and sound like science.' He explained why Cummins's point about 80 per cent of people already being immune to Covid-19 was not based on reality. 'If you have a disease coming into a country where 80 per cent of the population is already immune, then you already have herd immunity… so the virus couldn't spread.' Dr Shane Crotty, a virologist at the La Jolla Institute for Immunology who spoke to the *New York Times* about Cummins's claims, described the immunity theory as 'convenient arithmetic but … wrong arithmetic'.

The 'casedemic' theory, which became widespread among Covid and lockdown sceptics throughout 2020 and 2021, was also debunked and criticised by scientists and healthcare professionals. Although there are genuine challenges related to PCR testing, the claim that increased cases were driven by huge numbers of false positives simply doesn't add up. Using the UK as an example, Dr Pimenta explained that the number of daily PCR tests did increase by 60 per cent in the late summer and early autumn of 2020 – but in the same period, the number of positive tests increased by 1180 per cent. This increase, he said, 'simply cannot be explained by an increase in the false positive tests.'

Epidemiologist Gideon Meyerowitz-Katz explained further in a blog post.[23] Another reason why case numbers were so much higher for many countries during the second wave, he said, was that many cases were missed in the first wave. Testing had not been properly rolled out at the start of the pandemic and certain people weren't eligible for tests, so the true numbers infected in the first wave were likely significantly higher than what was officially reported.

Despite these facts, Cummins's September 2020 video went viral and catapulted him to fame among the growing communities of people who were not convinced of the dangers of Covid-19. His confident approach mixed with his use of data and scientific-sounding language meant that many regular people were easily persuaded of what he was saying, even when subsequent waves of Covid-19 killed millions of people throughout the world.

Cummins has been repeatedly shown to use the core tenets of science denial in many of his videos, including cherry picking research and poorly interpreting data. In an email replying to my request for comment, Cummins defended his position by saying that he discusses and debates his conclusions with a 'huge world-wide network of medical and scientific professionals'. With regards his viral September 2020 video that claimed the virus had largely run its course, he said that he was 'pleasingly correct on every major technical vector' he discussed, and directed me to watch a follow-up video where he revisited the claims he had made. In this video, he said that he was right about 80 per cent of the population being 'de facto immune', and maintained that he was correct on increasing case numbers being a 'casedemic'. He concluded the video by reiterating that he was 'overwhelmingly correct' and that 'all those academics and professors for whatever reason were largely incorrect and that's just the way it is'.

But there are also plenty of people who, despite having the correct qualifications and experience, choose to disregard much of what they know in favour of spreading information that is blatantly false. It is almost impossible to figure out the individual motivations that drive people to leave behind the world of rigorous scientific research in favour of science denial, but a few common traits seen in many of these bad experts can be used to recognise new ones as they pop up in the future.

The first is contrarianism. Of course, contrarianism is not always bad – far from it, in fact. In science, it is seen as essential. In order for science to progress, there has to be a certain number of people who are willing to disagree and challenge a consensus. This is necessary for discovering errors and oversights. When these challenges turn out to be right, they can lead to a breakthrough that would not have been discovered were it not for the contrarian.

But as with everything, there is a balance to strike. Contrarianism only works well when those who are challenging the consensus can admit when they've been wrong. Bad experts will never admit to being wrong, even when the evidence that they are mistaken is overwhelming. In some people, this is a personality trait. They will always go against the main-stream consensus, they will never admit to being wrong and they will dig their heels in when challenged.

We saw this with Dr Kory and Dr Lawrie in the ivermectin debacle. Instead of saying they may have been wrong about the miraculous effects of ivermectin, they doubled down on their position and maintained that they were right, even when the evidence showed something different.

The second trait is self-aggrandisement, which simply amounts to boasting. Bad experts will spend considerable time tooting their own horn, often speaking in jargon that the average person won't understand but which sounds impressive. This can be accompanied by exaggerating their experience and having a persecution complex for not being recognised for their perceived brilliance. Bad experts often go to great lengths to persuade people that their motives are good and that the people they are opposing are driven by greed and self-interest. Dr Robert Malone is a good example of this.

Dr Malone rose to fame in 2021, hailing himself as the 'inventor of mRNA vaccines', the technology used in the Pfizer and Moderna Covid-19 vaccines. However, he came to the public's attention not for his invention but for speaking out against the vaccines and saying they were harmful, despite all the evidence pointing in the opposite direction. You can see the appeal of a headline that reads, 'Inventor of mRNA vaccines says vaccines are dangerous'. Admittedly, this makes Dr Malone a very convincing bad expert.

Dr Malone is being more than economical with the truth by calling himself the inventor of mRNA vaccines. In reality, mRNA vaccines were the result of hundreds of researchers working over the course of around 40 years, each one playing a part in the technology that is used today.[24] There is no denying that Dr Malone contributed key research back in 1988, but his claim of being the sole inventor is far from the truth and eliminates the work of hundreds of people who came before and after him in the development of mRNA vaccines.

It's clear that Dr Malone feels like he has not been recognised for his achievements. 'I've been written out of history,' he told *Nature*. He claims that companies he worked for have profited from his work (they have denied this), which he told *The Atlantic* amounted to 'intellectual rape'. In contrast, others who also contributed important research to mRNA vaccines do not claim their contribution is more important than others and are just happy to see the technology being used as a force for good.

Dr Malone has an axe to grind with establishment science, and he was therefore welcomed with open arms into the anti-vaccine, Covid-sceptic and conspiracy circles. He joined the chorus of people claiming that ivermectin was an effective cure and that it was being suppressed in favour of dangerous vaccines.

The next trait of bad experts, quite predictably, is the use of conspiracy theories. In order to explain why their claims are not being listened to by those in charge, bad experts will say that there is a conspiracy at play to keep the truth hidden for some kind of nefarious purpose.

Dr Peter McCullough is a successful and well-established cardiologist who led early studies into the use of hydroxychloroquine for Covid-19. When the drug was found to be ineffective, Dr McCullough continued to promote a treatment containing the drug, which was rebutted by the medical and scientific communities. Dr McCullough soon became a regular on right-wing media, podcasts and conspiracy theory channels, promoting ineffective treatments and discouraging people from getting the vaccine.

Similarly to Dr Malone, Dr McCullough also feels that his work has not been recognised. On Joe Rogan's podcast in December 2021, Dr McCullough said that he saw himself as one of a handful of doctors who were brave enough to take risks, and he claimed that if people had listened to him in 2020, he could have prevented 90 per cent of Covid-19 deaths. Why does he think he was ignored? He believes it was because there was an 'intentional, very comprehensive suppression of early treatment in order to promote fear, suffering, isolation, hospi-talisation and death … to create acceptance for, and then promote, mass vaccination'.

This is almost verbatim the main theme of the conspiracy theory film *Plandemic*, a clear indication that Dr McCullough, once a respected cardiologist, had fallen head first into the conspiracy theory world. Instead of the reality that hydroxy-chloroquine was found to be ineffective, McCullough reasons that there must be a grand conspiracy in place, involving governments, healthcare authorities and even doctors and nurses who ignored treatments in order to deliberately cause suffering and death.

Bad experts whose views have been rejected by their peers can easily find a willing audience online who will support them. Social media rewards contrarianism, with controversial viewpoints receiving higher engagement because they rile people up and attract more attention. There's nothing special about someone saying that vaccines are safe, climate change is real and Covid-19 should be taken seriously – they're the same opinions you hear from the 'mainstream'. Saying the opposite is what gets you attention, and attention should not be under-estimated as a driving force behind bad experts.

The world of science denial will always welcome a confi-dent contrarian who feels like they have been rejected and silenced by the mainstream. Dr Malone's Twitter following went from 3,000 in January 2021 to half a million by December 2021, when he was removed for violating the platform's policies on Covid-19 misinformation.

Both Dr Malone and Dr McCullough bounced around the predictable online echo chamber: from Bret Weinstein's and Joe Rogan's podcasts, to slots on Fox News, and from interviews with well-known anti-vaccine and alternative health gurus, to InfoWars and Steve Bannon's *War Room*. These communities will not challenge them on their opinions; they will massage and feed their egos, constantly reassuring them that they are right and everyone else is wrong.

The last reason is the oldest reason in the world why people do things that seem to go against everything they believe in: money. The world of science denial can be a lucrative business for many. One of the most egregious examples of this is the man credited with founding the modern anti-vaccine move-ment: Andrew Wakefield. Wakefield is a British former doctor whose discredited 1998 study linking the three-in-one MMR vaccine to autism sparked worldwide alarm and triggered the kind of vaccine hesitancy that still affects the world today.

Wakefield called for suspension of the MMR vaccine and was given considerable media attention. An investigation by Brian Deer in the *Sunday Times* found that, in the two years before his paper was published, Wakefield had been paid £435,643 by a legal firm looking to find scientific evidence to support the claim that the vaccine caused autism. *The Lancet*, which had published Wakefield's research, then said the study was 'fatally flawed' and should never have been published.[25] In fact, the study's results had essentially been made up. There was absolutely no basis for Wakefield's claims that the vaccine caused autism. Deer also found that Wakefield had applied for a patent on a single-jab measles vaccine, so he stood to gain financially from the MMR vaccine being discontinued.

Wakefield has always denied any wrongdoing, incredulously stating, 'No fraud. No hoax. No profit motive.' He was eventually struck off the UK medical register but took his campaigning to the US, where he found a welcoming home among the anti-vaccination movement. He has since produced some of the most potent anti-vaccination documentaries ever made, making a fortune in the process.

Many of the leading anti-vaccine and alternative health activists are earning huge amounts of money doing what they do, getting paid for speaking engagements, selling bogus cures and treatments, collecting donations online, selling books and hosting anti-vaccine talk shows. They have scared their audiences into turning their backs on conventional medicine, leaving them vulnerable to the bogus advice and snake oil they offer as an alternative.

Ireland's best bad expert

Throughout the pandemic, a number of Irish doctors began making waves by pushing back against restrictions and lockdowns – none more so than Dr Dolores Cahill. With a degree in molecular genetics and a PhD in immunology, Dr Cahill was, until September 2021, a professor of translational science at University College Dublin (UCD). She had been on my radar for a number of years as the chairperson of the Irish Freedom Party. Prior to 2020, she campaigned in line with the party – promoting Euroscepticism, anti-immigration policies and freedom of speech. She had run for election twice – once during the 2019 European elections, coming 11th out of 23, and then as a candidate in the 2020 general election, when she secured just 521 votes.

In May 2020, Dr Cahill was interviewed by Dave Cullen on his YouTube channel in a video that went viral (before being removed from YouTube). This set the scene for the stance she would take throughout the pandemic.

Dr Cahill began the interview by talking about her credentials and experience, telling a perplexed but impressed Cullen about diagnostic assays, high-content protein arrays, adjuvants and proteomics. She explained how her research was of such a high standard that she then got involved in scientific integrity: 'All of my research was validated, but that does not happen often.' She discussed the awards she has received, the positions she held on both EU and Irish science advisory councils, the companies she founded, her work on vaccine development, and her experience running biosafety labs ('There's not many people who would have that expertise').

After almost 10 minutes, Cullen told Dr Cahill, 'The over-whelming thing I'm getting from you is that your career has been steeped in data integrity, in transparency and in trying to the best of [your] ability to engage in good, high-quality science.'

This is certainly the impression Cahill gives. There is no doubt that she has mountains of relevant experience and is more than qualified to speak on topics related to the pandemic, which is what makes the remaining hour of the interview so appalling.

With absolute certainty, Dr Cahill told Cullen that Covid-19 was not as dangerous as scientists were saying it was, that most people were already immune to the virus, that those who catch it will recover fully after 10 days and will then be 'immune for life', that people under 50 will have 'no issues' unless they have a chronic lung disease, and that illness could be prevented by simply boosting your immune system (even in people with chronic conditions). She encouraged people to 'go out and mingle', saying that hydroxychloroquine would cure them if they got sick. She said the current restrictions, masks, social distancing and lockdowns were putting the lives of Irish people in danger.

Dr Cahill also had a conspiracy theory to explain what was going on, again lifted almost wholesale from *Plandemic*, which had been released the previous week: 'The politicians and the media [are] using this as a fear-mongering propaganda tool to try and take away rights from people and to make them more sick and to force vaccination on us.'

Even in May 2020 these claims were preposterous and flew in the face of everything that was known about the virus. With the benefit of writing this two years later and knowing that Covid-19 has killed more than six million people and left many others with long-term health consequences, it is more than clear that Dr Cahill's claims were not only detached from reality but downright dangerous. I got in touch with Dr Cahill to see if she wanted to comment or retract any of the claims she made in the video, but she didn't reply to my request.

After her interview with Cullen, Dr Cahill shot to fame. She became a superstar in both Irish and international Covid-sceptic and conspiracy circles, lending her impressive expertise to the growing movement of people who did not believe in the basic truths of the pandemic. She started on the interview circuit, speaking with big names in the anti-vaccine world and becoming a regular on Irish, UK and European conspiracy community channels. She was invited to speak at rallies across Europe, telling thousands of people that everything they had been told about the pandemic and Covid-19 was a lie.

Dr Cahill set up a number of organisations and business ventures during 2020 and 2021, including a media company producing conspiracy theory documentaries and a travel agency. The latter promised unvaccinated people access to air travel and offered charter flights at up to $13,000 per hour – but first you had to become a member, at a cost of between $100 and $500 per year.

Dr Cahill was the founding member of an organisation called the World Freedom Alliance (€20 annual membership fee), which aims to 'promote freedom' and is linked to Robert F. Kennedy Jr's anti-vaccine movement. She also founded a World Freedom Alliance partner organisation called the World

Doctors Alliance, a group of 12 doctors and scientists from around the world who came together to spread false information about the pandemic. These include a doctor who claimed that the Covid-19 virus doesn't exist and another who had previously claimed that AIDS was a hoax. What's better than one bad expert? Multiple bad experts.

Throughout 2021, Dr Cahill's comments became more extreme. She claimed that the Covid-19 vaccines were lethal and that people would start to die soon after getting them. She encouraged people instead to take vitamins, zinc, hydroxychloroquine and ivermectin (and claimed that these cures were being suppressed). Her claims became too much for the Irish Freedom Party, which called for her to step down as chairperson after she told a crowd in Dublin that wearing a mask would lower children's IQs.

During the summer of 2021, Dr Cahill stood as a candidate in the Dublin Bay South by-election, receiving just 169 first-preference votes but securing herself in people's memories by engaging in a shameless confrontation with Gardaí outside the count centre, where she was refused entry for not wearing a mask. In August, a warrant was issued in London for Cahill's arrest after she failed to turn up to a number of hearings on charges related to holding an anti-lockdown gathering in Trafalgar Square the previous September. She was later fined £2,500 at a November hearing in Westminster Magistrates' Court.

In September 2021, Dr Cahill's employment at UCD was ended, and in December, her Facebook page, which had accrued 130,000 followers, was removed for repeatedly spreading false information. At this stage, Dr Cahill was calling herself 'the most censored Irish citizen'. She has since claimed that 'there is no basis for climate change', that 5G is 'causing huge harm to children' and that there are neurotoxins in drinking water, evidence of her further descent down the rabbit hole.

Dr Cahill's fall from grace is certainly something to behold. In 2004, at the first annual Science Summit, she spoke in front of then-taoiseach Bertie Ahern and tánaiste Mary Harney about her career to date. She had just taken a position at the Royal College of Surgeons as the founding director of the Centre for Human Proteomics and was optimistic about the opportunities that came with the state's decision to focus on investment in scientific research. It's difficult to figure out what happened in between, but 16 years later she chose to be at the centre of a campaign to destroy people's trust in the science that she once seemed so passionate about promoting.

* * * *

At the start of this chapter, I asked where we would be without our ability to understand science. A more relevant question might be: Where would we be if everyone *misunderstood* science? Science denial promotes a warped version of reality where vaccines are lethal, climate change isn't serious and 5G is frying us alive. The conspiracy theories that attempt to explain the core tenets of these movements claim that healthcare workers – people who dedicate their lives to helping others – are part of some evil, twisted plot to do the opposite. They claim that the vast majority of scientists and researchers are driven by selfish ends and have no integrity.

Science isn't perfect, but it isn't meant to be. It has allowed us to survive and thrive on this planet until now. But if we lose our grip on it, the consequences, as we have seen, would be deadly.

Chapter 6

The Fallout

ON 15 SEPTEMBER 2021, I was sent a video that stopped me in my tracks. It was recorded in Letterkenny Hospital in County Donegal, the hospital where I was born. Speaking into the camera, Antonio Mureddu, a far-right activist associated with the Italian anti-immigration party Lega Nord, announced that he had come to the hospital to rescue his friend Joe, 'because they [hospital staff] were trying to kill him' by putting him into ICU. The Joe he was referring to was Joe McCarron, a 67-year-old man who had recently contracted Covid-19 and was being treated in hospital for the disease.

In the video, as Joe is guided into a wheelchair, he is visibly struggling to catch his breath. A five minute stand-off ensues as medical staff in the hospital plead with Joe to stay. 'He's endangering your life,' a doctor tells Joe, referring to Mureddu. 'You're barely able to breathe ... I'm very worried about you and I want you to stay … It's a very difficult disease that you have, and I'm not lying to you, you could die.' Mureddu repeatedly and viciously accuses the staff of killing people. 'You will be held accountable,' he says, pointing his finger at them. 'You were trying to kill somebody here.'

Joe seems torn and unsure what to do. 'I don't know who's endangering whose life,' he says in between short breaths. He says that there's been 'mixed messages' and that the night before he was told he needed ICU, but then in the morning he was told he was improving. 'This disease comes in peaks and troughs and changes from hour to hour and day to day,' explains another healthcare worker. 'This happens all the time. Patients are considered for ICU, and then they don't need it.'

But despite the best efforts of doctors and nurses, Joe says he wants to leave and is led into the elevator and out of the hospital. 'Fair play, lads. Well done. We saved a life today,' says Mureddu as they get into the lift.

I couldn't believe what I had just watched. My first thought was, 'That man is going to die.' And he did. After spending two days at home, where he was treated with vitamins and ivermectin, Joe was rushed back into hospital after the disease spread to his brain, leaving him blind and deaf. On 24 September 2021 he passed away, leaving behind his wife Una, for whom he cared full time.

Joe's death, and the video showing the events that led to it, shone a spotlight on the real damage caused by promoting dangerous information and disregarding medical advice during the pandemic.

Joe himself didn't believe that the virus was real. Speaking to Rodney Edwards at the *Sunday Independent* in March 2022, his wife Una said that Joe thought Covid was a hoax and 'another way for the Government to make money'. He refused to wear a mask and turned down the vaccine, even though he suffered from chronic obstructive pulmonary disease (COPD), putting him at high risk from Covid-19.[1] Had he listened to public health advice, Joe might still be alive today.

During the summer of 2021, as vaccines were rolled out around the world, stories like these appeared in the news every day: people who had refused the vaccine and were sceptical about the dangers of Covid-19 were passing away from the disease. Here is a small sample of the stories I have collected since the middle of 2021.

In July, Francis Goncalves, a chef based in Wales, lost his mother, father and brother within one week after they all contracted Covid-19. Francis described his 40-year-old brother as the 'healthiest person' he knew, but all three had refused the vaccine because of their belief in anti-vaccine propaganda, he told *The Guardian*.

On 26 July, 34-year-old Matthew Keenan, a father, football coach and 'self-confessed vaccine sceptic' from Bradford, UK, died of Covid-19 after spending two weeks in hospital fighting the disease.

On 4 August, Dick Farrel, a 65-year-old conservative radio host from Florida, died of complications after contracting Covid-19. He had discouraged his listeners from getting the vaccine because they were 'promoted by people who lied … about masks [and] where the virus came from'. At least five conservative radio hosts touting similar false information died from Covid-19 in the space of a month in the US.

On 16 August, Lydia Rodriguez, a 42-year-old from Texas, passed away from the disease two weeks after her 49-year-old husband Lawrence also succumbed to it. They left behind four children.

On 11 September, 32-year-old Sammie-Jo Forde died in the Ulster Hospital in Belfast, leaving four children without a mother. Ten days earlier, two beds away in the same ward, Sammie-Jo's 55-year-old mother Heather had also passed away. Both Sammie-Jo and Heather worked caring for elderly people, and both had refused the vaccine. In the weeks before her death, Heather had shared a number of posts on Facebook referring to Covid-19 conspiracy theories.

On 19 September, Paul Hamill, a councillor for the Democratic Unionist Party (DUP), died after contracting Covid-19. The 46-year-old father of two had regularly shared anti-vaccine content online and was described as a 'disciple' of Ivor Cummins. When asked by *Belfast Telegraph* journalist Sam McBride whether he felt responsibility for Hamill's death, Cummins said, 'Sharing the actual science, data, risk quotients and logic of any issue would never cause one to "feel respon-sibility" for an individual's personal situation.'

Just after Christmas 2021, 77-year-old Billy Greenaway left behind a wife, three children and a grandchild when he passed away after spending weeks fighting Covid-19 in South West Acute Hospital in Enniskillen, County Fermanagh. Billy and his wife Veronica had refused the vaccine because they believed it caused heart attacks and strokes. Speaking to the *Sunday*

Independent in January 2022, Veronica said she had learned a lesson 'in the cruellest manner possible'. Before Billy's passing, they were hosting local meetings on their farm where anti-vaccine and Covid-sceptic influencers would speak. Two particular people had an impact on Veronica's stance on the virus and vaccine: a Derry GP named Anne McCloskey and Dr Dolores Cahill: 'Dolores was quite convincing. She and Anne McCloskey are the two people I looked up to, but I was wrong.'

This wasn't the first time Dr Cahill had been named as influencing people's poor health choices.

I fought the law

Una McCarron told the *Sunday Independent* that Joe's decision not to take the Covid-19 vaccine had a lot to do with Dr Cahill. She said he went to see her speak in Letterkenny, and he told Una that 'after listening to Dolores, I'm definitely not getting the vaccine.' But Dr Cahill's involvement in Joe's decision-making didn't stop there.

Back in Letterkenny Hospital, Antonio Mureddu made a point of thanking one particular person for their effort in making Joe McCarron's release from hospital a reality. 'Thank you so much [to] Dolores Cahill as well. She was on the phone all day long trying to sort out this one. Thank you so much, professor.'

Dr Cahill and Mureddu had known each other for some time. They were photographed together at a far-right rally in November 2019, when she was still the chairperson of the Irish Freedom Party, and Mureddu was present outside the count centre in Dublin during Dr Cahill's belligerent confrontation with Gardaí after the Dublin Bay South by-election in July 2021.

But in the hospital, Mureddu wasn't thanking her for her advice related to Euroscepticism or anti-immigration policies, or even her science denial or anti-vaccination propaganda. He was referring to her involvement in a very specific movement that she had been promoting in Ireland from the start of 2021. It is a convoluted pseudolegal ideology that goes by a number of different names – 'sovereign citizen', 'freeman on the land' or 'common law' movement, to name a few.

Supporters of this ideology believe in a warped interpretation of common law or natural law and claim that, unless they give consent through a contract, they are exempt from conforming to the law. Part of this belief includes reasoning that governments and government bodies are in fact illegitimate 'corporations' and that names written on legal documents such as birth certificates refer to a 'straw man', a fictional legal entity as opposed to a real 'sovereign' person. This allows them to claim that laws don't apply to them, or that they are under no legal obligation to pay debts.[2] Needless to say, these movements have no legal basis and have never been successful in a court of law.

According to Mureddu, when he heard about Joe's situation, he got in touch with Dr Cahill, who suggested creating a team to get him out of the hospital. 'In 30 minutes she was able to organise a team,' he said. Dr Cahill also rang Una McCarron, telling her that she needed to get her husband out of the hospital because they would kill him. She promised Una that there would be 'plenty of people to look after him'.

Dr Cahill, who claimed to be a 'common-law peace con-stable', had spoken at a number of common-law meetings throughout the country, including one in Donegal in July. The team she put together included Mureddu and members of this Donegal common-law group. They then gathered 'paperwork', which they believed gave them the right to take Joe out of hospital.

Followers of this ideology are known for their antagonistic interactions with law enforcement, their use of bogus legal documents and the belief that saying certain words will grant them immunity from the law. Before the pandemic, the move-ment appealed to people facing financial hardship, and for this reason it gained a fringe following in Ireland after the 2008 recession. At that time, one man in particular was involved in its promotion.

Ben Gilroy is an anti-government campaigner who has been described as a 'serial litigant', being involved in at least 16 High Court cases, mostly involving banks. He has also been imprisoned for contempt of court and been issued with the little-used Isaac Wunder order to prevent him from taking further frivolous cases. One of the leading figures behind the Irish Yellow Vest movement, Gilroy ran for the Irish Freedom Party in the 2020 election. In the post-recession era, Gilroy was promoting freeman-on-the-land ideologies through a minor political party called Direct Democracy Ireland, of which he was once the leader. In 2014, Joe McCarron had stood for local elections as a Direct Democracy candidate.

During the pandemic, Dr Cahill took the reins from Gilroy in promoting the freeman-on-the-land ideology in Ireland.

She encouraged people to break lockdown rules and refuse masks and PCR tests by using pseudolegal common-law language. She was involved in sending 'notices of liability' to leading politicians, the Garda Commissioner and the President of Ireland, accusing them of 'crimes against humanity'. She threatened to prosecute them in common-law kangaroo courts that she held in a castle she owns in County Kildare.[3] She also advised the public to perform citizen's arrests on teachers, pharmacists and doctors who were involved in administering vaccines.

A Garda investigation was launched into Joe's death and Mureddu was investigated for his role, but there was not enough evidence to bring charges against him. He was in court on multiple occasions on unrelated charges such as traffic offences and breaking lockdown restrictions. During one of these appearances, he wore a velvet cloak tied at the neck and presented to the court a number of documents in red lettering, one of which argued that the State had to pay him €50,000 for interfering with his 'God-given right to travel peacefully'. On another occasion, he curiously handed a silver coin to the court, to which the judge replied, 'It's a very nice coin, but I don't know why it has been lodged.'

Dr Cahill didn't respond to my query about whether she feels in any way responsible for Joe McCarron's death. When asked the same question by the *Sunday Independent* in October 2021, she said, 'That was nothing to do with me.' She also denied any involvement with the Donegal common-law group, despite the presence of photographs online that show her addressing a meeting there.

This use of sovereign-citizen theories wasn't just happening in Ireland. The transnational nature of the Covid-sceptic movement meant that the same strategies were being used across the world.

In the US, groups were employing 'paper terrorism', another strategy associated with sovereign citizens. This involves flooding organisations with endless amounts of bogus legal documentation to harass and intimidate them into changing rules or laws, even though the documents and claims are legally baseless. School boards, for example, were bombarded with spurious claims in order to force policy changes on masks, vaccine mandates and the teaching of issues related to race, sexuality or diversity.

In the UK, courses were being run around the country to train an 'army of common-law constables'; paper-terrorism tactics were also being used. Towards the end of 2021 and early 2022, anti-vaccine and common-law ideologues started turning up at police stations to present large amounts of false 'evidence' to supposedly prove that the Covid-19 vaccines were unsafe. Upon submission of the documents, police officers issued them with crime reference numbers (CRNs). A CRN is not an indication that an investigation has been opened, and it certainly does not mean that the police has confirmed that a crime has been committed. It is simply confirmation that an allegation has been recorded.

Despite these facts, the CRNs were widely spread online as 'proof' that police had opened an investigation into the safety of vaccines, and people were urged to submit further 'evidence'. Police officers were tasked with going through these documents, a laborious task that certainly resulted in a diversion of resources and staff away from more urgent matters. The Metropolitan Police has since confirmed that no further action would be taken after it found no evidence to support the claims.

Armed with these CRNs, anti-vaccine zealots turned up at Covid-19 vaccine centres claiming that the vaccines were under investigation and the centres were 'crime scenes' that had to be shut down. Again, they presented bogus legal documents as proof, intimidated healthcare workers and people who were there to receive vaccines, and in some instances damaged equipment used for vaccination.

In an incident similar to the one that resulted in Joe McCarron's death, at the end of December 2021, a group walked into the Covid-19 ward of a hospital in Liverpool, announced themselves as the 'constables under the common-law court' and tried to remove an elderly man, who was allegedly the father of one of the group. They threatened nursing staff with 'open arrest', accusing them of 'aiding and abetting geno-cide' while proclaiming 'there is no virus' – and, bizarrely, announcing that Boris Johnson had been arrested.

Nuremberg 2.0
The fusion of anti-vaccine groups with sovereign citizens was part of a wider phenomenon that I and other researchers were witnessing throughout the pandemic. Movements and ideol-ogies that were not linked previously were now coming together in a new hybridised force. New Age spiritualists,

anti-5G campaigners and alternative health practitioners were mingling with right-wing extremists while using the language of QAnon and the strategies of sovereign citizens. And most were convinced the pandemic was in fact a 'plandemic' for instigating the Great Reset/Agenda 21/2030/New World Order, and that the vaccines were killing people. Groups that used to live in their own online bubble and fight their own fringe causes were now working together and learning from each other – and it was happening on a global scale[4].

In Canada, in January 2022, a protest movement dubbed the 'Freedom Convoy' blockaded a busy US/Canada border crossing. Initially centred around vaccination requirements for truckers crossing the border, the protest ballooned into a movement against any and all Covid-19 precautions. A convoy of trucks and other vehicles descended on the capital Ottawa and occupied a section of the city for three weeks, attracting an estimate of up to 18,000 protesters at its peak. At times, trucks ran their engines and beeped their horns day and night in residential areas.

The organisers came from a cross section of Canada's burgeoning conspiratorial communities. A number had stated their support for QAnon. One of them, Pat King, had previously promoted the Great Replacement and said the only way to solve the pandemic was 'with bullets'. Another group closely associated with the convoy had previously spread Islamophobic and anti-5G conspiracy theories. Confederate flags and swastikas were also seen at the event, with attendees likening vaccine requirements to the struggles faced by Jews under the Nazi regime. This became a common rallying cry around the world, one that was condemned widely by Holocaust survivors and Jewish advocacy groups.

The Canadian protests were also heavily promoted within the US right wing, receiving support from GOP officials (including Donald Trump and Marjorie Taylor Greene), right-wing media like Fox News and conservative commentators. Fundraising campaigns that raised millions of dollars were shared among white supremacist communities online,[5] and networks of channels were set up internationally to promote similar actions around the world, with varying degrees of success.

Growing increasingly frustrated by what they saw as a worldwide cover-up being ignored by those in power, and by the vast majority of the public, the Covid-sceptic movement started adopting more extreme methods and rhetoric. This went well beyond acceptable criticism of pandemic measures, veering swiftly into dangerous hate-mongering.

Kate Shemirani, a former nurse who lost her job in 2020 for spreading conspiracy theories about Covid-19, told the crowd at a July 2021 rally in London that NHS doctors and nurses treating people for Covid-19 were no different from those convicted of mass murder at the Nuremberg Trials following World War II: 'Get their names. Email them to me … We are collecting all that. At the Nuremberg Trials the doctors and nurses stood trial and they hung. If you are a doctor or a nurse, now is the time to get off that bus… and stand with us the people.'

Citing the Nuremberg Trials became a common refrain for these movements, which regarded the actions of so-called

conspirators as comparable to the crimes of those who instigated the Holocaust. The only way many of them saw the
conspiracy finally ending was with the execution of those they
viewed as responsible. This is similar to the tale QAnon weaves,
which ends with the Storm, the execution of the deep state.
One user on Telegram wrote, 'If there aren't Nuremberg-style
tribunals (followed by mass hangings) after all is said and done
then there is no justice.' Another wrote, 'You have to ... grab
each politician, each cop, each doctor, each mainstream reporter,
rip them limb from limb in the streets and film it.'[6]

The pandemic radicalised a huge number of people. Many
who believe in these conspiracy theories see the conspirators
(politicians, scientists, the media, healthcare officials) as evil,
murderous monsters, who were working only in their own
self-interest or in the interest of those leading the plot. As a
result, advocating violence against them became acceptable.

Journalists covering the various Covid-sceptic, anti-
lockdown and anti-vaccine protests throughout the pandemic
were regularly subjected to violence, intimidation and threats.
Many journalists described facing a level of hostility they had
never encountered before, because they were believed to be
traitorous enemies working for a propaganda machine. Frank
Stoltze, a reporter working for a local NPR station, described
covering a pro-Trump, anti-vaccine rally in Los Angeles.
'Something happened to me today that's never happened in
30 yrs of reporting ... I was shoved, kicked and my eyeglasses
were ripped off of my face by a group of guys at a protest,'
Stoltze wrote on Twitter. At the same protest, journalist Tina-
Desiree Berg was physically attacked and had her mask ripped

off her face by a protester who had also been present at the storming of the Capitol.

Italian reporter Antonella Alba was physically attacked and called a 'terrorist journalist' while covering a protest in Rome. She said afterwards that in her 20 years of reporting she had 'never … been confronted with such immediate violence'. While covering an anti-vaccine mandate protest in Melbourne, 7News reporter Paul Dowsley was grabbed around the neck and had urine poured on him before being hit with a can in the back of the head. In the UK, *Newsnight* journalist Nicholas Watt was chased by a furious mob and repeatedly called a 'traitor' while covering a protest outside Westminster in June 2021.

Doctors, nurses and other healthcare workers, who dedicate their lives to treating and helping others, were also frequent targets, as seen in the confrontations described above with those touting common law. A doctor in Czechia who also held the position of president of the Czech Medical Chamber told the BBC that he was targeted by an angry mob who followed him home and shoved excrement through his letterbox. In Bulgaria, a doctor was beaten by an anti-vaccine conspiracy theorist and accused of killing people through the administration of the vaccine. In October 2021, a man in Baltimore was charged with the killing of his pharmacist brother and his sister-in-law. According to documents filed with the charges, the man told a number of people that he thought his brother was 'killing people with the Covid shot'.

In Ireland, this hybridisation was clear from the beginning. The first protests in 2020 were organised and promoted by established far-right and anti-government groups, including the Irish Freedom Party and Yellow Vests, in conjunction with Health Freedom Ireland, a group led by alternative health practitioners pushing traditional anti-vaccine tropes. Clashes with counterprotesters broke out at a number of these events, including one incident where National Party member Michael Quinn assaulted Izzy Kamikaze, a veteran LGBTQ+ campaigner, by striking her on the head with a plank of wood wrapped in a tricolour. He was subsequently sentenced to two years in prison.

By 2021, a movement called RiseUp Éireann, rooted in New Age spirituality, became a lead promoter of rallies against Covid restrictions. They were billed as events promoting peace, love and freedom, but extremist elements lurked beneath this layer. An anti-lockdown protest on 27 February 2021, organised by RiseUp Éireann, showed the country the real-life manifestation of those online communities. Dubbed 'Unite the Tribes', the rally was planned to take place in St Stephen's Green in Dublin city centre. At this time, Ireland was in the middle of its third and longest lockdown, which came into effect on Christmas Eve 2020. Level five restrictions meant that people were advised to stay at home, with exercise permitted only within five kilometres of where they lived. Funerals were limited to ten people. No organised indoor or outdoor events were permitted, and retail was restricted to essential services only. The number of daily Covid-19 deaths was at an all-time high throughout January and February and an announcement in the days before the protest had extended level five restrictions for a further six weeks, until 5 April. Tensions were at an all-time high.

From early in the day, posts were flooding into Telegram communities from people travelling from all corners of the country to attend the protest, which looked set to be the biggest anti-lockdown gathering yet. As protesters arrived in the city centre, they found St Stephen's Green closed, with barricades and Garda Public Order Units at the top of Grafton Street. As the crowd grew to an estimated 2,000 people, attendees became agitated. There was pushing and shoving in the crowd and bangers and fireworks were let off. Bottles of urine were thrown in the direction of Gardaí and chants of 'shame on you' came from the crowd. It was becoming clear that the 'peace and love' vibe promoted by RiseUp Éireann was quickly disintegrating.

As Gardaí with batons formed a line to contain the crowd, videos recorded from a building on Grafton Street captured the moment that a man lit a firework, made his way to the front of the crowd and propelled the firework directly at the Garda line. Gardaí baton-charged the crowd, causing panic as people fled down Grafton Street. Three Gardaí were injured and 23 people were arrested – including the protester who launched the firework, who was charged with a number of offences including assault and endangering life. Online, conspiracy communities lit up with their explanation for the violence. 'I think someone from the Gardaí made this happen,' one person said. Others reasoned that it was the work of 'antifa' or 'an agent provocateur' or 'George Soros'.

Although the scenes at the top of Grafton Street were shocking, around the corner on South King Street, a crowd including families with young children had gathered for a sing-a-long and speeches. Eventually, the entire crowd made its way to the GPO on O'Connell Street and the diversity of the attendees was on full show. The crowd was young and old, urban and rural. There were hippies smoking weed and groups of friends drinking cans. National Party members handed out flyers. Placards blamed various entities for the pandemic – Bill Gates, RTÉ, 5G. It was here that *Sunday Times* reporter Mark Tighe met the women promoting the fully formed Irish version of QAnon. It was clear that the pandemic, the strict lockdowns and the distrust people had in the 'mainstream narrative' had united this crowd and they weren't going away silently.

Following the introduction of vaccine passes in the summer of 2021, which allowed vaccinated people more freedom – including entry into bars and the ability to travel – many in the Covid-sceptic crowd became noticeably more desperate. *This* was what they had feared: an electronic system to track your health and vaccine status, a system that locked them out of social situations if they didn't comply. In Ireland, the vaccine passports were widely criticised for their infringement on people's rights. The Irish Council for Civil Liberties called them 'discriminatory' and said they would 'set a dangerous precedent'. All opposition TDs voted against the introduction of the passes, highlighting their discriminatory nature and issues around privacy.

Politicians became the primary targets of the angry vitriol after the introduction of vaccine passes, and there was a notable uptick in calls for violence. 'He should be ambushed and slaughtered in broad daylight,' said one comment on Telegram about Tánaiste Leo Varadkar. Gemma O'Doherty's former side-kick Dee Wall, who established her own following throughout the pandemic, told a July protest, 'You want your vengeance, you can have your vengeance. And I will not open my mouth if you storm the building we're going to, if you take every head out of it and fucking stand on it.'

From September 2021, a small group of militant protesters calling themselves 'sovereign people' mobilised online in Facebook groups. They had a new plan: take it to their doors. They began protesting outside the homes of politicians, health-care officials and broadcasters, accusing them of crimes against humanity. Demonstrators gathered outside the home of Minister for Health Stephen Donnelly, where he lived with his wife and three young children. Homophobic slurs were heard at protests held outside Tánaiste Leo Varadkar's home, which he shared with his partner Dr Matthew Barrett.

In an incident that exemplifies the lasting power of centuries-old theories mixed with extreme rhetoric and the use of conspiratorial pick and mix, on 18 September 2021, a group of around 50 protesters marched to the front of the Freemasons' Grand Lodge in Dublin chanting 'Freemasons out! No to the New World Order! Paedo! Paedo! Paedo!' A banner was unfurled, falsely claiming that there had been tens of thousands of deaths due to the Covid-19 vaccines.

Andy Heasman, a religious extremist and member of Síol na hÉireann, and Dara O'Flaherty, a far-right extremist, addressed the crowd. Heasman said that after two years of protesting around Dublin, they realised that it was the Freemasons they really needed to target. O'Flaherty said that, as the 'administrative arm of the British Empire', the Freemasons had caused the famine and that, as a result, Ireland was currently under British rule. He also instructed the crowd to 'live your life by the natural and common law' and said that all that had to happen to get the group to stop protesting was 'Nuremberg 2'.

'They [the Freemasons] are running the show ... Satanic rituals happen in this building ... We want every stone of this building taken down ... We want them gone out of our country,' said Heasman.

On New Year's Eve 2021, the same Freemasons' Lodge was targeted in an arson attack, and graffiti was scrawled on the pavement outside saying, 'Burn for the children you destroy', along with a reference to mRNA vaccines. The suspect was reported to be a follower of multiple conspiracy theories, including QAnon. He injured himself badly during the attack and was brought to hospital.

More than 230 years after the Freemasons first instilled the fear of God in people due to their promotion of enlightenment ideas – things like rationality, scientific reason and equality – here was the same group accused of planning a pandemic to kill children with a vaccine. Fear is the most powerful of weapons.

Where to from here?

If you asked me at the very start of 2022 where this hybridised conspiratorial movement would turn their attention to next, my answer would have been climate change denial. Denying the realities of climate change was already a commonly held belief in many of these groups, and it was easily planted into the wider Covid-19 conspiracy theory movement during the pandemic.

An analysis by my ISD colleagues found that the phrase 'climate lockdown' began to circulate and become popular in Covid-sceptic and anti-vaccine communities during 2021, spread by climate change sceptics who believed that the Covid-19 lockdowns were a test case for further lockdowns to tackle climate change.[7] This concept was in turn bolstered by right-wing media and political commentators and became enmeshed with the themes around the Great Reset.

Joe Ondrak, head of investigations at Logically.ai, a leading media organisation tackling the murky world of disinformation, agreed that climate narratives will be easily exploited within this movement: 'The seeds are there ... to prime the wider group to take a vocal anti-green energy or renewables stance.'

The stakes could not be higher when it comes to climate change. On 28 February 2022, the Intergovernmental Panel on Climate Change (IPCC), the leading global authority on the crisis, released its starkest warning to date. Plants and animals are dying off at a rate never seen before, sea level rise is accelerating, more than doubling the rate of 50 years ago, and extreme weather events are more frequent and deadly. Some of these effects have gone so far that we cannot reverse them. Put simply, we need to remove carbon dioxide (CO_2) from the atmosphere, 85 per cent of which comes from the burning of fossil fuels[8], in order to save our planet. We are living through a real-life *Don't Look Up* situation.

'Our assessment clearly shows that tackling all these different challenges involves everyone – governments, the private sector, civil society – working together to prioritize risk reduction, as well as equity and justice, in decision-making and investment.' This is what the IPCC says needs to happen. We need to cooperate, work as one across countries, across different industries, institutions, national and international bodies, and we need to do it to save our home. You can be sure that the conspiracy theory communities will be shouting 'Communism!', 'New World Order!' and 'Propaganda!' at the top of their lungs, but the stakes are too high to let them win.

Four days before the grave IPCC report was released, Russia invaded Ukraine and the new direction of these communities became clear. In a predictable move, the groups housing this new hybridised conspiratorial force became mouthpieces for spreading pro-Russian disinformation. The movement supposedly defending itself against authoritarianism turned to supporting and promoting Putin, an authoritarian.

If you think back to the three principles of the conspiratorial mindset – nothing happens by accident, nothing is as it seems, everything is connected – it is not surprising that this happened. What is agreed upon by the media, government leaders and much of the wider public in the West is that Putin is the aggressor invading a sovereign country, and Ukrainians are defending themselves against the invasion. The conspiratorial mindset will naturally go against this consensus.

The disbelief in the mainstream opinion, combined with the fact that many of these online ecosystems had been ingesting Russian disinformation for years, means it was a swift and easy pivot for these groups to support the Kremlin's position. Analysis of QAnon conversations on Telegram between January and November 2021 by Marc-André Argentino found that one website stood out above the rest: Russia Today, or RT, a

Kremlin-controlled international broadcaster. Many mainstream social media platforms blocked access to pro-Russian news organisations when the invasion began, but alternative platforms where conspiratorial communities live have no such restrictions. The right-wing media ecosystem is so useful to the Russian campaign that the Kremlin instructed Russian media to use clips from Fox News' Tucker Carlson to sell the war to its own people.

These communities became conduits for Putin's warped justification for the invasion: saving Ukraine from Nazi rule. This narrative took a grain of truth and contorted it into something unrecognisable. Yes, there are neo-Nazis in Ukraine. They are a fringe, albeit loud, movement, but they have very little public support. A militant far-right group, the Azov Battalion, was formed in 2014 to defend the areas of Donetsk and Luhansk from Russia-backed separatists, before they were embedded in the Ukrainian National Guard. They're thought to number around 1,000 members. Are Nazis running the country? Absolutely not. Ukrainian president Volodymyr Zelenskyy is Jewish and lost family members in the Holocaust, making this claim all the more absurd.

In the early months of the invasion, there were a number of different conspiratorial narratives circulating online. Some claimed the invasion wasn't happening at all – that it was all green screens, false flags, crisis actors and a well-oiled lying media machine. Others following the QAnon narrative believed that Putin had taken over from Trump in the battle against the deep-state cabal of child traffickers and paedophiles. In other instances, Putin was seen as standing up against the New World

Order or the Great Reset, or preventing the next pandemic by seizing control of Ukrainian 'biolabs'.

The war in Ukraine has resulted in millions of people being displaced from their homes and fleeing across Europe, with the EU granting these refugees the right to live and work in EU countries for up to three years. The support shown by many countries was encouraging, but it was quickly seized upon by many of the usual far-right voices. In Ireland, Rowan Croft touted an old favourite anti-immigrant trope, claiming that Ukrainian refugees would take diseases to the countries they were fleeing to. Dave Cullen, taking a leaf out of Fox News' Tucker Carlson's book, claimed that refugees were coming to the country to be 'used as a voting block'. Other figures couldn't quite fathom the fact that some people fleeing Ukraine to Ireland were non-white, giving them further reason to express their bigotry.

These communities becoming Russian mouthpieces is a significant development. As Joe Ondrak pointed out, the disinformation and conspiracy narratives being shared 'demonstrate an acute awareness of key issues that circulate rapidly and with high volume in this group.' Claims of 'crisis actors', 'biolabs' or mainstream media cover-ups are not new within these communities. 'I think the biggest impact of this development is that it signals for others, quite explicitly, how to exploit and leverage this conspiratorial force/cultic milieu or steer them to certain ends,' Ondrak told me.

Melanie Smith, Head of Digital Analysis at ISD, believes that this development signals an advancement in the 'post-truth environment' that came after Brexit and the 2016 US election. 'What we're seeing now is not just disinformation and conspiracy theories filling a vacuum of credible thinking and reporting, but rather winning in a battle between the two,' she said.

Who gains from this new global, hybridised, radicalised force? Melanie Smith put it simply: 'Chaos merchants. Any and all covert or overt networks operated by political actors (state-backed or not) stand to gain from the confusion sown by disinformation and conspiracy theories.' In other words, groups who wish to influence voting segments, and those who promote hate or distrust in institutions and governments, all stand to gain from pandering to these communities.

Joe Ondrak pointed to the 'transphobic streak [that] runs through the wider movement', which could also easily be seized upon by other groups wishing to promote an anti-trans narrative. Trans rights have become a wedge issue for political movements across the world who seek to exploit people's lack of understanding of the trans community to promote fear. For years, Putin and Russia have been framing LGBTQ+ rights as a threat to Russia's 'traditional values', and trans rights and gender issues are now at the forefront of this battle. In a nation-wide broadcast in March 2022, Putin even referenced the 'cancellation' of J.K. Rowling for her gender-critical stance, while Steve Bannon praised Putin for being 'anti-woke' and 'knowing how many genders there are in Russia'.

This new force is a real threat to the very foundations of liberal democracies worldwide. Melanie Smith agrees: 'The biggest impact of this more generally is the loss of belief and contentment with liberal democracy as a set of principles among some of the most developed and highly educated populations in the world.' To paraphrase Winston Churchill, democracy is not perfect, but compared to other forms of governance, it is the best option we have. It allows for individual rights and freedoms to be protected and for every citizen to be a part of the democratic process.

Liberal democracies are the hallmark of the most free and affluent countries in the world. Yet many within these online communities are convinced that they do not live in freedom and that granting minority communities the same rights as other citizens somehow infringes on their rights. Far-right groups and right-wing populist political figures confirm that their fears are well founded, dismissing the concern for less privileged groups as 'wokeism' or 'virtue signalling'. Playing on people's sense of nostalgia, they promise a return to the glorious days of the past – to make their country great again, or to take back control that has been supposedly lost. They tell them the whole system is corrupt and needs to be destroyed, that everyone you're meant to trust is lying to you and that you need to fight to win back your freedom.

In the US, the threat these forces wield against democracy is very real. Although Trump lost in 2020, the 2024 presidential race will likely see Trump himself, or a candidate in line with Trump's politics, running as the Republican candidate. The mid-term elections in November 2022, where dozens of people supporting the core tenets of QAnon are running for various positions, are predicted to see Republican gains in the House and Senate. In state elections, the stakes are arguably higher in states where candidates supporting Trump's 'Big Lie' about the election could be elected to secretary of state positions. This is the office that sets regulations for how elections are conducted at a state level.

Several countries across Europe have far-right parties in power or at least sitting in opposition in parliaments. Ireland has so far bucked this trend by rejecting far-right parties and candidates wholesale at the ballot box. But there are signs that some independent politicians are more than willing to pander to these groups. Mattie McGrath, an independent TD from Tipperary, for example, used the term 'scamdemic' in relation to Covid-19 restrictions and, on multiple occasions, compared pandemic meaures to events in 1930s Nazi Germany. He was also pictured accepting letters and petitions related to Covid-19 from religious extremist Andy Heasman in July 2021.

In 2020, after the killing of George Floyd in the US sparked another wave of Black Lives Matter protests across the world, Cork TD Michael Collins and Kerry's Danny Healy-Rae were criticised for invoking the phrase 'all lives matter' in response. The expression is widely used on the far right as a way to delegitimise the Black Lives Matter movement.

In 2021, during the controversy over an effort to appoint Katherine Zappone – the former Minister for Children and a gay woman – to a position at the UN, independent Senator Sharon Keogan claimed it was a sign of an 'organised takeover' in governments around the world to 'catapult' LGBTQ+ people into powerful positions. In response to the backlash she received for the comments, Keogan said that she had 'an established record' of support for the LGBTQ+ community and opposed what she saw as 'appointing personnel based on their sexual orientation'.

These sentiments and the beliefs of far-right and conspiratorial communities in Ireland do not have widespread support as it stands. Perhaps this is due to the island's history of conflict, still fresh in the memories of many: we know where hate and irrationality can lead. Perhaps the scars left by the authoritarian rule of the Catholic Church have allowed us to resist such movements. Ireland also does not have the partisan media present in other countries such as the US and UK, which is willing to pander to conspiracy theorists for views.

Nevertheless, complacency is ill advised. There are plenty of opportunities for these movements to seize on public discontent around issues such as the crumbling healthcare system or an ever-worsening housing crisis. The future could bring a referendum on Irish reunification, a question that is sure to cause division even without the influence of such irrationality. The opening years of the 2020s taught us that the world can change in the blink of an eye, so it's best to be prepared for what the future could throw at us.

Should we bin social media?

Frances Haugen took a job at Facebook for personal reasons. A close friend, someone who had assisted her when she was struck down with illness, had fallen into the world of conspiracy theories and white nationalism during the 2016 US election. She tried to intervene and pull him back, but it didn't work and their friendship ended. 'It's one thing to study misinformation, it's another to lose someone to it,' she told the *Wall Street Journal*.[9]

Haugen had worked at Google, Yelp and Pinterest before taking a position on Facebook's Civic Integrity team as a product manager in June 2019. This team, consisting of fewer than 200 people, worked on investigating ways the platform could be used for nefarious purposes, such as spreading political disinformation, hatred or incitement to violence, with a focus on the upcoming US election. It didn't take long for her to realise that the team was severely understaffed and under-resourced, with unrealistic targets assigned to them that they could not possibly achieve. The sheer number of vulnerabilities that could have impacted the election was overwhelming. Haugen was also soon exposed to the harm that Facebook was causing outside of the US, seeing that content that was going viral in 'at risk' countries, such as Ethiopia and Myanmar, was contributing to the risk of genocide.

Haugen started having panic attacks, unable to cope with the fact that it was her job to try to solve these issues, but she felt absolutely powerless to do so. She said that Facebook was making a choice. It was choosing not to invest properly in solving these problems. Facebook has denied this, telling the *Wall Street Journal*, 'We've invested heavily in people and technology to keep our platform safe, and have made fighting misinformation and pro-viding authoritative information a priority.'

In December 2020, one month after the US election, Facebook announced that they were shutting down Haugen's team. They also turned off a number of safety features they had added to the platform during the election, features that slowed down virality and made the platform less reactive. One month later, rioters stormed the US Capitol building, demanding that the election be overturned. Facebook played a key role in the mobilisation of Stop the Steal, the movement that brought together all the disparate Trump-supporting groups – from QAnon followers and white nationalists to militia groups and the regular MAGA crowd – in the belief that the election had been rigged.

With this news, Haugen made her own choice: she would become a whistle-blower and show the public what was going on behind the scenes. She spent her last few months at the platform copying thousands of internal documents, and in September 2021, with the aid of reporters from the *Wall Street Journal*, the public were able to see how decisions were being made at the world's biggest social media platform, a $1 trillion company that also owns WhatsApp and Instagram.

The documents delivered bombshell after bombshell, showing that the public image the company tried to portray, of a platform dedicated to creating a safe place for its users and tackling issues around misinformation, was completely at odds with what was going on behind the scenes.

One example detailed a pivotal change Facebook made in 2018 to its news feed algorithm, the artificial intelligence system that decides what content people see when they scroll through their feed. In many ways the algorithm is the money-making machine of any social media platform, but they are currently a black box for researchers who know little about how they work due to a lack of transparency from the platforms. In general, we know that data about a huge range of topics related to your friends, interests, location and online habits are fed into the algorithm, which then recommends content based on what it thinks you'll be interested in. Social media platforms also sell this information to advertisers in order to target users with ads. This is how platforms make the vast majority of their money.

The change to Facebook's algorithm was made to boost what the company calls 'meaningful social interactions', suggesting that the news feed would prioritise content from friends and family as opposed to that from media and businesses. At the time, Mark Zuckerberg publicly said this was to 'help us connect with each other' and to make sure Facebook's services were 'good for people's well-being'. It was seen as an effort to clean up the platform after years of criticism due to its role in spreading harmful, false and misleading content.

But the internal documents told a different story. There was panic at the company throughout 2017 because user engagement metrics were decreasing. Although time spent online hadn't diminished, people weren't posting, commenting or sharing as much. They weren't quite sure why this was happening, but there was a fear that people would start leaving Facebook. The news feed algorithm change was meant to address this issue by prioritising content in people's feeds that was likely to get high engagement.

According to the documents, this change was successful at addressing the engagement problem, but it quickly became apparent that it was also having a monumentally negative impact on the platform by making it an angrier and more divisive place. The content being prioritised was sensational and outrageous, including conspiracy theories and false, hateful information. That was the content the algorithm found was likely to drive engagement.

'Our approach has had unhealthy side effects on important slices of public content, such as politics and news,' said an internal memo. 'Misinformation, toxicity, and violent content are inordinately prevalent among reshares.'

When Facebook was asked about this, they admitted that any algorithm can be exploited to promote harmful content and that the company had a team – the data integrity team – dedicated to figuring out how to mitigate these problems.

Members of the data integrity team suggested ways to address these issues and reduce the spread of misinformation. One solution they proposed was quite radical, but research found that it could solve a lot of the platform's problems: get rid of the Share button. Unsurprisingly, that solution didn't fly, but neither did a number of other more moderate proposals, including reducing the amount of comments users could make from the cap of 300 per hour.

A number of minor changes were implemented, but only on specific kinds of content and only in certain countries. Generally, if the proposed solution contributed to lower user metrics, it would not be implemented. Facebook's priority was keeping users engaged on the platform for as long as they could.

The algorithm gave certain groups and businesses – namely, publishers and political parties – an incentive to create divisive content. The documents revealed that a political party in Poland changed its communication strategies to suit the fact that negativity was what drove engagement on Facebook: 'One party's social media management team estimates that they have shifted the proportion of their posts from 50/50 positive/negative to

80 per cent negative and 20 per cent positive, explicitly as a function of the change to the algorithm.'

One of documents released by Haugen gave some insight into how recommendation algorithms work. Facebook researchers created three personas. The first was Carol, an American conservative Christian living in North Carolina, who liked the pages of Donald Trump, Melania Trump and Fox News. The second user, Karen, was a liberal also living in North Carolina, and she followed North Carolina pages, including local news sites and the page of MoveOn, a liberal advocacy group. The third user was a female based in the Indian city of Jaipur but originally from Hyderabad.

The profiles followed whatever Facebook recommended to them, and the results were startling, to say the least. Within just two days, Carol, the conservative Trump supporter, was recommended QAnon groups to join. In five days, the recommendations were full of 'extreme, conspiratorial and graphic content'. Within one week, Karen, the liberal, was being recommended exclusively anti-Trump content, including derogatory memes featuring Melania Trump or referring to Republican Senator Mitch McConnell as 'Moscow Mitch'.[10] For content, the user based in India went to the Watch and Live tabs, which were initially full of soft-core porn. After a terrorist attack in Kashmir, however, the user's feed was brimming with anti-Pakistani hate speech, fake images of bombings, manipulated photos claiming to show people killed in the attack and images of beheadings. The Facebook researcher said, 'I've seen more images of dead people in the past three weeks than I've seen in my entire life total.'

In response to the information on the Karen and Carol

accounts being made public, Facebook said the research was 'a perfect example' of what the company does 'to improve our systems' and that it 'helped inform our decision to remove QAnon from the platform'. For context, this research was conducted in June 2019, and Facebook finally took decisive action against QAnon in October 2020, after it had broken away into the Save the Children movement and radicalised countless numbers of people during the pandemic. Issues with recommendation algorithms were highlighted even before this, when internal research in 2016 showed that '64 per cent of all extremist group joins are due to our recommendation tools'.[11]

Much of the content recommended to the Indian user was in Hindi and was therefore getting past regular content moderation, which is primarily focused on the English language. In response to this, Facebook said that the user test 'inspired deeper, more rigorous analysis of our recommendation systems, and contributed to product changes to improve them'. Facebook also said that the company was continuing to work on ways to counter hate speech, which included strengthening the algorithm used to detect hateful content to include four Indian languages. To put this into perspective, Facebook has approximately 330 million users in India, making it the company's biggest market, and India has 22 official languages and thousands of different dialects.

The documents also revealed what Facebook knew about the spread of vaccine misinformation on the platform. In 2019, after low vaccine uptake rates caused outbreaks of measles, the platform promised to tackle the problem but failed to get a grasp on it. When Covid-19 came and the vaccine roll-out began, vaccine misinformation was rampant on the site. According to internal documents, one out of every five posts related to vaccines was dissuasive of the jab, and comments on posts were even worse. The ability of the organisation to detect what was said in comments was described in one memo as 'bad in English, and basically non-existent elsewhere'.

A May 2021 memo from internal Facebook researchers revealed that one thing they were aware of was that the vast majority of anti-vaccine misinformation was coming from a small number of users: 'We found, like many problems at FB, this is a head-heavy problem with a relatively few number of actors creating a large percentage of the content and growth.'

In 2021, the platform implemented some changes to tackle the problem, including reducing the number of comments a user could make per hour and demoting certain content and comments. The platform also changed its policies on vaccine misinformation, expanding the list of claims that were prohibited and would be removed. But even with these changes, Facebook was ultimately failing to make headway on the problem.

In 2021, a number of ISD colleagues and I conducted research looking at this exact issue. We analysed content posted by, or mentioning, the World Doctors Alliance, one of the health misinformation groups set up by Dr Dolores Cahill. We found that the group and its members had reached over half a million followers on Facebook during the pandemic, an increase of a whopping 13,215 per cent from its follower numbers at the start of 2020.[12] The group's posts, which were riddled with all sorts of Covid-19 and vaccine-related misinformation, were clocking up millions of interactions on the platform, despite the fact that much of what they were saying went against Facebook's own policies, as well as the scientific consensus on the issues.

Facebook will often lean on its employment of artificial intelligence (AI) and its work with fact-checking organisations to give the impression that it is taking the issue of misinformation seriously. Our report into the World Doctors Alliance found that the group had been included in at least 189 articles from Facebook's fact-checking partners since the beginning of the pandemic. Content that had been fact-checked multiple times was still being shared on Facebook and receiving high engagement, with AI technology failing to find and remove even the most egregious examples. The fact-checkers were doing their work, but Facebook and the technology it uses were failing to act on it. Dr Dolores Cahill, for example, had been mentioned in 75 fact-checking articles in the 16 months since the pandemic began. Her Facebook page was removed a number of months after the release of our report, after she had amassed an audience of almost 130,000 followers, begging the question, how many strikes do you need to get before Facebook takes decisive action?

The examples I have outlined only scratch the surface of what Frances Haugen's whistle-blowing revealed. The documents also showed that internal research conducted by Facebook found that Instagram was making 'body images worse for one in three teen girls' and contributing to increased rates of anxiety, depression and toxic thoughts. It revealed the huge imbalance between resources dedicated to English-speaking countries and those to developing countries, where most of the platforms' new user base is coming from. In some instances, the company has few or no employees speaking the local language in regions it is expanding to, allowing drug cartels and human traffickers free rein of the sites.

Frances Haugen's revelations were stark, but this certainly wasn't the first time that Facebook had been dragged over the coals for living up to its founder's mantra of 'move fast and break things'. This was a motto that translated into one of the world's biggest companies seemingly having little ability to control what happens on its platform. In the words of a member of Facebook's leadership, 'We created the machine, and we can't control the machine.'

In 2018 it was revealed that British political consulting firm Cambridge Analytica (whose vice president was none other than Steve Bannon) had harvested data on Facebook users by getting them to use an app called 'This is Your Digital Life'. The app paid around 300,000 users to complete a personality test, telling them their data would be used for academic purposes; however, unbeknown to them, the app also accessed the Facebook data of the users' friends, resulting in around 87 million Facebook users having their data collected without their knowledge. This data was used to create psychological models of users and sold to political campaigns in order to target people with advertising. Both Senator Ted Cruz and former president Donald Trump used the data as part of their advertising campaigns during the 2016 election.

The issue of Facebook dedicating little to no resources to its operations in developing countries had been highlighted years before, when the social media platform expanded to Myanmar. In 2013, after being under a military dictatorship for years, Myanmar saw a relaxation of control. The arrival of tele-communications companies into the country allowed for affordable smartphones to fill the market. The phones came with the Facebook app preinstalled, which made the word 'Facebook' a synonym for 'internet' in Myanmar.

Facebook quickly became *the* source of news for many, who had lived for years ingesting state-sponsored propaganda. It didn't take long before the platform was being used to spread hate and advocate violence against the Rohingya, a Muslim minority population that had long been discriminated against in the country. Doctored videos and photos claiming to show Burmese people killed by Rohingya Muslims started to circ-ulate on Facebook, along with rumours that attacks from the population were imminent. Riots and killings broke out, based on false information spread on Facebook. It soon became apparent that the company had employed a single Burmese-speaking moderator to oversee Facebook's operations in a country with over 100 languages.[13] Since 2016, more than 25,000 Rohingyas have been killed in a genocide carried out by the Burmese military, and hundreds of thousands have been forced to flee the country.

It is easy to focus on Facebook as the source of the internet's problems due to the vast amount of information that has been made public about what goes on behind the scenes, but the truth is that many of these issues are found across every social media platform. Although the research I did with colleagues looking into the World Doctors Alliance focused on the group's presence on Facebook, we also found content that violated platform rules on Instagram, Twitter, YouTube and TikTok. Russia's interference in the 2016 election, swaying voters away from Clinton and towards Trump, utilised Facebook, Twitter, Instagram, Reddit, Tumblr, Vine, Google+, Pinterest and Medium.[14]

Twitter is arguably one of the angriest sites on the internet, but it was not always like that. It is thought that one particular function changed the culture of the site: the addition of the Retweet button. Before this, people had to retweet manually, copying and pasting the tweet they wanted to share into a new tweet, tagging the original person and adding 'RT' for retweet. This made people think about what they were sharing. The Retweet button removed these steps, giving people the ability to share immediately.

Chris Wetherell was the developer who built the Retweet feature. In 2019, he described it to BuzzFeed as similar to handing 'a four-year-old a loaded weapon'. Wetherell realised during Gamergate that the Retweet button was being used to coordinate attacks and spread misinformation, and that the platform had no way to push back. He described Gamergate as a 'creeping horror story' saying, 'It dawned on me that this was not some small subset of people acting aberrantly. This might be how people behave. And that scared me to death.'

Twitter has since added prompts asking people to read articles before retweeting them and has set up a community programme called Birdwatch to help tackle misinformation on the platform. These features may have some impact, but there is more than enough evidence on a daily basis that the platform, just like

Facebook, is failing at this mission, whether from a lack of ability to tackle misinformation and hate or from a lack of will.

YouTube has long been criticised as a pathway to radicalisation, as previously mentioned in the case of the 'Gamergate to alt-right' pipeline. A 2019 analysis by Bellingcat cited the platform as the most common source of red-pilling among fascist activists online. Just as Facebook's algorithm rewards the sensationalist, so too does YouTube; and like Facebook, YouTube prioritised engagement over user safety, even when employees spoke up about the dangerous pipelines their algorithms were leading to. According to the platform, 70 per cent of the time people are on YouTube is spent watching recommended videos.

In 2019, Caleb Cain told his story of YouTube radicalisation to *The New York Times*'s *Rabbit Hole* podcast, allowing them to analyse his YouTube data from 2015 to 2019. Cain had been looking for self-help videos initially, and he quickly came across men's rights activists and anti-feminists. As the algorithm fed him what it thought he wanted, he was soon watching videos on conspiracy theories and others featuring graphic violence. Before long, he was deep in the world of the alt-right and right-wing news content, before reaching neo-Nazis holding explicitly anti-Semitic views.

TikTok is a platform with one billion users that is particularly popular with children and teenagers. It is powered by an algorithm whose main aim is to keep users on the app for as long as possible by tracking the kind of videos watched, the length of time they're watched (or rewatched) and the interaction they have with them. With the flick of a thumb, the user is presented with the next video in the algorithmic For You feed, which plays automatically, meaning the user has little control over what appears on their screen. It is like the crack cocaine of social media. This mechanism has since been replicated by Instagram in its Reels feature.

Using over 100 bot accounts with different interests, the *Wall Street Journal* tested where the TikTok algorithm can take users, finding that it learns a user's interests within a few hours of them joining the app and can then take them down very specific rabbit holes. For example, the app can pick up on mental health vulnerabilities and lead users to posts about depression, eating disorders and suicide, or featuring sexual content.

Analysis by my ISD colleague Ciarán O'Connor found that TikTok is also hosting white supremacy content, ISIS content, terrorism videos, and videos promoting Holocaust denial and hate against minorities. What was once a fun dancing and singing app has gone the way of almost all other platforms, into an uncontrollable deluge of toxicity.

These examples have only scratched the surface to point out how parts of social media are inherently broken. One of the biggest issues is that we have allowed tech entrepreneurs with no understanding of sociological impacts to make us addicted to tools that are changing the way we view the world.

But as tempting as it might be to bin social media, it's here to stay. So the next question naturally is: can we fix it?

Can we fix social media?

It is clear that we need to make the internet a place that works for people instead of a place that contributes to harm and polarisation, and the regulation of social media platforms is essential for this to happen. Too many times in recent years we have seen that the platforms are unable, or unwilling, to regulate themselves, and regulation is a subject that seems to be supported across the political spectrum. There are a huge number of challenges when it comes to this kind of regulation, however.

First, the online world changes at a rapid rate, and policy making is painfully slow. The internet of 2016, when the subject of online harms started to receive attention from policy makers, was a very different place from what it is today. As Niamh Kirk from UCD's Centre for Digital Policy told me, 'Changes that are being implemented now are in response to six-year-old problems. The environment has completely changed [in that time] and malicious actors have changed their practices.'

Kirk also made the point that digital policy has to operate on a number of different levels: platform level (and across multiple platforms), national level and international level. All of this makes the environment for creating robust policy extremely complex.

Understanding the online world requires a certain level of technological knowledge – something that lawmakers are often lacking. This lack of knowledge was on full show when Mark Zuckerberg had to explain the basics of the internet to lawmakers during a Senate Committee in 2018, in a hearing that should have seen him hauled over the coals for Facebook's role in the Cambridge Analytica scandal. Frances Haugen's clear and concise explanations of these complicated subjects, and her willingness to speak to lawmakers around the world, however, has contributed to greater understanding across the board.

Without getting into the weeds, there are a number of things that certainly need to be taken into account to make tech regulation workable and fair. Regulation needs to be rooted in democratic principles around accountability and transparency, with the ability to protect human rights such as freedom of expression, privacy and the protection from discrimination and harassment.[15] Niamh Kirk says that a pro-active approach is needed, grounded in the questions of 'what are public informational needs?' and 'how do we enable people to engage with these needs while protecting them from harms online?' This is no easy challenge. An authoritarian approach using censorship and strict control of content and speech is not a useful framework, because it will only feed mistrust and suspicion and infringe on people's rights.

One of the most glaring issues related to digital policy is around transparency. As it stands, policy makers, academics, the media and researchers such as myself have only a narrow understanding about how harms are perpetrated online and how the online ecosystem functions. It is at the discretion of social media platforms to decide what kind of data they allow the public to access. Some platforms, such as Facebook and Twitter, allow very limited access to publicly available data for researchers. Others, like TikTok, do not allow any such access at all. In order to figure out how to fix social media, we need to know exactly how it works, and this begins with access to vital information that will both protect the privacy of online users in line with

General Data Protection Regulation (GDPR), while enabling a fuller understanding of the problems we face.

Not only does there need to be greater insight into how content is spread online, there is also a need for greater transparency from inside the platforms themselves. Each platform has community guidelines and policies about what they allow or do not allow on their sites, yet little is known about how these decisions are made or how policies are enforced. Even with limited access to data, researchers and members of the public are consistently finding grievous examples of policy violations and harmful content that are not being discovered and/or acted on by the platforms themselves. There is also little to no transparency from platforms about the impacts of interventions such as removing content, fact-checking or labelling content as misinformation.

Advertising is another area where more information is needed. The public should be aware of how and why they are targeted with certain advertisements, especially when personal data is used to target people in this way. This is especially pertinent when it comes to political advertising. After mounting pressure, in recent years platforms have taken some steps to address this, but advertising archives that are available to researchers fall way short of the mark as regards the information they provide related to microtargeting – that is, the targeting of individuals with ads using personal data gleaned from their online footprint.

What's clear to many researchers in this field is that algorithms that prioritise engagement are a significant part of the problem. Yet when it comes to understanding algorithms, researchers have been left in the dark. In 2019, YouTube said they had reduced the spread of 'borderline content and harmful misinformation' by 50 per cent, but it is impossible to verify this without the data to back it up.

A common expression used in tech policy spaces is 'freedom of speech is not freedom of reach'. In other words, we have the right to say what we want, but we don't have the right to automatically have what we say algorithmically amplified to millions of people. Understanding algorithms will translate into an ability to understand what goes viral, giving more options to stem the flow of harmful information than what exists today, which is a binary choice between platforming or deplatforming.

In general, social media platforms tend to make a lot of noise about what their technology (such as algorithms or AI) can do when it comes to tackling issues around disinformation and harmful online content. They expect the public, policy makers and the media to take them at their word when there is no mechanism to independently verify what they are saying, and when the vast majority of evidence shows that they are ultimately failing at these efforts.

When it comes to *who* should hold the responsibility for regulation, as already mentioned, it is quite clear that social media platforms are unable to regulate themselves and have acted in bad faith in this regard too many times. In 2018, platforms signed up to the EU Code of Practice on Disinformation, a voluntary programme with a range of commitments related to responding to disinformation. Dublin City University's Institute for Future Media, Democracy and Society (FuJo) conducted an analysis of the transparency reports provided by the platforms on their response to Covid-19 disinformation under this agreement. Dr Eileen Culloty, an assistant professor at FuJo and one of the report's authors, told me that the transparency reports were 'unbelievably vague' and 'often contained completely irrelevant information'.

Because self-regulation has proven to be a non-starter, new policies are aiming for a co-regulatory approach. The EU Digital Services Act (DSA) – the most comprehensive piece of legislation on internet safety and accountability to date – takes this sort of approach. The DSA aims to make sweeping changes to the way companies operate online, setting out a range of requirements that platforms will have to adhere to. An independent regulatory body will be responsible for ensuring the implementation of requirements at a national level. UCD's Centre for Digital Policy has called the DSA a 'light-touch approach' and said it gives the industry too much responsibility for shaping its own rules. Henry Tuck, Head of Policy & Programmes at ISD said that, overall, the DSA adheres to the principles of transparency, accountability and a human rights-based approach, but the complexity of implementing it and the changing nature of the tech industry likely mean it will take time to make the policy effective.

At home, Ireland has marched ahead with its own Online Safety and Media Regulation Bill. This legislation will propose the establishment of a new regulatory body, the Media Commission, to replace the Broadcasting Authority of Ireland, as well as an Online Safety Commissioner to focus on creating an online safety code. Although it is positive to see some moves being made, there are doubts as to whether it will be fit for purpose. FuJo has raised concerns over the bill's failure to include provisions around 'disinformation' and 'misinformation' – in fact, the bill doesn't even mention these words. FuJo also recommended the addition of algorithmic oversight and an individual complaints process for users who may not be satisfied with a platform's decision over a complaint. The focus on attempting to vaguely define 'harmful content' in the bill is quite problematic, and the Irish Council for Civil Liberties has raised concerns that the bill could infringe on freedom of expression for this reason. Policing content decisions, which can be extremely complex and subjective, could be a recipe for disaster. There is also a possibility that this bill will conflict with the EU legislation in the Digital Services Act.

In recent years, conversations about online regulation have frequently come around to the issue of anonymity. As the old meme goes, on the internet, nobody knows you're a dog, and there are many people who believe online issues related to harassment and abuse could be easily solved by taking away people's ability to post anonymously. This was raised in 2021 following the murder of British MP David Amess and, in Ireland, in March 2022 when a Sinn Féin bill proposed legislation to force social media platforms to disclose the identity of anonymous accounts engaging in defamation and abuse online.

This reasoning is quite understandable as anonymity provides a shield, allowing people to feel like they can say and do what they want without the fear of reprisal, which certainly leads to abuse and harassment. But this shield is also extremely beneficial for many, including whistle-blowers, journalists, researchers and people living in repressive communities. In authoritarian countries, especially, anonymity is of key importance to many. There are also many legitimate everyday reasons why people may wish to protect their privacy by being anonymous online. Teachers, for example, may not want their students to be able to find their social media profiles.

There is some evidence to suggest that getting rid of anonymity will not have the desired effect. A study conducted on comments posted on news articles found that the use of 'stable pseudonyms' (where a user had to authenticate their account but didn't have to reveal their real name), reduced abusive language and contributed to a healthier environment. An earlier study by Disqus, a commenting service for news websites, found that pseudonymous comments were of the highest quality. It's also worth noting that abuse is still rampant on platforms like Facebook, where people are more likely to use their real name.

In creating policies related to the online world, we need to be extremely careful of any idea that is seen as a magic wand. A sweeping move like getting rid of anonymity would have huge consequences, considering anonymity has been a cornerstone of the internet since its earliest days. There are also big questions to be answered about *how* authenticating identities would work. Are we going to trust social media platforms – which make their money by selling personal data to advertisers – to hold the information carried on your personal ID? Will people trust their governments to hold that information? Authoritarian regimes would no doubt quickly take advantage of this. It would also make systems with that much personal information prime targets for hacking.

It's easy to focus only on trying to fix the blatantly bad parts of the online world, but we also need to make sure that efforts to mitigate harm don't end up inadvertently destroying the parts of the online world that make it unique, useful and enjoyable for the majority of people who use it. The onus should be on the platforms to create online spaces where abuse isn't part of the furniture.

Facebook is now investing in the metaverse, a virtual reality world, and lo and behold, the place is rampant with online abuse, harassment and rape threats. The platforms continue to grow, drawing people's attention to their latest, shiniest new toy, while doing little to make their online spaces safer. By withholding data that would allow us to see what is really going on behind the scenes, they are holding the whole planet hostage. If we allow platforms to continue to make their own rules, govern themselves, put profit over people and refuse to take responsibility for the situations they have created, the problems outlined in this book will likely continue to get worse.

Prevention is the best cure

Admittedly, we're not going to fix the internet overnight, but there are other things we can do to try to prevent people from falling for false information and stop the radicalising effect of online rabbit holes filled with conspiracy theories, extremism and hate.

Our information ecosystem has completely changed in the space of around 15 years. When smartphones became a must-have product, in the early 2010s, people suddenly had the internet in the palm of their hand. It was truly revolution-ary, but we are clearly still reeling from this swift and sudden change in our information consumption habits, not to mention the proliferation of social media platforms that have been built to be addictive. Lies have always travelled faster than the truth, but now lies are attached to an algorithmically powered rocket ship delivered to screens that we take with us everywhere we go.

Multiple studies have shown that conspiratorial belief is linked to low news consumption and higher consumption of social media. The news media as an industry has been decimated in recent years as publishers struggle to find a business model that works in the digital age while trying to maintain their standards. Many journalists are underpaid, overworked and trying to keep up with a 24-hour news cycle.

News providers have not always worked to gain people's trust. We should have a certain level of scepticism about what is reported in the media, since it is vulnerable to mistakes, bias and sensationalism. The media is also susceptible to a phenomenon known as 'false balance'. This is when, in the name of avoiding accusations of bias, the media will platform a position that is not supported by evidence. An example would be a debate about climate change including a climate change sceptic in order to 'balance' the conversation. This is extremely problem-atic and gives the impression that evidence of both positions is equally valid, when that is far from the case. Similarly, poor reporting around conspiratorial and extremist movements can often serve to promote their causes and amplify fringe views into the mainstream.

The media is not perfect. There is no doubt that the industry holds immense power and there are many reasons to be critical of it. However, the media operates within a code of practice that most journalists take very seriously. Journalists are trained to check their sources and back up the information they are receiving. The news media has gatekeepers such as editors and legal teams, whose job is to make sure a story is accurate, and there are consequences when they get things wrong, whether legal ramifications or in terms of loss of public trust. None of these things are present in the world of social media influencers or those who present themselves as online citizen journalists.

Understanding how the media works – including how it's funded, how editorial standards differ across publications and how news is produced – is a concept known as media literacy. Dr Eileen Culloty explained that the basic idea of media literacy is that people 'should have a better understanding of how media is made, which will leave them more able to evaluate it for themselves'. This involves empowering people with the skills to assess the news they are seeing by helping them to identify and understand the differences between good and bad information. It enables people to identify things like bias and sensationalism and to understand the effect that these can have on news stories. Media literacy and information literacy programmes, run in schools and libraries, can certainly help direct people towards trusted sources and empower them to make educated choices over the information they consume.

But as well as people learning about the media, the media needs to learn from the people. Many media companies are stuck in the past, writing and reporting as if people still pick up a newspaper every day and read it cover to cover. There has been an unwillingness at times to embrace the digital age, and many publications have fallen behind the times as a result. As Dr Culloty pointed out, 'It's astounding to me how many news articles don't even use links to other sites to show where their work has come from, or point readers to where they could find more information.' There are simple changes that can be made to move the somewhat stagnant media industry forward.

The relationship between news organisations and social media has been fraught for many years, because the platforms have effectively acquired all the advertising revenue that once kept newspapers afloat. But failing to create content designed to reach people on social media is a big miss. For example, 2.1 million Irish people are now using TikTok, but at the time of writing, not one of the daily print newspapers is active on the platform. Media organisations and journalists need to be looking to the future and changing with the times. If not, they will be left behind.

My colleagues at ISD, in partnership with YouTube, developed a curriculum for schools called Be Internet Citizens, a digital citizenship programme that teaches children from the ages of 13 how to be responsible citizens online and provides them with the skills to identify online harms. This includes teaching them how to recognise misinformation, disinformation and conspiracy theories; how to identify bias and sensationalism in the media; and how to understand how algorithms can create filter bubbles and echo chambers online. They are also taught to recognise their own biases in relation to stereotyping, how to avoid an 'us versus them' mentality and the effects of things like hate speech. Conspiracy theorists will call this indoctrination and right-wing pundits will call it 'wokeism', but it's hard to see how teaching children to be careful online and to be considerate people can be a bad thing.

Media Literacy Ireland, an alliance of different organisations and individuals working voluntarily to promote online safety, has had great success in recent years with its Be Media Smart campaign.[16] This suggests a few simple instructions to help people become aware of what they are reading online.

The basic messaging is to stop, think and check – in other words, look beyond a headline, and don't assume that an image or video is telling you the whole story, or that just because something has high engagement online that it is true. Think about what the information is telling you. Is it news? Is it satire? Is it an ad? Think about whether your biases are playing a role in what you're reading. Are you tempted to share it because it's shocking, or because it's made you angry? Perhaps think twice about sharing if so. Check the source. Is it a news organisation? Is it someone qualified to speak on the subject? Or is it simply a random person speculating and giving their opinion?

A quick Google will often tell you what you need to know, and Wikipedia, once frowned upon as a source for information, is one of the most valuable tools on the internet (but check the references on the page you're reading). Another easy trick is to Google the claim being made along with the words 'fact-check' or 'debunk' in order to see if the claims have been picked up by fact-checkers. The 'News' tab on Google is also extremely handy for filtering Google results to show you only news content.

Another method that has shown some promise is called prebunking, or inoculation, which uses the same principles as vaccination but applies it to information.[17] As John Cook, the climate change communicator from Monash University, explained to me, 'If you expose people to a weakened form of misinformation, this builds up their cognitive immunity, so that they're less likely to be influenced when they encounter the actual misinformation.' He compared this to someone showing you how a magician does a magic trick. If you can explain the tricks that are used to fool people into falling for misinformation, they will recognise it more easily when they encounter it. This can be fact-based – explaining the facts to people so they know the truth before they encounter a myth; it can be source-based – where people are shown how to identify credible and non-credible sources of information; or it can be logic-based – where a critical thinking approach is taken and the techniques used to spread misinformation are explained.

John Cook has taken this idea further, into a technique he calls Fact-Myth-Fallacy, which he uses in a free online course he runs to inoculate people against the most common climate change myths. He presents a fact about climate change, followed by a myth and then by an explanation of what science denial technique or fallacy is used to spread the myth – for example, bad experts, cherry picking or unrealistic expectations.

Cook is also developing ways to implement these methods at scale, which is a huge challenge. 'Inoculation is a very versatile method and can be applied in a lot of ways,' he told me. He believes there are ways to integrate inoculation into social media, or even develop web tools like plugins to detect misinformation as you browse.

Additionally, Cook has created a game called *Cranky Uncle* (available to download as an app), which has gamified these techniques by getting people to guess what kind of logical fallacies, bad arguments and denial techniques are being used. Not only does this inoculate people against these arguments, it also develops their critical thinking skills.

None of these things alone – be it media literacy, digital literacy, critical thinking or inoculation – are going to solve this problem, but when used in combination they can hopefully go some way towards empowering people to make informed decisions about the information they are seeing.

* * * *

We're living at a very precarious and disruptive time in history that will no doubt be studied and scrutinised for years to come. Since the turn of the millennium, the world has witnessed harrowing terrorist attacks, brutal campaigns of war, a global recession, a life-changing pandemic, political leaders intent on polarising their populations and the stark, looming realities of climate change. Before being able to draw a breath and recover from one disaster, another seems to strike. We have been trying to navigate each puck life has fired in our direction while also coming to terms with a complete overhaul in the way we consume and share information. There are no instructions to follow, only our knowledge and instincts guiding us through the dark in the hope that we make it out the other side unscathed.

In the hyper-connected online world, there is a constant battle to secure people's attention. As it stands there are few, if any, rules around how this can be done, but those who wish to use sensationalism, shock, outrage and lies have the power of the algorithm on their side, feeding some of the worst parts of human nature. Trails of red pills are leading vulnerable and unsuspecting people down a deadly virtual path by providing them with warped explanations for the turbulent nature of the world. Good intentions are twisted into nefarious schemes set to destroy the world, and deep seeds of doubt are sown in agreed-upon facts. This alternate reality dismisses the pillars of scientific research in favour of science denial and ignores the rule of law that works to keep us safe, instead turning to its own flawed legal interpretations and weaponising lies, slander and stereotypes as a means of spreading hate.

For those who are targeted by these movements, the fight to push back is constant and exhausting. Migrants trying to live their lives face the threat of harassment and violence, are accused of being criminals or scroungers, or part of an elaborate plot to 'replace' or eradicate native populations. The LGBTQ+ community, in their efforts to promote acceptance and tolerance, are branded 'paedophiles' and 'groomers' who wish to indoctrinate children, sending strides for equality back decades. Women speaking about their lived experiences in a world built by men are harassed and intimidated into silence. People who choose careers in healthcare or medical research are painted as evil puppets who are happy to relinquish the morals and ethics of their jobs. Decent politicians working for positive changes, and journalists standing by the mission of the job, are all seen as self-serving, corrupt criminals.

For those who follow the trails of red pills and get sucked into this alternative reality, the outcomes can be deadly. It was deadly for Joe McCarron and the countless others who believed medical and scientific myths only to suffer the ultimate consequences. For others, such as Jen's friend Shaun and Andy's brother Jason, it has transformed good, well-meaning people into shadows of their former selves, costing them friendships, damaging family ties and isolating them from the realities of the world around them.

But as dark as the rabbit hole gets, there is a path out for those who choose to take it and there are a variety of ways people can decide to follow the escape route. For Lydia Greene, the former anti-vaxx mother that I spoke with, it was the fear of what the pandemic could bring and the realisation that her choices and beliefs might end up harming her children that jolted her back to reality. This fear caused her to question whether the path she was on was the right one and allowed her to steer herself towards reliable and trustworthy sources of information. For others, it can be the discovery of a single piece of information that casts doubt on their convictions – a blue pill, as such – which could trigger a re-evaluation and unravelling of their entire belief system.

Some people find their way out because someone in their life guided them in the right direction. This is why the single best piece of advice I can give to people struggling to maintain friendships and relationships because of a loved one's belief in these movements is to try, if you can, to keep them in your life. This may involve setting boundaries, by telling your loved one that certain subjects that may lead to arguments, such as politics or vaccines, are off the table when spending time together.

Simply maintaining this connection can act as a lifeline to pull them back into reality if they happen to find their blue pill. For those who have disconnected completely from their loved ones and only maintain a social circle with other 'true believers', this journey back to reality can often be impossible.

If you wish to try to help a loved one back to the surface, it is critical to approach this in an empathetic manner and without judgement. Conspiracy theory debunker Mick West covers this topic in his book *Escaping the Rabbit Hole*, which gives practical advice to people wishing to help a loved one find the exit path.[18] West's work is based on his interactions with hundreds of conspiracy theorists and former conspiracy theorists, and he maintains hope that a way out is possible, but, he says, it takes great amounts of patience and time.

Maintaining effective communication is the main pillar of West's advice. Arguments and heated debates that are meant to force people to change their minds rarely produce worthwhile results and can cause further friction. Listening to your loved one explaining their beliefs and developing an understanding of why they believe in them is key. You don't have to agree with them, but it is important to be honest about your feelings on the subject without resorting to insults. This can help in finding common ground, fears or anxieties that you both share, which are often the root basis of conspiratorial belief. Perhaps they have health concerns or are worried about decreasing levels of privacy due to technological developments. These are genuine grievances and it's important to validate these to build trust.

Many people jump straight to trying to contradict their loved ones' beliefs by sending fact-checking articles or research that proves their beliefs to be false or inaccurate. This step, according to West, should only take place after a solid foundation of trust has been developed, which can make supplying them with reliable information more effective. He suggests finding information that shows that your loved ones' beliefs have been mistaken, or information about the subjects they believe in that they may have missed, and providing them with these details in a non-judgemental way. This can also work for exposing the inconsistencies in their sources of information. If they get a lot of information from InfoWars, for example, show them the times when Alex Jones was unequivocally wrong about something. Generally, West says it is about supplying your loved one with information to give them a broader perspective on how the world works. This can include talking about how politics works, or how laws are developed or the history of vaccines. Many people who fall for conspiracy theories do so because they lack this wider world perception.

It can be a slow process, and West is adamant that you should not expect immediate results. Instead, see the process as a way of slowly building a more rational understanding of the world for your loved one and guiding them towards a moment of realisation that can pull them back to reality.

From where I stand, the work that West does is some of the most important in this entire field of research. Throughout the many interviews I did in the course of researching this book, I asked almost everyone what they think can be done about this situation the world has found itself in. Many answered with the points I outlined earlier in the chapter – social media regulation, media literacy, better critical thinking, better communication – but some also answered with what I think are the most important points.

Logically.ai's Joe Ondrak said, 'Rather than asking how to combat or push back against disinformation, we should be asking what leads people to want to believe in these narratives to begin with, and how we address what may trigger the desire to move from participating in consensual reality to the epistemological framework of conspiracies.'

This was echoed by Dr Annie Kelly, who said, 'We need to know what it is about these messages that are often so appealing to people. It's rare that you see someone fall into a conspiratorial or reactionary sphere when everything is going great in their lives.'

The only way to push back effectively against the onslaught of lies and deception is to tackle the root causes of the problem – satisfying the unmet psychological needs that draw people to conspiracy theories in the first place. These are: the need for knowledge; the need to feel safe, secure and in control of their lives; and the need to feel good about themselves and accepted in their social groups. We have more information in the palm of our hands than ever before, yet people's need for reliable information is not being satisfied. Healthcare crises, housing crises, food shortages and the rising cost of living mean that many people do not feel safe, secure or in control of their lives, and are enticed by the simple answers offered by conspiracy theories. Poor mental health services mean that many people who do not feel happy in themselves, or in their social circles, are turning to the online communities that conspiracy theories offer in order to find acceptance.

As Melanie Smith told me, 'We have to find a way to leverage those human instincts for community, belonging and knowledge to make the truth the more desirable version of the story again.'

No one knows what the future will bring or what obstacles we'll have to manoeuvre around next, but we can be sure that there will be people and groups hoping to disrupt all reasonable attempts to overcome them. To counter that, we need to fight for a future built on reason, rationality and compassion for all living people.

I'll leave you with the wise words of a good friend of mine that sum this up nicely: 'Don't fall for the bullshit. It's everywhere and it stinks.'

Acknowledgements

First of all, to the dozens of people who took the time to speak to me, and to the countless researchers whose work I was able to cite to put this book together: I am forever grateful to you for sharing your stories, knowledge and expertise.

I would like to say a huge thanks to everyone at Gill Books, especially commissioning editor Seán Hayes, whose unrelenting confidence in my ability allowed me to believe that I could actually write a book.

To all those at ISD who have become my biggest cheerleaders throughout the last year, thank you so much for your unwavering support. Special thanks to Jacob Davey, Melanie Smith, Henry Tuck, Sarah Kennedy and Sasha Havlicek. Shout out to all my former Storyful colleagues, who gave me an invaluable grounding in the world of journalism and online research: I wouldn't be here without you.

A special thanks to Joe Galvin, Ciarán O'Connor, David Robert Grimes, Brian Hanley and Tim Squirrell for their notes and feedback.

Lastly, to everyone in my life who listened to my rants about the 'goddamn book', provided support when the going got tough and reassured me that it would all be worth it – you all know who you are and I truly couldn't have done it without you. I am especially grateful to those who cooked my meals, washed my clothes and reminded me to get fresh air after long and unrelenting hours at my computer.

Notes

Chapter 1

1   Uscinski, J.E. (2019). *Conspiracy Theories and the People Who Believe Them*. Oxford University Press.

2   Butter, M. (2020). *The Nature of Conspiracy Theories*. Polity Press.

3   Grimes, D.R. (2021). 'Medical Disinformation and the Unviable Nature of Covid-19 Conspiracy Theories'. *PLOS ONE* 16(3), e0245900.

4   Richards, A. [@abbieasr]. (2021). *Conspiracy theories are everywhere and people don't understand how harmful they are* [Tweet]. *Twitter*. https://twitter.com/abbieasr/status/1462953203067240450

5   Allington, D. (2021). 'Conspiracy Theories, Radicalisation and Digital Media'. [online] *Global Network on Extremism & Technology*. https://gnet-research.org/wp-content/uploads/2021/02/GNET-Conspiracy-Theories-Radicalisation-Digital-Media.pdf

6   Bartlett, J. and Miller, C. (2010). 'The Power of Unreason'. *Demos* [online]. https://demosuk.wpengine.com/files/Conspiracy_theories_paper.pdf?1282913891 [accessed 26 February 2022].

7   Berger, J.M. (2018). *Extremism*. The MIT Press.

8   Van Prooijen, J-W. (2018). *The Psychology of Conspiracy Theories*. Routledge.

9   Barkun, M. (2013). *A Culture of Conspiracy: Apocalyptic Visions in Contemporary America*, 2nd ed. University of California Press.

10 Taylor, L.E., Swerdfeger, A.L. and Eslick, G.D. (2014). 'Vaccines Are Not Associated with Autism: An Evidence-Based Meta-Analysis of Case-Control and Cohort Studies'. *Vaccine* [online] 32(29), pp.3623–9. https://www.sciencedirect.com/science/article/pii/S0264410X14006367

11 Oliver, J.E. and Wood, T.J. (2014). 'Conspiracy Theories and the Paranoid Style(s) of Mass Opinion'. *American Journal of Political Science* 58(4), pp.952–66. http://www.jstor.org/stable/24363536

12 Festinger, L., Riecken, H.W. and Schachter, S. (1967). *When Prophecy Fails: A Social and Psychological Study of a Modern Group that Predicted the Destruction of the World*. Harper & Row.

13 Ward, C. and Voas, D. (2011). 'The Emergence of Conspirituality'. *Journal of Contemporary Religion* 26(1), pp.103–21.

14 Johnson, S.B., Park, H.S., Gross, C.P., and Yu, J.B. (2018). 'Complementary Medicine, Refusal of Conventional Cancer Therapy, and Survival Among Patients with Curable Cancers'. *JAMA Oncol.* 4(10):1375–81. doi:10.1001/jamaoncol.2018.2487

15 Wood, M.J., Douglas, K.M. and Sutton, R.M. (2012). Dead and alive: Beliefs in contradictory conspiracy theories. *Social Psychological and Personality Science*, 3(6), pp.767–773. doi:10.1177/1948550611434786.

Chapter 2

1 Stauffer, V. (1918). *New England and the Bavarian Illuminati*. Columbia University Press.

2 Jacob, M.C. (2006). *The Origins of Freemasonry: Facts & Fictions*. University of Pennsylvania Press.

3 Wilson, M. (2020). 'The Eye of Providence: The symbol with a secret meaning?' https://www.bbc.com/culture/article/20201112-the-eye-of-providence-the-symbol-with-a-secret-meaning.

4 Hofman, A. (1993). 'Opinion, Illusion, and the Illusion of Opinion: Barruel's Theory of Conspiracy'. *Eighteenth-Century Studies* 27(1), 27–60. https://doi.org/10.2307/2739276

5 Fitzpatrick, S. (2017). *Russian Revolution*, 4th ed. Oxford University Press.

6 Lee, Martha F. (2005). 'Nesta Webster: The Voice of Conspiracy'. *Journal of Women's History* 17(3), pp.81–104.

7 Levy, Richard Simon (2006). *Antisemitism: A Historical Encyclopedia of Prejudice and Persecution*, Vol.1, A–K. ABC-Clio.

8 Beller, S. (2015). *Antisemitism: A Very Short Introduction*. Oxford University Press.

9 Dunning, B. (2012). 'Deconstructing the Rothschild Conspiracy'. *Skeptoid Podcast*. Skeptoid Media, https://skeptoid.com/episodes/4311

10 Douglas, R.M. (2009). *Architects of the Resurrection: Ailtirí na hAiséirghe and the Fascist 'New Order' in Ireland*. Manchester University Press.

11 Keogh, D. (2002). *Jews in Twentieth-Century Ireland: Refugees, Anti-Semitism and the Holocaust*. Cork University Press.

12 Davitt, M. (1903). *Within the Pale: The True Story of the Anti-Semitic Persecutions in Russia*. Barnes.

13 Hanley, B. (2020). '"The Irish and the Jews Have a Good Deal in Common": Irish Republicanism, Anti-Semitism and the Post-War World'. *Irish Historical Studies* 44(165), pp.57–74.

14 Hagemeister, M. (2008). 'The Protocols of the Elders of Zion: Between History and Fiction'. *New German Critique* 103, pp.83–95. http://www.jstor.org/stable/27669221

15 Bernstein, H. (1921). *The History of a Lie: A Study*. General Books.

16 Herf, J. (2006). *The Jewish Enemy: Nazi Propaganda During World War II and the Holocaust*. The Belknap Press of Harvard University Press

17 Schrecker, E. (2004). 'McCarthyism: Political Repression and the Fear of Communism'. *Social Research* 71(4), The New School, pp.1041–86. http://www.jstor.org/stable/40971992

18 Delaney, E. (2011). 'Anti-Communism in Mid-Twentieth-Century Ireland'. *The English Historical Review* 126(521), pp.878–903. Oxford University Press. http://www.jstor.org/stable/41238799

19 Newsinger, J. 'Blackshirts, Blueshirts, and the Spanish Civil War.' *The Historical Journal* 44(3), 2001, pp. 825–44. *JSTOR*, http://www.jstor.org/stable/3133586 [accessed 25 May 2022].

20 McGarry, F. (2001). 'Ireland and the Spanish Civil War'. *History Ireland* vol.9, no.3, pp.35–40. Wordwell Ltd. http://www.jstor.org/stable/27724902

21 Delaney, E. (2001). 'Political Catholicism in Post-War Ireland: The Revd Denis Fahey and *Maria Duce*, 1945–54'. *The Journal of Ecclesiastical History* 52(3), pp.487–511. https://doi.org/10.1017/S0022046901004213

22 Madden, G. (2017). 'McCarthyism, Catholicism and Ireland'. *History Ireland* 25(3), pp.46–9. Wordwell Ltd. http://www.jstor.org/stable/90014539

23 Barkun, M. (2013). *A Culture of Conspiracy: Apocalyptic Visions in Contemporary America*, 2nd ed. University of California Press.

24 Toy, E.V. (2004). 'The Right Side of the 1960s: The Origins of the John Birch Society in the Pacific Northwest.' *Oregon Historical Quarterly* 105(2), Oregon Historical Society, pp. 260–83, http://www.jstor.org/stable/20615422.

25 Berlet, C., and Lyons, M.N. (2000). *Right-Wing Populism in America: Too Close for Comfort*. Guilford Press.

26 Lenz, R. (2013). 'Agenda 21 and the Jews'. [online] Available at: https://www.splcenter.org/fighting-hate/intelligence-report/2013/agenda-21-and-jews#.UaZIUvKoBHl [accessed 21 May 2022].

Chapter 3

1 Lien, T. (2013). 'No Girls Allowed'. *Polygon* [online]. https://www.polygon.com/features/2013/12/2/5143856/no-girls-allowed [accessed 8 May 2019].

2 Ging, D. (2017). 'Alphas, Betas, and Incels: Theorizing the Masculinities of the Manosphere'. *Men and Masculinities* 22(4), pp.638–57.

3 Berkowitz, B. (2003). '"Cultural Marxism" Catching On'. Southern Poverty Law Center [online]. https://www.splcenter.org/fighting-hate/intelligence-report/2003/cultural-marxism-catching [accessed 29 September 2021].

4 Kelly, A. (2020). 'Fear, Hate and Countersubversion: American Anti-Feminism Online'.

5 Evans, R. (2018). 'From Memes to Infowars: How 75 Fascist Activists Were "Red-Pilled"'. *Bellingcat* [online]. https://www.bellingcat.com/news/americas/2018/10/11/memes-infowars-75-fascist-activists-red-pilled/ [accessed 24 September 2020].

6 Eagly, A.H. (n.d.). 'Does biology explain why men outnumber women in tech?'

[online] *The Conversation*. Available at: https://theconversation.com/does-biology-explain-why-men-outnumber-women-in-tech-82479

7   Beran, D. (2019). *It Came from Something Awful: How a Toxic Troll Army Accidentally Memed Donald Trump into Office*, p.38. All Points Books.

8   Schreckinger, B. (2017). 'World War Meme'. *Politico* [online]. https://www.politico.com/magazine/story/2017/03/memes-4chan-trump-supporters-trolls-internet-214856/ [accessed 9 February 2022].

9   Bernstein, J. (2017). 'Here's How Breitbart and Milo Smuggled Nazi and White Nationalism into the Mainstream'. *BuzzFeed News* [online]. https://www.buzzfeednews.com/article/josephbernstein/heres-how-breitbart-and-milo-smuggled-white-nationalism [accessed 28 May 2020].

10 Noteworthy (2021). 'Eyes Right'. *Noteworthy News*. [online] Available at: https://www.noteworthy.ie/eyes-right/news/ [accessed 27 Apr. 2022].

11 Tighe, M., and Siggins, L. (2019). 'Far-Right Activists Incite and Spread Uproar Online over Oughterard Asylum'. *The Times* [online]. https://www.thetimes.co.uk/article/9821d63a-dc9f-11e9-b3b4-45ac47bac696 [accessed 29 April 2022].

12 Fanning, B. (2021). *Diverse Republic*. University College Dublin Press.

13 Mudde, C. (2019). *The Far Right Today*. Polity Press.

14 Davey, J., and Ebner, J. (2019). '"The Great Replacement": The Violent Consequences of Mainstreamed Extremism'. *Institute for Strategic Dialogue*. https://www.isdglobal.org/isd-publications/the-great-replacement-the-violent-consequences-of-mainstreamed-extremism/ [accessed 29 January 2022].

Chapter 4

1   Rothschild, M. (2021). *The Storm Is Upon Us: How QAnon Became a Movement, Cult, and Conspiracy Theory of Everything*. Monoray.

2   Richardson, J.T., Best, J., and Bromley, D.G. (eds) (2012). *The Satanism Scare*. Transaction Publishers.

3   Nathan, D., and Snedeker, M. (2001). *Satan's Silence: Ritual Abuse and the Making of a Modern American Witch Hunt*. Author's Choice Press.

4   Robb, A. (2017). 'Anatomy of a Fake News Scandal'. *Rolling Stone* [online]. https://www.rollingstone.com/feature/anatomy-of-a-fake-news-scandal-125877/

5   Wong, J.C. (2020). 'Down the Rabbit Hole: How QAnon Conspiracies Thrive on Facebook'. *The Guardian* [online]. https://www.theguardian.com/technology/2020/jun/25/qanon-facebook-conspiracy-theories-algorithm [accessed 25 June 2020].

6   Gallagher, A., Davey, J., and Hart, M. (2020). 'The Genesis of a Conspiracy Theory'. *Institute for Strategic Dialogue*. https://www.isdglobal.org/wp-content/uploads/2020/07/The-Genesis-of-a-Conspiracy-Theory.pdf

7   Contrera, J. (2021). 'A QAnon Con: How the Viral Wayfair Sex Trafficking Lie Hurt Real Kids'. *Washington Post* [online]. https://www.washingtonpost.com/dc-md-va/interactive/2021/wayfair-qanon-sex-trafficking-conspiracy/ [accessed 11 February 2022].

8   Tiffany, K. (2020). 'The Women Making Conspiracy Theories Beautiful'. *The Atlantic* [online]. https://www.theatlantic.com/technology/archive/2020/08/how-instagram-aesthetics-repackage-qanon/615364/ [accessed 8 March 2021].

9   Wolak, J., Finkelhor, D. and Sedlak, A.J. (2016). 'Child Victims of Stereotypical Kidnappings Known to Law Enforcement in 2011'. [online] *US Department of Justice.* Available at: https://ojjdp.ojp.gov/sites/g/files/xyckuh176/files/pubs/249249.pdf [accessed 20 May 2022].

10   Hobbes, M. (2020). 'The Futile Quest for Hard Numbers on Child Sex Trafficking'. *Huffington Post* [online]. https://www.huffpost.com/entry/futile-quest-hard-numbers-child-sex-trafficking_n_5f6921cac5b655acbc6e9e70 [accessed 27 April 2022].

11   Thomas, C. (2021). 'Move Quickly and Misinform: How Direct Provision Centres Became a Catalyst for Far-Right Activism in Ireland'. *The Journal/Noteworthy News* [online]. https://www.thejournal.ie/eyes-right-pt1-5364809-mar2021/ [accessed 27 April 2022].

12   Gallagher, A., and O'Connor, C. (2021). 'Layers of Lies: A First Look at Irish Far-Right Activity on Telegram'. *Institute for Strategic Dialogue.* https://www.isdglobal.org/wp-content/uploads/2021/04/Layers-of-Lies.pdf

13   Goldstein, D. (2022). 'Opponents Call It the "Don't Say Gay" Bill. Here's What It Says.' *The New York Times.* [online] Available at: https://www.nytimes.com/2022/03/18/us/dont-say-gay-bill-florida.html.

14   Turban, J. (2020). 'The Disturbing History of Research into Transgender Identity'. *Scientific American* [online]. https://www.scientificamerican.com/article/the-disturbing-history-of-research-into-transgender-identity/

15   Bustos, V.P., Bustos, S.S., Mascaro, A., Del Corral, G., Forte, A.J., Ciudad, P., Kim, E.A., Langstein, H.N., and Manrique, O.J. (2021). 'Regret After Gender-Affirmation Surgery: A Systematic Review and Meta-Analysis of Prevalence'. *Plastic and Reconstructive Surgery – Global Open* [online] 9(3), p.e3477. https://journals.lww.com/prsgo/fulltext/2021/03000/regret_after_gender_affirmation_surgery__a.22.aspx

16   Turban, Jack L et al. 'Factors Leading to "Detransition" Among Transgender and Gender Diverse People in the United States: A Mixed-Methods Analysis.' *LGBT Health* 8(4), (2021): 273–80. doi:10.1089/lgbt.2020.0437

17   Knox, L. (2019). 'Media's "Detransition" Narrative is Fueling Misconceptions, Trans Advocates Say'. *NBC News* [online]. https://www.nbcnews.com/feature/nbc-out/media-s-detransition-narrative-fueling-misconceptions-trans-advocates-say-n1102686

18   National Survey on LGBTQ Youth Mental Health 2021. (2021). [online] *The Trevor Project.* Available at: https://www.thetrevorproject.org/survey-2021/?section=Introduction.

Chapter 5

1   Grimes, D.R. (2020). *The Irrational Ape: Why Flawed Logic Puts Us All at Risk, and How Critical Thinking Can Save the World.* Simon & Schuster Ltd.

2 History of Vaccines: A Vaccine History Project of The College of Physicians of Philadelphia (2019). https://www.historyofvaccines.org/

3 Cook, J., Oreskes, N., Doran, P.T., Anderegg, W.R.L., Verheggen, B., Maibach, E.W., Carlton, J.S., Lewandowsky, S., Skuce, A.G., Green, S.A., Nuccitelli, D., Jacobs, P., Richardson, M., Winkler, B., Painting, R., and Rice, K. (2016). 'Consensus on Consensus: A Synthesis of Consensus Estimates on Human-Caused Global Warming'. *Environmental Research Letters* [online] 11(4), p.048002. http://iopscience.iop.org/article/10.1088/1748-9326/11/4/048002

4 Cook, J. (2020). 'Deconstructing Climate Science Denial', in Holmes, D., and Richardson, L. M. (eds), *Research Handbook on Communicating Climate Change*. Cheltenham, UK: Edward Elgar.

5 FDA (2019). Thimerosal and Vaccines. *FDA.* [online] Available at: https://www.fda.gov/vaccines-blood-biologics/safety-availability-biologics/thimerosal-and-vaccines#:~:text=A%20vaccine%20containing%200.01%25%20thimerosal.

6 Baker, J.P. (2008). 'Mercury, Vaccines, and Autism: One Controversy, Three Histories'. *American Journal of Public Health* 98(2), pp.244–53.

7 Institute of Medicine (2001). *Immunization Safety Review: Thimerosal-Containing Vaccines and Neurodevelopmental Disorders.* [online] nap.nationalacademies.org. Available at: https://nap.nationalacademies.org/catalog/10208/immunization-safety-review-thimerosal-containing-vaccines-and-neurodevelopmental-disorders.

Hviid A, Stellfeld M, Wohlfahrt J, Melbye M. (2003). 'Association Between Thimerosal-Containing Vaccine and Autism'. *JAMA* 290(13):1763–1766. doi:10.1001/jama.290.13.1763

Ball, L.K., Ball, R. and Pratt, R.D. (2001). 'An assessment of thimerosal use in childhood vaccines'. *Pediatrics*, [online] 107(5), pp.1147–1154. doi:10.1542/peds.107.5.1147.

8 Frei, P., Poulsen, A.H., Johansen, C., Olsen, J.H., Steding-Jessen, M., and Schüz, J. et al. (2011). 'Use of Mobile Phones and Risk of Brain Tumours: Update of Danish Cohort Study'. *BMJ* [online] 343, d6387. https://www.ncbi.nlm.nih.gov/pmc/articles/PMC3197791/

9 Ibid.

10 Ernst, E., Pittler, M.H. (1998). 'Efficacy of Homeopathic Arnica: A Systematic Review of Placebo-Controlled Clinical Trials'. *Archive of Surgery*. 133(11):1187–1190. doi:10.1001/archsurg.133.11.1187

11 Ernst, E. (2002). 'A Systematic Review of Systematic Reviews of Homeopathy'. *British Journal of Clinical Pharmacology* 54(6), pp.577–82.

12 Zadrozny, B., Nadi, A., and Kaplan, A. (2019). 'How Anti-Vaxxers Target Grieving Moms and Turn Them into Crusaders Against Vaccines'. *NBC News* [online]. https://www.nbcnews.com/tech/social-media/how-anti-vaxxers-target-grieving-moms-turn-them-crusaders-n1057566

13 'National Vaccine Injury Compensation Program Data Report'. (2022). [online] *Health Resources & Services Administration.* Available at: https://www.hrsa.gov/sites/default/files/hrsa/vaccine-compensation/data/vicp-stats-03-01-22.pdf.

14   Belluck, P., and Abelson, R. (2019). 'Vaccine Injury Claims Are Few and Far Between'. *The New York Times* [online]. https://www.nytimes.com/2019/06/18/health/vaccine-injury-claims.html [accessed 15 October 2019].

15   Cullen, P. (2017). 'The HPV Propaganda Battle: The Other Side Finally Fights Back'. *The Irish Times* [online]. https://www.irishtimes.com/life-and-style/health-family/the-hpv-propaganda-battle-the-other-side-finally-fights-back-1.3221166

16   Jarry, J. (2021). 'Finding a Paper on PubMed Does Not Mean the Paper Is Any Good'. Office for Science and Society. McGill University [online]. https://www.mcgill.ca/oss/article/critical-thinking-health-and-nutrition-general-science/finding-paper-pubmed-does-not-mean-paper-any-good [accessed 4 March 2022].

17   Howard, J., Huang, A., Li, Z., Tufekci, Z., Zdimal, V., Westhuizen, H.-M. van der, Delft, A. von, Price, A., Fridman, L., Tang, L.-H., Tang, V., Watson, G.L., Bax, C.E., Shaikh, R., Questier, F., Hernandez, D., Chu, L.F., Ramirez, C.M. and Rimoin, A.W. (2021). 'An evidence review of face masks against COVID-19'. *Proceedings of the National Academy of Sciences*, 118(4). doi:10.1073/pnas.2014564118.

      Brooks, J.T., Butler, J.C. (2021). 'Effectiveness of Mask Wearing to Control Community Spread of SARS-CoV-2'. *JAMA*. 325(10):998–999. doi:10.1001/jama.2021.1505

      Abboah-Offei, M., Salifu, Y., Adewale, B., Bayuo, J., Ofosu-Poku, R. and Opare-Lokko, E.B.A. (2021). 'A rapid review of the use of face mask in preventing the spread of COVID-19'. *International Journal of Nursing Studies Advances*, 3, p.100013. doi:10.1016/j.ijnsa.2020.100013.

18   Davey, M., Kirchgaessner, S., and Boseley, S. (2020). 'Surgisphere: Governments and WHO Changed Covid-19 Policy Based on Suspect Data from Tiny US Company'. *The Guardian* [online]. https://www.theguardian.com/world/2020/jun/03/covid-19-surgisphere-who-world-health-organization-hydroxychloroquine [accessed 3 April 2022].

19   Davey, M. (2021). 'Huge Study Supporting Ivermectin as Covid Treatment Withdrawn over Ethical Concerns'. *The Guardian* [online]. https://www.theguardian.com/science/2021/jul/16/huge-study-supporting-ivermectin-as-covid-treatment-withdrawn-over-ethical-concerns

20   Lee, S.M., and Bensinger, K. (2021). 'A Prominent Study Said Ivermectin Prevents Covid, but the Data Is Suspect'. *BuzzFeed News* [online]. https://www.buzzfeednews.com/article/stephaniemlee/ivermectin-covid-study-suspect-data [accessed 27 April 2022].

21   Lawrence, J.M., Meyerowitz-Katz, G., Heathers, J.A.J., Brown, N.J.L., and Sheldrick, K.A. (2021). 'The Lesson of Ivermectin: Meta-Analyses Based on Summary Data Alone Are Inherently Unreliable'. *Nature Medicine* 27, pp.1853–4. https://doi.org/10.1038/s41591-021-01535-y

22   Reis, G., Silva, E.A.S.M., Silva, D.C.M., Thabane, L., Milagres, A.C., Ferreira, T.S., dos Santos, C.V.Q., Campos, V.H.S., Nogueira, A.M.R., de Almeida, A.P.F.G., Callegari, E.D., Neto, A.D.F., Savassi, L.C.M., Simplicio, M.I.C., Ribeiro, L.B., Oliveira, R., Harari, O., Forrest, J.I., Ruton, H. and Sprague, S. (2022). 'Effect of Early Treatment

with Ivermectin among Patients with Covid-19'. *New England Journal of Medicine*. doi:10.1056/nejmoa2115869.

23 Gideon, M-K. (2021). 'There is no "Casedemic"'. *Medium* [online]. https://gidmk. medium.com/there-is-no-casedemic-c6b0ba8b9fec

24 Dolgin, E. (2021). 'The Tangled History of mRNA Vaccines'. *Nature* [online] 597(7876), pp.318–24. https://www.nature.com/articles/d41586-021-02483-w [accessed 17 September 2021].

25 Deer, B. (2004). 'Revealed: MMR Research Scandal'. *The Times* [online]. https://www.thetimes.co.uk/article/revealed-mmr-research-scandal-7ncfntn8mjq

Chapter 6

1 Edwards, R. (2022). '"My Husband Was Killed by a Disease He Didn't Believe Was Real" – Joe McCarron's Widow on His Death from Covid'. *Independent.ie* [online]. https://www.independent.ie/irish-news/news/my-husband-was-killed-by-a-disease-he-didnt-believe-was-real-joe-mccarrons-widow-on-his-death-from-covid-41491378.html [accessed 28 April 2022].

2 Southern Poverty Law Center. (2010). 'Sovereign Citizens Movement'. [online] Available at: https://www.splcenter.org/fighting-hate/extremist-files/ideology/sovereign-citizens-movement

3 Edwards, R. (2022). 'The Strange World of Dolores Cahill: Gardaí Probe Covid-Denier Links to Donegal Patient Removal'. *Independent.ie* [online]. https://www.independent.ie/irish-news/news/the-strange-world-of-dolores-cahill-gardai-probe-covid-denier-links-to-donegal-patient-removal-40911635.html [accessed 28 April 2022].

4 *Institute for Strategic Dialogue*. (2021). 'New Series Tracks Online Anti-Lockdown Activity Internationally'. [online] Available at: https://www.isdglobal.org/digital_dispatches/new-series-tracks-online-anti-lockdown-activity-internationally/ [accessed 28 Apr. 2022].

5 O'Connor, C. (2022). 'Examining US Support & Funding for the Canadian Trucker Convoy'. *Institute for Strategic Dialogue*. https://www.isdglobal.org/digital_dispatches/examining-us-support-funding-for-the-canadian-trucker-convoy [accessed 28 April 2022].

6 Yeomans, E., Lombardi, A., and Mitib, A. 'Kill Health Workers, Antivax Campaigners Demand in Telegram Chats'. *The Times* [online]. https://www.thetimes.co.uk/article/kill-health-workers-antivax-campaigners-demand-in-telegram-chats-mk87kpcsd [accessed 28 April 2022].

7 Maharasingam-Shah, E., and Vaux, P. (2021). '"Climate Lockdown" and the Culture Wars: How Covid-19 Sparked a New Narrative Against Climate Action'. *Institute for Strategic Dialogue*. https://www.isdglobal.org/wp-content/uploads/2021/10/20211014-ISDG-25-Climate-Lockdown-Part-1-V92.pdf [accessed 4 April 2022].

8 Pereira, J., Howden, M., and Sánchez, R. 'Mass Starvation, Extinctions, Disasters: The New IPCC Report's Grim Predictions, and Why Adaptation Efforts Are Falling Behind'. *The Conversation* [online]. https://theconversation.com/mass-starvation-extinctions-disasters-the-new-ipcc-reports-grim-predictions-and-why-adaptation-efforts-are-falling-behind-176693 [accessed 28 April 2022].

9 Horwitz, J., Wells, G., Seetharaman, D., Hagey, K., Scheck, J., Purnell, N., Schechner, S., Glazer, E., (2021). 'The Facebook Files'. *Wall Street Journal*. [online] Available at: https://www.wsj.com/articles/the-facebook-files-11631713039.

10 Zadrozny, B. (2021). '"Carol's Journey": What Facebook Knew About How It Radicalized Users'. NBC News [online]. https://www.nbcnews.com/tech/tech-news/facebook-knew-radicalized-users-rcna3581

11 Seetharaman, J.H. and D. (2020). 'Facebook Executives Shut Down Efforts to Make the Site Less Divisive'. *Wall Street Journal*. [online] 26 May. Available at: https://www.wsj.com/articles/facebook-knows-it-encourages-division-top-executives-nixed-solutions-11590507499.

12 Gallagher, A., Hart, M., and O'Connor, C. (2021). 'Ill Advice: A Case Study in Facebook's Failure to Tackle Covid-19 Disinformation'. *Institute for Strategic Dialogue*. https://www.isdglobal.org/isd-publications/ill-advice-a-case-study-in-facebooks-failure-to-tackle-covid-19-disinformation/

13 Frenkel, S. and Kang, C. (2021). *An Ugly Truth: Inside Facebook's Battle for Domination*. The Bridge Street Press.

14 Howard, P.N., Ganesh, B., Liotsiou, D., Kelly, J. and Francois, C. (2018). 'The IRA, Social Media and Political Polarization in the United States, 2012-2018'. [online] *Computational Propaganda Research Project*. Available at: https://demtech.oii.ox.ac.uk/wp-content/uploads/sites/93/2018/12/The-IRA-Social-Media-and-Political-Polarization.pdf.

15 Colliver, C., Comerford, M., King, J., Krasodomski-Jones, A., Tuck, H. and Schwieter, C. (2021). 'Digital Policy Lab '20 – Companion Papers'. [online] *Institute for Strategic Dialogue*. Available at: https://www.isdglobal.org/isd-publications/digital-policy-lab-20-companion-papers/.

16 Be Media Smart (2020). 'Stop / Think / Check'. https://www.bemediasmart.ie/tips

17 Cook, J., Lewandowsky, S., and Ecker, U.K.H. (2017). 'Neutralizing Misinformation through Inoculation: Exposing Misleading Argumentation Techniques Reduces Their Influence'. *PLOS ONE* 12(5), p.e0175799. https://journals.plos.org/plosone/article?id=10.1371/journal.pone.0175799

18 West, M. (2020). *Escaping the Rabbit Hole: How to Debunk Conspiracy Theories Using Facts, Logic, and Respect*. Skyhorse Publishing.